This book is dedicated to my father, Mark Creswell Skipper TD; as a child he took me to the Major General's Review of Trooping the Colour, igniting in me a lifelong love of cavalry.

Trooping the Colour
The Household Division at War and Peace

Ben Skipper AMRAeS

AN IMPRINT OF PEN & SWORD BOOKS LTD.
YORKSHIRE – PHILADELPHIA

First published in Great Britain in 2025 by
Pen & Sword History
An imprint of
Pen & Sword Books Ltd
Yorkshire – Philadelphia

Copyright © Ben Skipper AMRAeS, 2025

ISBN 978 1 39906 944 1

The right of Ben Skipper AMRAeS to be identified as Author of this work has been asserted by him in accordance with the Copyright, Designs and Patents Act 1988.

A CIP catalogue record for this book is available from the British Library.

All rights reserved. No part of this book may be reproduced, transmitted, downloaded, decompiled or reverse engineered in any form or by any means, electronic or mechanical including photocopying, recording or by any information storage and retrieval system, without permission from the Publisher in writing. No part of this book may be used or reproduced in any manner for the purpose of training artificial intelligence technologies or systems.

Typeset in Aldine 401 12/15 by
SJmagic DESIGN SERVICES, India.
Printed and bound in the UK by CPI Group (UK) Ltd, Croydon, CR0 4YY.

The Publisher's authorised representative in the EU for product safety is Authorised Rep Compliance Ltd., Ground Floor, 71 Lower Baggot Street, Dublin D02 P593, Ireland.
www.arccompliance.com

For a complete list of Pen & Sword titles please contact

PEN & SWORD BOOKS LIMITED
George House, Beevor Street, Off Pontefract Road, Hoyle Mill,
Barnsley, South Yorkshire, England, S71 1HN
E-mail: enquiries@pen-and-sword.co.uk
Website: www.pen-and-sword.co.uk

or

PEN AND SWORD BOOKS
1950 Lawrence Road, Havertown, PA 19083, USA
E-mail: uspen-and-sword@casematepublishers.com
Website: www.penandswordbooks.com

CONTENTS

Acknowledgements		7
Introduction		8
Chapter One	*Dieu et mon droit*	11
Chapter Two	Supporting State Ceremonial	58
Chapter Three	Royal Service	85
Chapter Four	Preparing for Parade	113
Chapter Five	The Relationship between Monarch and Guards	168
Chapter Six	Trusted Guardians	209
Chapter Seven	A World at War	242
Afterword		286
Bibliography		288
List of Monarchs from 1066		293
Index		298

Acknowledgements

This book wouldn't have been possible without the kind help, patience and support of the following, whose library services, knowledge and sharing of personal experiences have brought an almost overwhelming subject to life. Thank you. Royal Communications of the Private Secretary's Office of the Royal Household of the Sovereign of the United Kingdom; Brigadier Stuart Williams OBE, Royal Artillery; Colonel Tim Richmond OBE TD DL, Royal Artillery; Colonel Nick Hile DL, Royal Artillery; Lieutenant-Colonel Mark Houghton, the King's Troop, Royal Horse Artillery; Major Harry Wallace and the men and women of the King's Troop, Royal Horse Artillery; His Honour Jonathan Teare DL, Honourable Artillery Company; Jonathan Solomon; Sally and John Mitchell, Museum of the Horse, Tuxford, Nottinghamshire; the Guards Museum, London, the Household Cavalry Museum, Windsor … and every drill instructor and Warrant Officer who has ever had the misfortune to encounter me on their drill square; your patience and unique humour was noted.

Ben Skipper
The Dumbles, 2024

Introduction

On the morning of 14 October 1066, some six miles northwest of Hastings, the Anglo-Saxon forces of Harold Godwinson (1022–1066) stood on the high ground of Senlac Hill. There they overlooked the gathering invasion force of William of Normandy (1028–1087). William had landed at the village of Pevensey, East Sussex, on 28 September, three days after Harold's success against the forces of the King of Norway, Harald Hardrada (1015–1066), at the Battle of Stamford Bridge. Harold and his men felt confident that the Norman force that numbered around 7,000 could be easily beaten. Despite their wearisome southward march of some 300 miles, the Anglo-Saxons felt confident that they would repeat their victory as they looked down on the gathering Norman forces.

Sadly, this was no battle among equals, and despite the Anglo-Saxons fielding a force of 9,000, this was split into two very differing types of soldiers. The professional housecarls, who were armed with the vicious two-handed Danish battleaxe and equipped with armour, including shields for protection that could be used as a defensive wall against direct assault or artillery fire from archers. Their distinctive armour and shields gave the housecarls the same appearance as their Norman opponents. Alongside the housecarls were the fyrd, a locally gathered militia who often arrived on the field with very little military experience, but their presence brought extra metal and muscle to the fight.

Harold's forces were primarily infantry, with the forward ranks supported by archers and javelin throwers; as such Harold took advantage

Introduction

of the terrain, positioning his forces on the high ground between woodland and marsh. There he formed a C-shaped defensive shield wall to face the Normans, who would be attacking up the forward slope. This formation was able to hold off the initial Norman assaults, with the housecarls using their experience and weapons to great effect, keeping the Norman forces at bay with little loss.

However, William's forces were completely different to those of Harald Hardrada whom Harold had defeated only two weeks ago. William was fielding a combined-arms force of fifty per cent infantry, twenty-five per cent archers and most importantly, twenty-five per cent cavalry. Although the Normans were still tasked with assaulting a defensive position from a forward slope, they utilized combined-arms tactics.

While the initial use of archers was ineffectual, it would be the combination of the advancing infantry and cavalry that would break the Anglo-Saxon line. At one point the battle was close to going Harold's way, aided by a rumour of William's death, but victory was ultimately lost as the right flank of the English force broke free from the line to chase down withdrawing Normans. Harold tried desperately to maintain order over this momentary lapse in discipline, but to no avail and William seized his moment. Pinned between Norman cavalry and infantry the Anglo-Saxons, despite being armed with the deadly Danish battleaxe, were literally carved to pieces by the Normans from all sides. Cavalry and infantry clashed, clawing, biting, slashing and slamming into one another. The ensuing bloodshed turned this small area of East Sussex into a scene of bestial carnage.

After an early afternoon lull, William began to use his cavalry to feign a series of assaults and withdrawals, drawing Harold's housecarls out, and slowly thinning the Anglo-Saxon lines as the fyrd tried desperately to fill the gaps left by fallen and fighting housecarls. The battle raged on, with almost continuous cavalry assaults against the remaining Anglo-Saxon lines. Such was the determination of the Anglo-Saxons' defence that William had at least two horses killed under him, demonstrating how dangerous close-quarter fighting could be for a mounted soldier.

As the afternoon progressed the two sides remained locked in a battle from which neither could claim absolute victory. Suddenly Harold fell.

Although his death is popularly portrayed as being caused by an arrow, there remains uncertainty, fuelled in part by the Bayeux Tapestry's own ambiguity. Its depiction of Harold's death shows a man being felled by a mounted knight at the same time as another's eye is pierced by an arrow. Except for Harold's personal guard, and the defenders of the ominous sounding Malfosse, or 'Evil Ditch', the English line disintegrated, with men fleeing the field, ruthlessly pursued by the Normans.

A little over two months later, William was crowned King of England on Christmas Day 1066, at Westminster Abbey, thus beginning a millennia-long union between the Royal Household and the abbey. This moment also marked the start of a series of changes in how England, and subsequently Britain and the United Kingdom, would be governed. It also shaped how the military was used, not only for fighting, but as an expression of regal and national prestige, helping to define the nation's political, social and martial landscape over the next ten centuries.

The high point of this expression of nationhood is summed up in the annual State Ceremonial event of Trooping the Colour. Every June, the men and women of the Household Division gather to celebrate the birth of the Sovereign. This act of celebration is not only a visual representation of regal power but also the essence of what it is to be British.

The histories of the individuals and units of the Household Division are inexorably entwined with the history and development of the Royal Household and the United Kingdom of Great Britain and Northern Ireland itself. From bitter civil wars to overseas adventures, Trooping the Colour marks the culmination of 1,000 years of Guards, glory and majesty.

Chapter One
DIEU ET MON DROIT

'In all these ranks, whether they are Regimental Sergeants Major, Company Sergeants Major, Colour Sergeants or Sergeants, we have this one word which is common to all: Sergeant, which is derived from the word "to serve". We are the servants of the regiment. We are the servants and proud to be so. We cannot claim to be members of the family, but we do proudly claim to be the retainers and to serve the family to the best of our ability. We are responsible to the country, to parents and to relatives that no effort of ours shall be spared to fit these young men for their first duty as an officer. Because we are dealing with simple, straightforward and good soldiering things. Therefore, you could say that the Regimental Sergeant Major is the chief servant of the regiment and is the link between Commanding Officer and the others.'

On Discipline, lecture given to Officers Army Staff College, Camberley, by RSM John C. Lord (Grenadier Guards/PARA), Academy Sergeant Major, Sandhurst, July 1963

The moment has arrived. The mud, sweat and fears of the Combat Infantry Course carried out at the Infantry Training Centre Catterick, North Yorkshire, all seem like a distant memory. The numerous drill sessions, inspections and rehearsals of the past few months are now coming together. Weapons are drawn and last-minute buddy checks are carried out on tunics, boots and bearskins. Immaculate is no longer a byword, it is a way of life. Excellence is the goal and pride is your salve.

Soon you find yourself forming up, your lips are dry and your throat is tight. You strain for the word of command, the moment when you and your company begin your duties. You're vaguely aware of tourists looking through the wrought-iron fence that separates the parade square from Birdcage Walk, your mind races, you check off all the details, remembering what to do and when. Sage advice from the experienced Guards reminds you to prevent fainting by not locking your knees and wiggling your toes. Courtesy of experience you also know a simple mistake will stand out; don't tick-tock, don't overthink it. The band is forming up, you remember to step on the beat of the bass drum, you listen to its rhythm as it guides your step, and more importantly, later, your halt.

The officers march out, a hush descends. The Company Sergeant Major strides out confidently, undoubtedly the master of his domain, his confidence lending strength to those around him. A hush descends and the concentration intensifies. Your heart is in your throat, you can almost hear your heartbeat. Your ears strain as they listen out for the words of command that will take you to your place of duty. The Drum Major gives his command and raises his mace. The band comes to attention. Moments later the command rings out: 'By the left. Quick march!'

The band strikes up, you swing your left foot forward, you swing your left arm shoulder-high a step later, as you proceed forward the swagger grows. You are part of something special. Your Company leaves the barrack square, advancing toward Buckingham Palace. Throngs of excited tourists follow in your wake. You have become a symbol of something more than your regiment, today you are in the service of the Crown, providing the King's Guard. You are a symbol of nationhood, envied by so many, emulated by many more, and eclipsed by none. You are a Guard and this is your moment.

THE ROYAL HOUSEHOLD OF THE UNITED KINGDOM

'The ceremonies you have seen today are ancient, and some of their origins are veiled in the mists of the past. But their spirit

Dieu et mon droit

and their meaning shine through the ages never, perhaps, more brightly than now.'

Princess Elizabeth, 21 April 1947

When writing about State Ceremonial and Public Duties, it is crucial to understand that their roots are firmly founded in the history and traditions of the Royal Household of the United Kingdom of Great Britain and Northern Ireland, known simply as the Royal Household. These events are organized, supported and carried out by offices and organizations that, in some instances, are almost a millennium old. The events have witnessed changes in the Royal Household itself, and in the birth of Great Britain and the United Kingdom, the expansion and contraction of the empire, and multiple social changes. They have endured war, plague and revolution. Today they remain visual expressions of the United Kingdom's royal, military and civic identity, securing them in the popular consciousness.

Today the Royal Household provides the necessary support to the Royal Family to enable it to function as the base organization of the head of state. Its chief duties include assisting the monarch in carrying out the responsibilities of the head of state, organizing ceremonies involving the Royal Family or Royal Residences, and maintaining and presenting the Royal Collection.

SUPPORTING THE ROYAL HOUSEHOLD

The start of any State Ceremonial, such as Trooping the Colour, or a public event, such as the Buckingham Palace Garden Party, is the Royal Household. In the twenty-first century, this organization mirrors the most contemporary of large organizations, seamlessly merging current management practices with traditional tasks. Heralds rub shoulders with IT managers, while Generals mingle with curators, all working together to maintain an institutional excellence that remains the world's envy.

Within the Royal Household, there are five key departments led by the Private Secretary's Office which provides support and advises the sovereign, as the head of state, in crucial constitutional, governmental and political duties. These services include organizing the domestic and overseas official programmes as well as dealing with speech writing and correspondence. These duties sit alongside sourcing official presents and drafting and sending congratulatory communications to members of the public.

The next office is the Privy Purse and Treasurer's Office, providing the day-to-day professional business support for the Royal Household. These services include finance, human resources, technical communication, internal audit and property management services. Alongside the Privy Purse and Treasurer's Office, but working separately, is the Master of the Household's Department. This department manages the official and private entertainment events across the Royal Residences. The Master of the Household's Department is responsible for all the hospitality, catering and housekeeping services, and manages a diverse team of experienced hospitality professionals.

The Lord Chamberlain's Office is responsible for organizing State Ceremonial and public-facing events for the Royal Household, including the Opening of Parliament and the biannual honours awards ceremonies. The Lord Chamberlain's Office also manages the Royal Mews at Buckingham Palace, and is responsible for all road travel arrangements, be it horse-drawn or motor car, for all members of the Royal Family.

Finally, the Royal Collection Trust is a charitable organization responsible for the care and presentation of the Royal Collection, one of the world's most important art collections. All maintenance is funded by the public through admission charges to official residences of the Sovereign and His Royal Highness, the Prince of Wales.

Great Officers of State

As the early medieval European monarchies matured from a fractured mass of almost endless feuds, they gradually developed a system of government that not only led a country, but also kept quarrelsome parties in line. To do this, the Royal Court and Household centralized their powers through the Sovereign's chief and personal attendants, who, with the occasional nudge from the Church, became the realm's key administrators.

In the new Norman court, the Lord Great Chancellor was initially responsible for overseeing the Sovereign's communications. Over time the Lord Great Chancellor became the Keeper of the Great Seal and, as such, was responsible for the authentication of all significant state documents, thus becoming the principal officer of state. Today, such work is carried out by five departments within the Royal Household, replacing a host of principal officers of state, referred to as the Great Officers of State, including the Lord Chancellor. Perhaps the size of these five departments alone is testimony to the talents and energies of the Great Officers of State who preceded them.

The Great Officers of State includes all nine of the principal ministers of the Royal Household. Strictly speaking, the term is only applicable to the Lord High Steward, the Lord High Chancellor, the Lord High Treasurer, the Lord President of the Privy Council, the Lord Keeper of the Privy Seal, the Lord Great Chamberlain, the Lord High Constable, the Earl Marshal and the Lord High Admiral. Of these nine posts, two are held by serving United Kingdom government cabinet ministers; the Lord High Chancellor, and the Lord President of the Council, while the Lord Privy Seal can occasionally be held by a non-cabinet minister. Two of these posts, the Lord High Chancellor and the Lord Keeper of the Privy Seal, also belong to the Lords Commissioners.

The Lords Commissioners are drawn from the Privy Council, consisting of Privy Counsellors (PCs) appointed by the monarch as advisers and split into participating and non-participating members. They also exercise certain functions relating to Parliament, that otherwise requires the monarch's attendance at the Palace of Westminster when necessary. Such occurrences can include the opening and prorogation of parliament and the granting of Royal Assent. Collectively the Lords Commissioners are known as the Royal Commission, which includes up to five Lords Commissioners. Currently, the commissioners include the Lord High

Chancellor, the senior Lord Chancellor, the Archbishop of Canterbury, who do not participate, and the leaders of the three major parties in the House of Lords. They are joined by the Convenor of the House of Lords Crossbenchers and the Lord Speaker. Occasionally there are substitutions by deputies should commissioners be unavailable for duties.

While undertaking the State Opening of Parliament, the Lords Commissioners enter the chamber of the House of Lords, taking seats on a temporary structure for the duration of the ceremony. The Lord Chancellor or Leader of the House of Lords, as the most senior Lord Commissioner, then commands the gentleman/lady usher of the Black Rod to summon the members of the House of Commons. Representatives of the House of Commons then arrive at the Bar of the House of Lords but wait to enter the Lords' Chamber, bowing three times as they do so. After each bow, the male Lords Commissioners doff their hats to the Members of Parliament. By contrast, female Lords Commissioners bow. The Reading Clerk of the House of Lords will then read the Monarch's Commission, authorizing the Lords Commissioners. Finally, after the appropriate business has been transacted, representatives of the House of the Commons again bow thrice and depart.

The Great Officers of State represent the traditional Ministers of the Crown who have either inherited their positions, or are appointments that exercise certain ceremonial functions, or are political.

The four offices of the Lord High Steward, the Lord Great Chamberlain, the Lord High Constable, and the Earl Marshal were once heredity, with only the Lord Great Chamberlain and the Earl Marshal remaining so. However, all four offices are now purely ceremonial alongside that of Lord High Admiral, a post that has remained vacant since the passing of Prince Philip, Duke of Edinburgh (1921-2021), the last incumbent, in 2021.

The nine Great Officers of State in the Royal Household of the United Kingdom, are:

- Lord High Steward of England.
- Lord High Chancellor of Great Britain, preceded by the Lord High Chancellor of England (1068–1707).

Dieu et mon droit

- Lord High Treasurer of the United Kingdom, preceded by the Lord High Treasurer of England (c. 1126–1714) and the Lord High Treasurer of Great Britain (1714–1817).
- Lord President of the Council.
- Lord Keeper of the Privy Seal.
- Lord Great Chamberlain of England.
- Lord High Constable of England.
- Earl Marshal of England, preceded by the Lord Marshal of England (1135–1386).
- Lord High Admiral of the United Kingdom, preceded by the High Admiral of England, Ireland and Aquitaine (1385–1512), Lord (High) Admiral of England (1512–1707) and the Lord High Admiral of Great Britain (1707–1800).

Lord High Steward of England

> Where words are scarce, they are seldom spent in vain,
> For they breathe truth that breathe their words in pain.
> He that no more must say is listen'd more
> Than they whom youth and ease have taught to glose;
> More are men's ends mark'd than their lives before:
> The setting sun, and music at the close,
> As the last taste of sweets, is sweetest last,
> Writ in remembrance more than things long past:
> Though Richard my life's counsel would not hear,
> My death's sad tale may yet undeaf his ear.
> John of Gaunt, *Richard II*, William Shakespeare

The Lord High Steward of England was a role that first emerged with the Norman ducal household in 1066. From 1153 it was held by the Earls of Leicester and then of Lancaster until John of Gaunt, Duke of Lancaster (1340–1399), was appointed Regent for the then 10-year-old Richard II (1367–1400) in 1377. Gaunt, the third surviving son of Edward III

(1312–1377) and the father of Henry IV (1367–1413) professionalized his office's role, ordering minutes of official proceedings he oversaw, including claims from those wishing to participate in the coronation ceremonies. The resulting judgments from these meetings became precedents for the Court of Coronation claims held before the Steward and his successors. The court remains part of the official coronation proceedings but is now presided over by Lords Commissioners.

During Gaunt's tenure the Good Parliament of 1376 attempted to reverse its image as a corrupt establishment, a view held by most of the population at the time. Any progress for reform was not helped by Gaunt's dogmatic view of the infallibility of royalty and the growing power of the church in secular matters that Gaunt, through reformer and dissident Catholic Priest John Wycliffe (1328–1384), tried to rein in. Despite being the richest man in England, success eluded him when it came to domestic political dealings, regardless of his involvement and success in the French peace negotiations. The pressure of the domestic situation, ignored as Gaunt and his brothers made war in France, was spiralling out of control. Perhaps feeling cornered, Gaunt shut down parliament on 10 July 1376. Up to that point, parliament had been supported by his brother Edward of Woodstock, also known as the Black Prince (1330–1376) but was now beginning to revolt against the high taxes demanded by the Crown for fighting wars. Gaunt, increasingly isolated, must have felt immense anger and frustration as his grip on power slipped from his grasp. However, his father's increasingly poor health left Gaunt in a position of considerable power, resulting in Gaunt going from cornered to King in a very short period. In a display of blatant abuse of power, Gaunt used Edward's ailing health to pardon officials impeached by parliament. He then turned on Wycliffe and his associates, arresting them on a range of charges, bringing his wrath against a group who hitherto had been lucky to have the protection of his father and the Black Prince. On 27 January 1377, Gaunt established the Bad Parliament.

The new parliament overturned all previous anti-corruption work and introduced a Poll Tax, levied on everyone regardless of income. Supported by Sir Thomas de Hungerford (d.1397), the first person to be formally

Dieu et mon droit

identified as the Speaker of the House of Commons, Gaunt was able to strengthen his political position. The perceived increase of regal power was exactly that. Rioting, and acts of civil disobedience, especially due to the Poll Tax, started to become a serious threat to the security of the state and to Gaunt himself. He now faced increasing chaos and doubts regarding his desire to ensure the Crown passed to Richard II.

Gaunt's popularity rapidly waned and despite his efforts, best or otherwise, he found himself increasingly unpopular. The 1381 Peasants' Revolt, led by Wat Tyler (b. 1341) that sought to behead Gaunt upon arrest, also saw Gaunt's Savoy Palace, and all its contents, destroyed. Gaunt fled to Scotland during the revolt seeking the protection of Robert II of Scotland (1316–1390), thereby keeping his head. Around the same time, the Crown ironically added to Gaunt's woes by confiscating his property, including a ship, to pay off debts accrued by Sir Robert de Crull (1329–1378), Clerk of the King's Ships, to help build the navy. Richard II would crush Tyler's Peasants' Revolt most brutally, with Tyler dragged from his hospital bed and beheaded on 15 June 1381, his followers driven from London and hunted down.

By 1386 Gaunt had left England to claim the throne of Castile, a throne that he erroneously believed was his through right of marriage to his second wife, Constance of Castile (1354–1394). With Gaunt's absence, Richard II rapidly proved incapable of leading the country, bringing England to the verge of civil war within a year of Gaunt's departure. Gaunt gave up his campaign in Castile and returned to England to restore order between Richard and a group of five nobles known as the Lords Appellant. The five nobles sought to impeach five of Richard's favourites to prevent their behaviours from destroying the kingdom and restore a semblance of order and normality. This resulted in the skirmish of Radcot Bridge, outside Oxford, on 19 December 1387. The Lords Appellant defeated a force led by Robert de Vere, Earl of Oxford (b. 1362), who had been made the Marquess of Dublin in 1385, the first person to be awarded the title. After the defeat, de Vere abandoned the field, fleeing to self-imposed exile, where he died while hunting in Louvain, Flanders, in 1392.

With the defeat of the Earl of Oxford, Richard's reign was once again interrupted by the implementation of regency rule, this time by the Lords Appellant. This was followed by Richard attempting a simultaneous coup against the Lords Appellant while trying to negotiate peace with the Kingdom of France. The Lords Appellant responded with the establishment of the Merciless Parliament that governed from 3 February to 4 June 1388, overseeing the trials of many of Richard's court for treason. Those found guilty were executed, with a few exiled. Parliament and the Lords Appellant soon clashed over the latter's lack of interest in governing the country, preferring to concentrate on fighting the French and asking for parliament for the money to do so. On his return in 1389, Gaunt faced an almost Herculean task, including managing the discord between the Lords Appellant and Richard.

In 1397 John of Gaunt, now fully rehabilitated in the eyes of Richard's court, established another notable tradition by presiding as Lord High Steward at the trial of Richard FitzAlan (1346–1397), Earl of Arundel and Surrey held before parliament. Richard was keen to exact a brutal vengeance on the group of five nobles, resulting in the strangulation of Thomas of Woodstock, Duke of Gloucester (1355–1397), and the beheading of Richard FitzAlan. These two were singled out because they refused to side with Sir Simon de Burley (1336–1388), a favourite of the king, who had been impeached by the Merciless Parliament for treason. Of the other members of the Lords Appellant, Thomas de Beauchamp, 12th Earl of Warwick (1338–1401), was exiled to the Isle of Man, his lands and title removed. Henry Bolingbroke, Earl of Derby (1367–1413) and Gaunt's son, who would be crowned Henry IV within two years, and Thomas de Mowbray, Earl of Nottingham (1366–1399), died in exile in Venice.

Despite his best intentions to be rid of the Lords Appellant, Richard soon found himself falling foul of Bolingbroke, who returned from exile in June 1399 after the death of Gaunt in February. Bolingbroke's main reason for his return was to reclaim his lands and his title as the Duke of Lancaster from Richard, who was campaigning in Ireland at the time of Bolingbroke's return. The pair finally met at Flint Castle, Wales,

Dieu et mon droit

where Richard surrendered and abdicated, providing his life was spared. Bolingbroke agreed, with the pair returning to London, where Richard was imprisoned in the Tower on 1 September. On 1 October, Richard formally abdicated, with Henry IV crowned on 13 October. Richard died of starvation after plotting to remove Henry from the throne by nobles loyal to him around 14 February 1400.

The role of Lord High Stewardship remained a permanent post until 22 March 1421 with the death of the post holder Thomas of Lancaster, Duke of Clarence (b. 1387), the second son of Henry IV, at the Battle of Baugé, Anjou, France. After that, the Lord High Steward became an ad hoc appointment for a short period to allow him to preside over the Court of the Lord High Steward and bear St. Edward's Crown at the proceeding coronation.

A further role of the Lord High Steward that was abolished with the Criminal Justice Act of 1948 was that of president of impeachment trials of peers through the Court of the Lord High Steward when Parliament was not in session. The Criminal Justice Act of 1948 consequently abolished this privilege of Peers to face trial by their peers. As a result, the judicial function of the Lord High Steward ended.

Today the Lord High Steward of England is revived for coronation only, with General Sir Gordon Messenger (b. 1962), 161st Constable of His Majesty's Tower of London, carrying St Edward's Crown at the coronation of Charles III.

Lord High Chancellor of Great Britain

'Those who tread among serpents, and along a tortuous path, must use the cunning of the serpent.'

Thomas Becket

The office of the Lord High Chancellor is one of the few that dates back to the reign of Edward the Confessor (1003–1066) and, until the fourteenth century, was invariably held by a priest, including the Archbishop of

Canterbury Thomas Becket (1120–1170) and Cardinal Thomas Wolsey (1473–1530). Becket would die a particularly gruesome martyr's death at the hands of four knights, who believed they were carrying out the will of Henry II (1133–1189) after Henry had cried out in despair at Becket's control of the legal rights of the clergy.

The crux of the disagreement between the Church and the Crown was Becket's claim that if a Church official was accused of a crime, only the Church could place the accused on trial. Henry saw this as an attempt to increase the Church's power, therefore a threat to his own. On 29 December 1170 four knights, Reginald FitzUrse (1145–1173), Hugh de Morville, Lord of Westmoreland (d. 1173), William de Tracy (d.1189) and Richard le-Breton (fl. 1170), arrived at Canterbury Cathedral, attacking Becket during Vespers. They were aided by a cleric who ensured Becket was dead by scattering his brains across the cathedral's floor. All four knights were excommunicated the following Easter by Pope Alexander III (born Roland, c. 1100/5–1181). They were further ordered to undertake penitentiary pilgrimages as knights to the Holy Land for fourteen years. Alexander canonized Becket on 21 February 1173, and Henry publicly carried out an act of penance at Becket's tomb at St. Dunstan's, which became a popular pilgrimage site.

Thomas Wolsey was another holy man and Lord High Chancellor who fell foul of regal ire and frustration. Initially entering service as Henry VIII's (1491–1547) Almoner in 1509, Wolsey climbed the ladder quickly and by 1515 was arguably among the most powerful men in Tudor England. Not only was he Archbishop of York, the second most senior Church position in England, but he also served as the Papal Legate and as such was appointed Cardinal by Pope Leo X (Giovanni di Lorenzo de' Medici, 1472–1521). This made Wolsey the head of the English Catholic Church, a position with immense spiritual, political and economic power. That year Henry made Wolsey his Lord Chancellor, a role he would fulfil until 1529.

Wolsey was instrumental in establishing England as a key European power in the Renaissance through several diplomatic coups, including organizing the famous Field of the Cloth of Gold meeting of Francis I of France (1494–1547) and Henry in 1520. This event led to the signing

Dieu et mon droit

of a series of treaties, including one with Spain. Regardless of Wolsey's statecraft, he became unstuck with the attempted annulment of Henry's marriage to Katherine of Aragon (1485–1536). Despite his best efforts, the annulment was not forthcoming with the Cardinal Protector of England, Lorenzo Campeggio (1474–1539) causing such delays that the case was suspended. Despite Wolsey's reputation and experience, his future was bleak, and Henry removed him from office, and sent him north to York. Wolsey was stripped of his government property and articles of office. To placate Henry, Wolsey gifted him Hampton Court as his new residence. On 29 November 1530, after being summoned to return to London to face charges of treason, Wolsey fell ill and died at Leicester.

Wolsey was succeeded by Sir Thomas More (1478–1535), who was canonized for his refusal to take the Oath of Supremacy which recognized Henry as the Supreme Governor of the Church of England. More's commitment to his Catholic faith and his refusal to recognize the annulment of Henry's marriage sealed his fate. He was executed on charges of treason, a method favoured by Henry to remove those who stood in his way, regardless of the validity of the charge.

As well as being the Chancellor, the incumbent also served as the Royal Chaplain and the monarch's secretary in secular matters. All the secretarial work of the Royal Household was managed by the Chancellor and his staff, with accounts kept by the Justiciar and Treasurer, writs were drawn up and sealed, and any royal correspondence was responded to. Today the Lord Chancellor retains the role of the Keeper of the Great Seal of the Realm and is the chief seal of the Crown, used to show the monarch's approval of important state documents. This combination of duties, characteristic of the early Middle Ages, remained a responsibility of the Chancellorship into the early twenty-first century. However, most of the office's political power had long ceased to exist.

A further responsibility of the Chancellor as Speaker, or Prolocutor, of the House of Lords was started during the reign of the early English Norman kings when the ministers of the Curia Regis or King's Court sat *ex officio* in the Great Council known as the Commune Concilium and parliament. As the Speaker of the House of Lords, the Chancellor's role differed considerably, in terms of powers and duties, from those held by the Speaker of the House of Commons. Although they can call for a vote, they have no power to rule on points of order. However, they can participate in debates, unlike the House of Commons' Speaker. When present in the House of Lords, the Chancellor presided over his duties from a woolsack seat, a practice introduced by Edward III that symbolized England's prosperity. As time progressed, the woolsack was stuffed with wool from the British Commonwealth member states. The responsibilities of the Lord Chancellor often led to absences from the House of Lords; in these instances, the House was chaired by a Deputy Speaker.

Increasing administrative business left modern Chancellors with little time for judicial duties. At the start of the Plantagenet era (1154–1485) under Henry II, the Chancellor was responsible for processing all judicial work and petitions set before the king. Over time the role and office of the Chancellor developed into a more defined judicial function, so that by the start of Edward III's reign in 1327 the Chancellor's Court no longer followed the Royal Court. As the task of the Chancellor's Court grew, it became the direct precursor of the Court of Chancery and was fused into the High Court of Justice in the Judicature Act of 1873. The Chancery Division of the latter became responsible for equitable jurisdiction. The Chancellor also had certain powers of ecclesiastical patronage. Roman Catholics were barred from holding the office for many years, however, after parliamentary clarification in 1974, a bill announced that Roman Catholics could be appointed Lord Chancellor.

By the early twenty-first century, there were calls to abolish the Lord Chancellorship, as the office led by the Lord Chancellor held several essential responsibilities in different branches of government. To help counter concerns, a new post, the Secretary of State for Constitutional Affairs, was created to replace the Lord Chancellorship in 2003. However, establishing the new position was not widely embraced, and considerable support remained for retaining the Lord Chancellorship. As a result, parliament approved the Constitutional Reform Act 2005, which preserved the Lord Chancellor's office but redefined its role. Further changes followed, and since 2007, the Lord Chancellor has also

Dieu et mon droit

held the title of Secretary of State for Justice, while the Secretary of State for Constitutional Affairs position was abolished. At the same time, most of the Lord Chancellor's judicial functions were transferred to the Lord Chief Justice of England and Wales, with the post of the Lord Speaker becoming an elected office. These changes allowed the Lord Chancellor to concentrate on constitutional affairs. A final role of the Lord Chancellor is to continue to care for the Great Seal of the Realm.

Lord High Treasurer of the United Kingdom

> 'Counsel and conversation is a good second education, that improves all the virtue and corrects all the vice of the former, and of nature itself.'
>
> Edward Hyde, 1st Earl of Clarendon,
> Commission of the Treasury

The origin of the Lord High Treasurer of the United Kingdom can be dated to around 1126, in the reign of Henry I when it was part of the Royal Household, responsible for the safekeeping of the king's money. In 1216, a treasurer, later known as the King's Treasurer was appointed to take control of the treasury in Winchester, with the incumbent becoming an Officer of the Exchequer supervising the Royal accounts. By the sixteenth century, the office had evolved, and the post holder became known as the Lord High Treasurer, a post that was added to the Great Officers of State during the Tudor period. In terms of court precedence, this placed the Lord High Treasurer beneath the Lord Chancellor and above the Master of the Horse. Given the post holder's prestigious place, both at court and in the Royal Household, specific protections were put in place, and his murder was considered an act of treason under the Treason Act 1351. The Lord High Treasurer's importance cannot be understated, with the post holder considered the most crucial government official, becoming a de facto prime minister. Around this time, the Lord High Treasurer began to use a white staff as his symbol of office.

Initially, the post was held by high-ranking members of the Catholic Church in England, signifying its importance, particularly during the Plantagenet era. During the era of the Cadet Houses of York and Lancaster, the role became increasingly secular, with Bishop of Ely William Grey (d. 1478) being the last clergyman to hold the title, albeit for a short period from October 1469 to July the following year. Grey's appointment was perhaps the most unusual, given his father's role in the Southampton Plot to overthrow Henry V (1386–1422) on the eve of his departure to France in 1415 during the Hundred Years' War (1337–1453).

Grey's appointment was inspired considering the domestic turbulence of the period, and during the short-lived tenure of Edward IV (1442–1483). Grey's intellect, religious and political experience, alongside his love of learning, perhaps endeared him to Edward, who was besieged by the simultaneous economic crisis of the Europe-wide Great Bullion Famine (1457–1464) and the domestic Great Slump (1430–1480). Although his tenure was short, he brought wisdom and short-term political stability.

Throughout the Tudor period (1485–1603) the role of Lord High Treasurer remained functional until the beginning of the Stuart period (1603–1714) during which the first series of Commissions of the Treasury was established in 1612. The Stuart period also saw the return of the bishop into the role, with William Juxon (1582–1663), Bishop of London, serving from March 1636 to May 1641. At the same time, Juxon was made First Lord of the Admiralty by Charles I (1600–1649). Juxon's tenure was marked by balancing the books and dealing with an ever-changing political situation. On leaving as Lord High Treasurer Juxon retired to Fulham Palace where he continued to provide counsel to an increasingly besieged Charles. Such was the high esteem in which Charles held Juxon, that he requested Juxon's presence on the scaffold so that he could give Charles the last rites on the cold winter's morning of his execution on 30 January 1649.

The post and commissions continued in various forms throughout the Stuart period, including the Interregnum of Cromwell's Commonwealth, and into the restoration of Charles II (1630–1685). For some incumbents, the role also included taking on the task of Chancellor of the Exchequer. At the end of July 1714, on the eve of the death of Queen Anne (1665–1714) Charles Talbot, 1st Duke of Shrewsbury (1660–1718), became Lord High Treasurer. Talbot was known as a shrewd political operator, previously belonging to a group known as the Immortal Seven, who grew increasingly concerned over James II's (1633–1701) pro-Catholic policies. This group, consisting of six nobles and one bishop, wrote to Stadtholder William, Prince of Orange (1650–1702) in the summer of 1668. The letter they sent was the culmination of secret talks that had been ongoing since April of the previous year. They asked William to use military force against James to place his eldest daughter, Mary (1662–1694), William's Protestant wife, upon the throne. The letter was far from unsolicited having been written in response to William's own political manoeuvrings, when he realized that the English people would not take kindly to an incursion by an overseas antagonist.

William had been preparing his assault on England since the spring of 1688 but matters took on a life of their own in June when Mary of Modena (1658–1718), wife of James, gave birth to a son and heir, James (d. 1766). The birth of James saw Mary lose her position as heir. The Immortal Seven's letter alleged that the newborn James was supposititious – an imposter – and asked for William's protection as they felt their Protestant faith was at risk by James's pro-Catholic stance. To add fuel to the smouldering embers of discontent seven Protestant bishops were prosecuted for seditious libel. On 30 June 1688, the seven were acquitted, but instead of calming the situation it inflamed it, with sectarian violence culminating in anti-Catholic violence. Seizing their moment, the Immortal Seven sent their letter to William, using the disguised Admiral Arthur Herbert, 1st Earl of Torrington (1648–1715), who had been dismissed by James for not voting for his reforms, as their courier. To further sweeten the deal the letter pledged support to any landing, stating that it would be unopposed and that any landing force would be fully supported. So confident were the Immortal Seven of their scheme that they also included details of the logistical support they were prepared to offer William.

On 5 November 1668 William made his landing at Brixham, Devon. With a force numbering 20,000 William advanced on London, over 200 miles away. The Royal Army disappeared as William advanced, most probably as part of the deal brokered by the Immortal Seven; the ensuing revolution was relatively bloodless.

James fled to France on 23 December and on 11 April 1689 William and Mary were made joint monarchs by parliament of England and Ireland, with a separate agreement for Scotland the following June. There would be continued pro-Stuart dissent in Scotland and Ireland for several years leading to a series of battles whose legacy continues to shape British politics.

Talbot, who had accompanied William on his voyage across the channel and subsequent march to London, would later add his voice to the Revolution Settlement, arguing in favour of William and Mary's Coronation. By 1690 Talbot was in ill health, which, combined with political disagreements, led to his resignation from government. Talbot would return four years later, and would see the continuation of political intrigues and flirting with the Stuarts. Ill health saw Talbot resign from government in 1698 only to return less than a year later, before resigning once more in 1700.

There followed a five-year period of self-imposed exile and in 1710 Talbot returned once more to politics, supporting efforts to negotiate an end to the War of the Spanish Succession (1701–1715). In November 1712 Talbot was appointed the French ambassador and the Lord Lieutenant of Ireland, returning to England in June 1714. From 30 July to 13 October 1714 Talbot served as the Lord High Treasurer, but with the death of Queen Anne, the ascension of George I, and the installation of the new Whig government, Talbot's position remained untenable. Talbot was forced to resign all his government posts, although he remained George's Groom of the Stool, until he died in early 1718, an appointment that could be interpreted in a variety of ways.

After Talbot's resignation, the Lords Commissioners of His Majesty's Treasury were established as a presentment commission, with the sitting prime minister becoming the First Lord of the Treasury.

Dieu et mon droit

LORD PRESIDENT OF THE COUNCIL

'The preservation of every Government depends upon an exact adherence unto its Principles, and the essential Principle of the *English* Monarchy, being that well proportioned distribution of Powers, whereby the Law doth at once provide for the Greatness of the King, and the Safety of the People; the Government can subsist no longer, than whilst the Monarch enjoying the Power which the Law doth give him, is enabled to perform the part it allows unto him, and the People are duly protected in their Rights and Liberties.'

John Somers, 1st Baron Somers,
Lord President of the Council, 1708–1710.

The role of the Lord President of the Council is to formally direct the Privy Council, a body descended from the Curia Regis, that initially consisted of the monarch's tenants-in-chief, household officials and other advisers. The Curia Regis performed government functions in small groups, becoming the King's Council, or larger groups, growing into the Great Council and eventually developing into parliament.

By the reign of Henry VII, the King's Council had become a vital instrument of the crown. It comprised the Privy Council and the Prerogative Courts of Chancery, overseeing all matters of equity, including trusts, land law and the guardianship of infants. It was also responsible for the Star Chamber, a body that supplemented the judicial activities of the common law, the High Commission and their local subsidiaries. This system worked well, and it was staffed by capable individuals until the beginning of the Stuart period. For whatever reason, the Court was unable to find a suitable candidate for these vital appointments resulting in chaos that alarmed parliamentarians and common lawyers. This led to inevitable religious and constitutional irritation culminating with the Long Parliament's abolition of the council system in 1641.

Interestingly the Privy Council escaped formal abolition and was revived by Charles II. Despite its reformation, the Privy Council was a shadow of its former self and influence, with the Crown increasingly seeking

Cabinet advice on matters previously covered by the King's Council. In 1679 the office of Lord President of the Council became permanent, taking over the duty from the Lord Great Chancellor, the Lord Keeper of the Seal.

An attempt to restore the Privy Council was made via the Act of Settlement of 1701, when William took gravely ill, and a suitable heir was required. Despite there being fifty-seven Stuarts with hereditary claims to the throne the Act identified Princess Sophia of Hanover (1630–1714), the granddaughter of James I as the new monarch. The key rationale for making Sophia monarch was her Protestant faith, and her six sons who would provide a more stable line of accession, should she be enthroned. The Act was also a first step in moving Britain towards a constitutional monarchy, albeit in a limited sense. It also established that the appointment of the monarch was now a gift of parliament rather than a matter of birth and divine right.

Given Sophia's age, her eldest son, Georg Augustus (1660–1627) was made an English subject in 1705, as an insurance policy, should she die before Queen Anne. Sophia died exactly two months before Anne, making Georg Augustus George I of Great Britain and Ireland. Within a year of his coronation, George was dealing with an increasingly belligerent House of Stuart, gathering under the banner of the Jacobites in open rebellion. This situation was not helped by the fact that George was culturally isolated and unable to speak English; he often communicated with government representatives in French or Latin.

George's next test came with the collapse of the South Sea Company in 1720, known as the South Sea Bubble, which he had been governor of since 1718. The company had been established in 1711 as a private venture to take over the growing national debt, but its collapse took most of its investors' money. The crisis looked as though it would claim George and the new Hanoverian dynasty as a scalp. It was Sir Thomas Walpole (1676–1745) whose statecraft and astute political manoeuvring retained the crown of George and the legacy of the House of Hanover. Despite Walpole's politics as a Whig, for which George cared little, the South Sea Bubble had revealed Walpole's abilities and an increasingly isolated George made Walpole the First Lord of the Treasury a year later. Walpole's

Dieu et mon droit

appointment not only showed his quality but further consolidated parliamentary supremacy. At the same time, George withdrew from domestic politics as much as possible, engaging in a life of cards, horses and trips to his beloved Hanover, of which he had proclaimed himself king. Walpole was now George's key political contact and became his first point of consultation for all matters arising from the Houses of Parliament. Walpole was also invaluable in helping to navigate Britain's political scene, which remained turbulent long after the demise of the Stuart dynasty. Walpole had become George's prime minister, the first among equals. Other changes included making the Privy Council a formal body but with none of its previous influence on government.

Upon Geroge's death in Hanover in 1725, his son, George (1683–1760), with whom he had a tempestuous relationship, acceded the throne. Unlike his father, George II was keen to be more involved in his kingdom but was astute enough to recognize the political support network established by his father and headed by Walpole. This was remarkable given that he had established a rival court during his tenure as Prince of Wales. This theme of father and son rivalry continued between George II and heir apparent Frederick, Prince of Wales (1707–1751), with George openly despising his son, referring to him as 'the greatest ass, the greatest liar … and we heartily wish he was out of it'.

Like his father, Frederick established a parallel court, one which was politically active, extremely expansionist and sought to challenge French colonialism with British expansionism. Such musings led to concerns from Walpole who was desperate to avoid further political and military tensions with France, especially while the British–Dutch–Austrian–Hanoverian alliance fought against France in what was to become the War of Austrian Succession (1740–1748). By 1742 Walpole was out, his demise hastened by the Royal Navy's defeat at the Battle of Cartagena de Indias (1741). A year later George would feed his belligerent nature, by becoming the last British monarch to lead his troops at the Battle of Dettingen in Bavaria.

It was clear that George would need a suitably placed advisor, someone who was politically, and more importantly, militarily astute. In 1642 William

Stanhope, 1st Earl of Harrington (1683–1756) was appointed Lord President of the Council. Initially, Stanhope had been commissioned as a lieutenant into the 2nd Foot Guards (Coldstream), before transferring to the 3rd Foot Guards (Scots) who were fighting in the War of the Spanish Succession (1701–1715). Stanhope was a gifted individual and by 1710 was a lieutenant-colonel, becoming Colonel of Lepell's Regiment of Foot the following year. His command was short lived as the regiment was disbanded in November 1712 as part of the reduction of the British Army in the run up to the signing of the Peace of Utrecht in 1713 that brought about the conclusion of the War of the Spanish Succession.

Stanhope then served as a diplomat in Spain, where he joined the French Army under James FitzJames Duke of Berwick (1670–1734) as a volunteer during the War of the Quadruple Alliance (1718–1720). Stanhope remained with Berwick until the end of the war, after which he was reappointed British ambassador to Spain. Although Stanhope's active military career ended here he was awarded the Colonelcy of the 13th Light Dragoons. Stanhope would retain his position in Spain until the Anglo-Spanish War (1727–1729), having established himself as a talented diplomat, during what was a difficult period.

Stanhope's efforts were rewarded during the negotiations of the Treaty of Seville which ended the war; he was bequeathed the title of Baron Harrington in January 1730. Later the same year, he replaced Lord Charles Townshend (1674–1738) as Secretary of State for the Northern Department under Walpole. Despite policy differences, with Walpole in particular, over British involvement in the 1733–1735 War of the Polish Succession, Stanhope retained his position as Secretary of State until 1742. With the resignation of Walpole, Stanhope became Lord President of the Council. He brought immense diplomatic and military experience to this role, garnered from one of the more turbulent periods in European history, that George would have greatly appreciated. At the same time, Stanhope was created Earl of Harrington and Viscount Petersham.

Stanhope remained in post for almost three years, during which he was restored as Secretary of State for the Northern Department with the support of Thomas Pelham-Holles Duke of Newcastle (1693–1768).

This time Stanhope's tenure would be short, and he resigned in February 1746 over his inclination to end the War of the Austrian Succession (1740–1748) as soon as possible. Regardless of the grounds for his resignation, he was made both a full general and the Lord Lieutenant of Ireland from 1747 to 1751, before dying in London on 8 December 1756.

Today the Privy Council can call upon the collective knowledge of its 300 members. The council is comprised of those with political, judicial or ecclesiastical expertise and eminent individuals in science or letters who support the monarch as required. Meetings of the Privy Council focus on making orders within the council and issuing Royal Charters, primarily to municipal corporations and charitable bodies engaged in education, research, and encouraging the arts. Another critical role carried out by the Judicial Committee of the Privy Council is to hear appeals from the United Kingdom, British Crown Colonies, and members of the Commonwealth that have yet to abolish this final appeal from their courts. The Lord President of the Council has no role in this council.

Finally, the Privy Council is responsible for drawing up the minutes of the council on subjects that don't belong to any other Department of State. As such, the office is often held in conjunction with other ministerial posts. The Lord President of the Council is generally a member of one of the Houses of Parliament, with the office typically being a Cabinet position.

At the Coronation of Charles III in 2023, the Lord President of the Council, the Right Honourable Penny Mordaunt carried the Sword of State in The King's Procession. The Sword of State symbolizes the monarch's power to use the might of the state against its enemies as well as the monarch's duty to preserve rights and peace.

LORD KEEPER OF THE PRIVY SEAL

> 'When it is not *necessary* to change, it is necessary *not* to change.'
> Lucius Cary, 2nd Viscount Falkland,
> Lord Keeper of the Privy Seal

The Lord Keeper of the Privy Seal, also known as the Lord Privy Seal, has custody of the Privy Seal. Initially, its holder was responsible for the safety of the monarch's personal (privy) seal, used to authenticate the monarch's personal communications. Before the appointment of William Melton (d. 1340), 43rd Archbishop of York as the first Lord Keeper of the Privy Seal in 1307, the Privy Seal was kept by the Controller of the Wardrobe, who oversaw the expenditure of the Royal Household. Melton served Edward II (1284–1327) between 1307 and 1312.

Many holders of the Privy Seal have led interesting lives, but perhaps the most noteworthy incumbent was Henry Howard, 1st Earl of Northampton (1540–1614). Howard's life bridged the reigns of no less than five monarchs, each presiding over periods of unprecedented social, political and spiritual changes in the British Isles. These changes had been driven by the Reformation, which started in 1517 with the publication of the *Ninety-five Theses* by Martin Luther (1483–1546).

Throughout his life, Howard was suspected of being a Roman Catholic and would experience periods of Royal disfavour that harmed his reputation. Despite these challenges, Howard was renowned for his learned, cultured nature and his work with public charities; perhaps driven by his exposure to a cosmopolitan curriculum that had been instigated by his aunt Mary Howard, Dowager Duchess of Richmond (1519–1557). Mary had taken charge of the Howard children's education after the death of their father Henry Howard, Earl of Surrey (1516/17–1547).

Surrey was a prominent courtier of the time, serving as a soldier in France and Scotland, but it was his belligerent nature that would be his undoing. His seemingly limitless ability to be involved in intrigues, including using his sister Mary to seduce the ageing Henry VIII to gain favour at court, would be his downfall. His sister, mortified by the suggestion, would lend her testimony to Surrey's trial for treason. This was supported by the Seymours, who were staunch Protestants and felt Surrey's plan was part of a wider Catholic plot that included Surrey's father, Thomas Howard, 3rd Duke of Norfolk (1473–1554), a Privy Counsellor, to usurp Henry. While Surrey lost his life at the scaffold nine days before Henry's death, his father was spared in an armistice that

Dieu et mon droit

ushered in the reign of Edward VI. The 3rd Duke would remain in the Tower for a further six years until released by Mary I after the nine-day reign of Lady Jane Grey.

His father's actions would certainly taint Howard in court, bringing him under constant suspicion, but his aunt, perhaps aware of what the future might hold for Howard, assigned the tutoring services of John Foxe, a Protestant theologian well versed in Greek and Latin, which he passed on to his charges. Upon his release the 3rd Duke took over the education of Howard's children, dismissing Foxe, who fled to Europe in a self-imposed exile, to escape the brutal anti-Protestant measures that Mary had unleashed.

There followed a period of patronage and upheaval, until 1564 when Howard graduated from King's College, Cambridge followed by an incorporated Masters in 1568 from Oxford. Remarkably, this was funded by Elizabeth I. The same year that Howard graduated from Oxford he protested that his Catholic religious views were needlessly suspected and two years later entered court. This should have been the beginning of a more settled life, but his brother Thomas became embroiled in royal intrigue as the Duke of Norfolk (1536–1572). His father's son, Thomas had sought to marry the Catholic Mary Queen of Scots (1542–1587). Thomas was quick to implicate Henry, who was able to establish his innocence to Elizabeth's satisfaction. While his brother was executed for treason, Henry received a yearly pension and was readmitted to court.

Howard now directed the education of his nephews Philip, Thomas and William, and his niece Margaret, while trying to remain in Royal favour through letters to Elizabeth's closest ministers. Howard also maintained contact with Mary Queen of Scots, supplying her with political information and advice. To ensure no accusations were thrown at him, Howard maintained an almost paranoid record of his actions that may have been excessive but proved vital in keeping him alive. Despite this Howard would be arrested in 1582 after a quarrel with his cousin Edward de Vere, 17th Earl of Oxford (1550–1604), on charges of heresy and treasonable correspondence with Mary. Forced to defend himself once more Howard admitted his continued practising of Catholicism but denied any relationship, other than a professional one, with Mary. His letters of innocence to Elizabeth worked and Howard was freed from yet another period which would have pushed the resolve of any other courtier.

A year later, Howard again found himself under suspicion of treason, this time as part of the investigation into the Throckmorton Plot. Led by Sir Francis Throckmorton (1554–1584) the plot sought to overthrow Elizabeth, aid an invasion of the south of England, instal Mary as Queen and restore Catholicism in England. Howard was sent to the notorious Fleet Prison in London where he experienced harsh treatment. Initially, Howard's complaints were ignored, and it wasn't until the kindly intervention of Sir Robert Cecil (1563–1612), son of Secretary of State William Cecil, 1st Baron Burghley (1520–1598), that Howard was granted parole to the house of Sir Nicholas Bacon at Redgrave, Suffolk.

Howard used his letter-writing skills to leave his parole house and visited numerous locations in England and Europe for his health. Despite the treatment, accusations and doubts he faced, Howard was quick to offer his services to the defence of the realm in 1587. His requests, no doubt well intentioned, were refused and he continued to live off his small pension, whose payment was erratic at best.

Howard maintained his friendship with Cecil and became friends with the ambitious Robert Devereux, 2nd Earl of Essex (1565–1601), a favourite of Elizabeth, who would meet his demise after a failed coup. It was through Essex that Howard was once again admitted to Court in 1600, where he joined Cecil in courting the grace of James VI, King of Scotland (1566–1625) to persuade the atter to become James I of England. It was on James's accession in 1603 that Howard received payments for his work in preparing the throne for James. This included membership of the Privy Council and becoming 1st Earl of Northampton and Baron Marnhull, Dorset.

Howard would be one of the judges at the trials of Walter Raleigh (1552–1618) and Henry Brooke, 11th Baron Cobham (1564–1619) in 1603, Guy Fawkes (1570–1606) in 1605, and Henry Garnet (1555–1606) in 1606, in each case pressing for a conviction. In 1604 Howard was one of the commissioners who composed the treaty of peace with Spain, and from that date, he received from the Spanish Court a pension of £1,000. In 1608, Howard was made Lord Keeper of the Privy Seal, despite being out of favour with the king's wife, Anne of Denmark (1574–1619), taking over from Cecil, a position he held until he died in 1614. Howard's legacy was not only a tale of fortitude but also testimony to his ability to be capable of outwitting intrigue.

Howard's appointment was one of the last of those which established the office as a non-hereditary role within the Royal Household when the Commissioners of Parliament's Great Seal took over. With the Restoration of Charles II, the role of the Lord Keeper was reinstated and remains in use today.

Understandably, as the role of government has developed the need for a permanent Lord Keeper slowly disappeared as the Privy Seal became obsolete. Since the mid-1940s, the position of Lord Privy Seal has frequently been combined with either the Leader of the House of Lords or the House of Commons. However, the office does not confer membership in the House of Lords. In addition, the Office of Lord Keeper, unlike those of Leader of the Lords or Commons, is eligible for a ministerial salary under the Ministerial and Other Salaries Act 1975. This resulted in the Lord Keeper fulfilling what may be regarded as a traditional sinecure, with the incumbent invariably given a seat in the cabinet fulfilling the role of Minister without Portfolio.

The Lord Privy Seal also fulfilled the role of President of the Court of Requests between 1493 and 1685. This court was established by Richard III (1452–1485) to hear cases from those with low incomes and from servants of the king.

Lord Great Chamberlain of England

> 'A valiant mind no deadly danger fears.'
> Edward de Vere, 17th Earl of Oxford,
> Lord Great Chamberlain

The office of Lord Great Chamberlain is distinct from the non-hereditary office of Lord Chamberlain of the Household, a position in the monarch's household. This office arose in the fourteenth century, as a deputy to the Lord Great Chamberlain, to fulfil the latter's duties in the Royal Household. The office was initially held by Robert Malet (1050–1130), a son of one of the leading companions of William the Conqueror, William Malet (d.1071), who, as chronicled by William of Poitiers (c.1020–1090) had been present at the Battle of Hastings. Regarding the date of his appointment, there appears to be some disagreement, with some records stating 1126 and others 1130. The latter date may confuse, given that this is the year of Malet's death. To show how unreliable records were, it's also recorded that Malet the Younger died at the Battle of Tinchebray, fought between Henry I and his elder brother Robert Curthose, Duke of Normandy.

In 1133, Henry declared Malet's numerous estates and titles, held by another William Malet, an undefined blood relative, indefinite forfeit, most likely due to the conflict between Henry I and Louis VI (1081–1137). The office of Lord Great Chamberlain now passed to Aubrey de Vere (1085–1141). As well as being the Lord Great Chamberlain, de Vere also created the Justiciar to both Henry and Stephen of Blois, acting as the monarch's Chief Minister. It came with considerable responsibility, deputizing for the monarch while the latter was out of the country. This led to the creation of a peerage, passed to his son Aubrey, who became the 1st Earl of Oxford (1115–1194).

After that, the Earls of Oxford held the title with three forfeitures for treason until 1526, when John, 14th Earl of Oxford (b. 1499) died, leaving his aunts as his heirs. The earldom was inherited by a more distant heir, his second cousin. As sovereign, Henry VIII decreed that the office belonged to the Crown and was therefore not transmitted along with the earldom. Subsequently, the 15th Earl, John (b. 1482), was appointed to the office, but this was not hereditary. With John's death in 1540, Thomas Cromwell (1485–1540), Henry's Principal Secretary, was appointed the Lord Great Chamberlain between 17 April and 10 June 1540. After Cromwell's execution on 28 July, the office was filled by several courtiers until 1553, when it was passed back to the de Vere family, with the 16th Earl of Oxford, John (1516–1562), taking up the

Dieu et mon droit

role as a life appointment. As a reward for his support in her accession to the throne in 1553, Mary I decreed that the Earls of Oxford were indeed entitled to the office of Lord Great Chamberlain on a hereditary basis.

The death of Henry, 18th Earl (b. 1593) in 1625 left only a distant male relative as heir. As a result, the House of Lords ruled that the office belonged to the heir general, Robert Bertie, 14th Baron Willoughby de Eresby (1582–1642), who later became Earl of Lindsey. Once again, the office was awarded to Bertie on a hereditary basis and remained vested in the Earls of Lindsey, who became the Dukes of Ancaster and Kesteven. The death of Robert Bertie (b. 1756), 4th Duke of Ancaster and Kesteven in 1779 from scarlet fever, left two sisters, Priscilla and Georgina, and an uncle, leaving the House of Lords with an intriguing situation. Their solution was to allow the uncle, Brownlow Bertie (1729–1809), to become the 5th and final Duke, with the two sisters jointly acting as Lord Great Chamberlain and able to appoint a deputy to fulfil the functions of the office.

Priscilla was eventually granted the Barony of Willoughby de Eresby to become Priscilla Bertie, 21st Baroness Willoughby de Eresby. The sisters' portions were further divided when Priscilla's share was split between two of her granddaughters, with subsequent divisions. By contrast, Georgina's share has been inherited by a single male heir each time, with the individual becoming the Marquess of Cholmondeley, a title created for Georgina's husband George. The two parties remained joint office holders until 1902 when the House of Lords ruled that the then joint office holders, Gilbert Henry Heathcote-Drummond-Willoughby (1830–1910), 1st Earl of Ancaster, George Henry Hugh Cholmondeley (1858–1923), 4th Marquess of Cholmondeley, and Charles Robert Wynn-Carington (1843–1928), Earl Carrington, later Marquess of Lincolnshire, had to agree on a deputy to exercise the office, subject to the approval of the Sovereign. Should an agreement not be forthcoming, the sitting monarch would appoint a deputy until the triumvirate reached a consensus.

In 1912 the three parties reached an agreement, and the office, or right to appoint the person to exercise the office, rotated among the three office holders and their heirs at the start of each successive reign.

Now Cholmondeley and his heirs would serve every other reign, with Ancaster and Carrington each serving one reign in every four. This arrangement allows each party to decide to act as Lord Great Chamberlain or to nominate the individual to act as Lord Great Chamberlain.

The Carrington share was divided among his five daughters and their heirs when he died. It has been further divided, with eleven holding shares as of September 2022. At the accession of Charles III on 8 September 2022, the turn fell to the Carrington heirs, who named their cousin Rupert Carrington (b. 1948), 7th Baron Carrington, to act as Lord Great Chamberlain.

The House of Lords Act 1999 brought many changes to how hereditary peers worked within government, the fundamental change being the removal of their automatic right to sit in the House of Lords. Interestingly the Act contained a provision for the persons holding the office of the Lord Great Chamberlain, like the Earl Marshal, to temporarily continue to have seats to carry out their ceremonial functions in the House of Lords.

At the coronation, Lord Great Chamberlain, Lord Carrington, presented the Golden Spurs representing knighthood and chivalry to Charles III as part of the ceremony. Each gold spur features a Tudor Rose button and a velvet-covered strap with gold embroidery. The gold spurs were first included among the English coronation ornaments in 1189 at the coronation of Richard I (1157–1199). Their use derived directly from the initiation ceremony of a knight. The spurs used in the 2023 ceremony were made in 1661 for Charles II after parliamentarians destroyed the originals. These were altered in 1820 for George IV (1762–1830) when the earlier bootstraps were replaced.

Traditionally they were fastened to the sovereign's feet, but since the Restoration, they have been held to the ankles of kings or, in the case of queens regnant, and most recently the coronation of Charles III, presented to the monarch and placed on the altar. After the investiture, the sovereign is crowned.

On formal state occasions, the Lord Great Chamberlain wears a distinctive scarlet court uniform, with black overalls, featuring a broad, gold lace seam dressing. As well as carrying a sword, the Lord Great Chamberlain bears a gold key and white staff as the symbol of his office.

Dieu et mon droit

LORD HIGH CONSTABLE OF ENGLAND

'I will be correspondent to command, and do my spiriting gently.'
The Tempest, William Shakespeare

The office of the Lord High Constable of England is now only used to celebrate coronations. The role of Lord High Constable was established in 1139 when Stephen of Blois combined the posts of the commander of the Royal Armies and the Master of the Horse. In conjunction with the Earl Marshal of England, the Lord High Constable was the President of the Court of Chivalry or Court of Honour. During the feudal period, the Court the Lord High Constable was also responsible for the administration of martial law.

The constableship was granted as a Grand Serjeanty with the Earldom of Hereford by Empress Maude to Miles FitzWalter of Gloucester, 1st Earl of Hereford (d. 1143). Through a series of co-heirs including the Bohuns, it descended to the Staffords and Dukes of Buckingham, with Edward Stafford, 3rd Duke of Buckingham (1478–1521), being the last hereditary Lord High Constable of England between 1504 and 1521 In 1522, Henry VIII merged the office of the Lord High Constable of England with the Crown, with the result that the office would only be used during coronations. Most recently, Admiral Sir Tony Radakin (b. 1965) Chief of the Defence Staff, acted as Lord High Constable of England for the coronation of King Charles III.

Perhaps the most famous Lord High Constable of England was Arthur Wellesley, 1st Duke of Wellington (1769–1852). Wellesley was born in Dublin in 1769, and his early life was marked by familial upheaval and awkwardness often experienced by teenagers. It was his enrolment at the French Royal Academy of Equitation that introduced Wellesley to contemporary French culture, and most importantly, the French language. Wellesley excelled at equitation and his mother's early worries over her listless son's future were alleviated.

In March 1787, after the intervention of a family friend, Charles Manners, 4th Duke of Rutland (1754–1787), the Lord Lieutenant of

Ireland, Wellesley was commissioned as an ensign into the 73rd Regiment of Foot, an antecedent regiment to the Royal Regiment of Scotland (Black Watch). By October, with the help of his brother, Wellesley was appointed as aide-de-camp to the new Lord Lieutenant of Ireland, George Nugent-Temple-Grenville, 1st Marquess of Buckingham (1753–1813), who had created the Order of St Patrick in 1783.

This was followed by a period of development within Wellesley's military career, seeing him serve in the 18th Light Dragoons. Wellesley hoped his political career would allow him to influence martial matters and in 1789 he was elected as Member of Parliament for the rotten borough of Trim. In 1793 Wellesley, now a Lieutenant-Colonel, led the 33rd Regiment, later to become the Duke of Wellington's Regiment (West Riding), against Republican French forces in what was to become the Low Countries theatre of the war for the First Coalition (1719–1795). Wellesley's first taste of action occurred at the Battle of Boxtel, 14–15 September 1794, where the 33rd held off enemy forces, allowing neighbouring units to withdraw.

In 1795 Wellesley returned as MP for Trim, hoping to become the Secretary of War, but the Lord Lieutenant of Ireland, John Jeffreys Pratt, 1st Marquess Camden (1759–1840), could only offer him Surveyor-General of the Ordnance. Wellesley saw Camden's offer as second best and returned to his regiment. Within two years Wellesley had been made full Colonel and was serving in Calcutta, seeing action in the Fourth Anglo-Mysore War (1798–1799) against the Tipu Sultan, the Sultan of Mysore (1751-1799). Of note, Wellesley changed the spelling of his surname from 'Wesley' to Wellesley 19 May 1798, after his elder brother, Richard Lord Mornington (1760–1842) had become the Governor General of India. Wellesley's period of service in India covered what was one of the most intense during the British East India Company's involvement in Indian affairs, with Wellesley being involved in a period of almost unceasing conflict.

Wellesley's request to leave India in 1804 was granted, and he left with his brother, a small fortune made from prize money, and as a Major-General. Wellesley's Indian experience had been tough but gave him an immense amount of experience which he would employ against the French in particular. Wellesley now recognized the importance of both self- and whole-force discipline, logistics and diplomacy, both overt and covert.

There followed a period of domestic political service which saw a return as an MP, this time serving as the Tory representative for Rye, and later as the MP for Newport, Isle of Wright. It also saw Wellesley serve as chief secretary for Ireland under General Charles Lennox, 4th Duke of Richmond (1764–1819), Lord Lieutenant of Ireland.

Despite his political responsibilities, Wellesley was soon keen to see action again; in 1808, he was involved in the British expedition to Denmark and Norway. This short campaign would see him command an infantry brigade and become a Lieutenant General. He later set sail from Ireland to fight French forces in the Iberian Peninsula and begin a period of service that would cement his reputation and name. The Peninsula Wars (1808–1814) would not only shape the British Army's fortunes, ushering a period of enhanced prestige, it also firmly placed Britain on a global stage it would dominate by the end of nineteenth century. Wellesley would finish the campaign leading an experienced army, and with the title to which he became wedded: Duke of Wellington. He would also be appointed British ambassador to France.

On 26 February 1815 an exiled Napoleon returned to France, and by early summer he looked set to fracture and destroy allied forces in Northern Europe. On 18 June, at a site Wellington had come across a year earlier, south of the small Belgian town of Waterloo, Napoleon and Wellington clashed directly for the first and last time. It was here that the Foot Guards defended the Chateau of Hougoumont and adopted their famous bearskin caps.

After his victory at Waterloo, Wellington became a household name and a return to politics beckoned. His appointment as the Master-General of the Ordnance in 1818 was followed by an appointment as Commander-in-Chief of the British Army and Constable of the Tower of London in 1827. Wellington's tenure as army commander was short lived and the following year he resigned to become prime minister. Wellington was a great reformer. He championed Roman Catholic emancipation to restore civil rights to Roman Catholics in the United Kingdom of Great Britain and Ireland.

Such was Wellington's belief in the importance of this cause that he threatened to resign as prime minister if George IV did not give royal assent to the Roman Catholic Relief Act of 1829. This demonstrated that Wellington's convictions extended beyond the battlefield and that he exerted immense influence at Court. It was during this period that Wellington earned the nickname the 'Iron Duke'.

He was replaced as prime minister in 1834 by Robert Peel (1788–1850) but would remain active in government until 1846 when he retired as the leader of the Conservative Party in the House of Lords.

Field Marshal Arthur Wellesley, 1st Duke of Wellington died at home on 14 September 1852 and received a State Funeral before being laid to rest in St Paul's Cathedral, London. Wellington fulfilled the role of Lord High Constable of England at three coronations: George IV, William IV and Queen Victoria. On 18 June 1853 Wellington's old regiment, the 33rd Regiment of Foot, was granted the title 33rd (The Duke of Wellington's) Regiment by Queen Victoria on the thirty-eighth anniversary of the Battle of Waterloo. There is no finer epitaph for a great soldier and leader.

The office of the Lord High Constable of Ireland, established in the twelfth century, was abolished with the creation of the Irish Free State in 1922, while the office of Lord High Constable of Scotland, established in the early fourteenth century, remains a hereditary, albeit ceremonial, office in Scotland. The current Lord High Constable of Scotland is Merlin Hay, 24th Earl of Erroll (b. 1948).

EARLS MARSHAL OF ENGLAND

> 'A stubborn horse walks behind you, an impatient horse walks in front of you, but a noble companion walks beside you.'
>
> Unknown

Earls Marshal of England (alternate spellings include Marschal or Marischal) is a hereditary royal office holder and chivalric title held by the Dukes of Norfolk since 1672. Originally known as the Marshal of the Horses, then becoming the Lord's Marshal, the incumbent worked alongside the Lord High Constable. Together they shared the responsibility of managing the monarch's horses and stables, including mounts and tack associated with military operations, and the overall protection of the monarch and the Royal Household. The office became hereditary under John FitzGilbert who served around 1130–1165, during and after a period known as The Anarchy. The Anarchy marked the period of a civil war of succession, taking place in England and Normandy between 1138 and 1153, pitting Stephen of Blois against his cousin Empress Matilda, upon whose side FitzGilbert fought.

The Treaty of Wallingford, agreed in the summer of 1153, ended The Anarchy and allowed Stephen to retain the throne until his death. Upon his death on 25 October 1154 and as per the treaty, Stephen was succeeded by Matilda's son Henry II. By the time of his death in 1165, not only was FitzGilbert known as a Chief or Master Marshalcy, but his role had become hereditary. Upon his death, FitzGilbert was succeeded as Marshal by his first son, John 'Marshal' (1145–1194), who held the title until his death. The title was then conferred on FitzGilbert's second son, William 'Marshal', who was named first Earl of Pembroke by Richard I. William proved to be a more than capable Marshal serving five kings in various roles, including that of crusader and regent during Henry III's childhood, during which he signed the Magna Carta, in 1217.

The Lords of Pembroke retained the title of Lords Marshal until the death of the childless Anselm in 1245 when Pembroke's title went into abeyance and the office of Lord Marshal passed to his eldest sister Maid Bigod (1192–1248), then the Countess of Norfolk and Warenne. The role of Lord Marshal was then passed to Roger (1209–1270), the firstborn of her marriage to Hugh Bigod, 3rd Earl of Norfolk (c. 1211–1266). In 1386 the title was changed to Earl Marshal of England, retaining the *Earl* in its title even though Norfolk had become a Dukedom that year with the appointment of Thomas de Mowbray, 1st Duke of Norfolk. De Mowbray was banished in 1398 for rebelling against Richard II, dying in exile a year later.

De Mowbray was replaced by Thomas Holland, 1st Duke of Surrey and 3rd Earl of Kent (1372–1400), who was replaced in 1399 by Ralph

Neville, 1st Earl of Westmorland (1364–1425) after plotting to restore a deposed Richard II. Holland's treachery saw him beheaded by Henry IV on 7 January 1400 after his involvement in what became known as the Epiphany Rising. Neville's appointment as Earl Marshal was a reward for his loyalty to Henry IV during the Epiphany Rising. Neville also fulfilled the role of Warden of the West March (1403–1414), becoming responsible for the security of the border between England and Scotland. He later became a member of the Council of Regency during the early years of King Henry VI's reign.

The title of Earl Marshal was returned to John de Mowbray, 2nd Duke of Norfolk (1392–1432), by Henry IV in 1412, perhaps as an act of reconciliation for the family's part in the attempted restoration of Richard II thirteen years earlier. The role of Earl Marshal remained with the Norfolks, aside from a pause in service during the Interregnum between 1652 and 1661 and a period of Commission between 1662 and 1672. As the monarchy progressed from absolute rulers to a constitutional monarchy, the role and work of the Earl Marshal and the Lord High Constable declined in importance.

One fundamental change that did occur was the Earl Marshal becoming head of the College of Arms. This body was concerned with all matters of genealogy and heraldry. Along with the Lord High Constable, the Earl Marshal held the Court of Chivalry responsible for administering justice following the law of arms. Such laws were mainly concerned with military matters, such as ransoms, soldiers' wages and the misuse of armorial bearings.

In 1672, the office of Marshal of England and the title of Earl Marshal of England were once more hereditary and were held by the Howard family. On 16 June the following year, a declaration was made by Arthur Annesley, 1st Earl of Anglesey (1614–1686), the Lord Privy Seal, in response to a dispute over the exercise of authority over the Officers of Arms that saw Annesley quickly confirm the Earl Marshal's authority. As if to demonstrate his trust in the judgement of the Earl Marshal, the Lord Privy Seal made it clear that no patents of arms or any ensigns of nobility should be granted, with no augmentation, alteration or addition to arms, without the Earl's explicit consent. Today the Earl Marshal remains the leading Officer of Arms overseeing the work of the College of Arms and acting as sole judge of the High Court of Chivalry, dealing with matters of heraldry. As such, no coat of arms may be granted without his warrant.

Aside from his work with the College of Arms, the Earl Marshal is also responsible for organizing State Ceremonial such as the Coronation, State Funerals and the State Opening of Parliament. As a symbol of his office, the Earl Marshal carries a baton of gold with a black finish at either end.

The House of Lords Act 1999 brought many changes to how hereditary peers worked within government, the fundamental change being the removal of their automatic right to sit in the House of Lords. However, the Act contained a provision for the persons who hold the office of Earl Marshal and, if a peer, the Lord Great Chamberlain, to temporarily continue occupying seats to carry out their ceremonial functions in the House of Lords.

Interestingly, in the general order of precedence, the Earl Marshal retains the highest hereditary position in the United Kingdom outside the Royal Family, disputing other state and ecclesiastical officers outranking him; they are not hereditary. The single exception is the office of Lord Great Chamberlain, one considered notionally higher than that of Earl Marshal which remains hereditary. The office of the Earl Marshal also secures the Duke of Norfolk's traditional position as the First Peer, raising him above other dukes.

Until 1846 the Earl Marshal had a deputy: the Knight Marshal. Initially this role, established in 1236 by Henry III, was a standalone post with the incumbent and his men responsible for maintaining order within the king's court and for a twelve-mile boundary around it known as the Verges. It was during the reign of Henry VIII that the Knight Marshal became the Earl Marshal's deputy, with the role being a Crown appointment and paid as such. Prior to an Act of Parliament in 1824, the Knight Marshal was expected to be Protestant when the Earl Marshal was Roman Catholic, a frequent occurrence due to the Catholicism of the Norfolks. The office of Knight Marshal was abolished in 1849.

The office of Earl Marshal of Ireland has been in abeyance since 1697. An Earl Marischal of Scotland was forfeited in 1715 because of George Keith's, the last Earl Marischal's, participation in the Jacobite Rising of 1715–1716.

LORD HIGH ADMIRAL OF THE UNITED KINGDOM

'I'd much rather have stayed in the Navy, frankly.'
Prince Philip, Duke of Edinburgh

Today the Lord High Admiral is the ceremonial head of the Royal Navy. Most incumbents are courtiers or members of the Royal Family and are not necessarily professional Royal Navy officers. The office was established in 1385 with the appointment of Richard Fitzalan, 4th Earl of Arundel and 9th Earl of Surrey, as Admiral of England, combining the offices of Admiral of the North and Admiral of the West established in 1294. However, this unification of roles was short lived. In 1388 the offices of Admiral of the North and the West were re-established. However, the same man often held both positions, until 1406 when the Admirals of England were appointed continuously.

Initially, the titles High Admiral and Lord Admiral were used but were later combined to Lord High Admiral. Despite the grand name, the Lord High Admiral was not a command appointment, but it did have jurisdiction over maritime affairs and the authority to establish Courts of Admiralty, dealing with naval contracts, torts, injuries and naval-related offences.

By the time of Henry VIII, the navy had grown so large it couldn't be managed by a single Lord High Admiral, resulting in the establishment of the Navy Board on 24 April 1546, the same year the Royal Navy (RN) was founded. The board took responsibility for the day-to-day running of the navy. It later ran alongside the Board of Admiralty, established by Charles I in 1628. The Board of Admiralty supplied six Lords Commissioners to replace the loss of the previous Lord High Admiral, George Villiers, 1st Duke of Buckingham (1592–1628). However, Army Lieutenant John

Felton (1595–1628) assassinated Buckingham as revenge for being wrongly passed over for promotion. This charge has never been confirmed.

From the early eighteenth century onwards, when an individual Lord High Admiral was appointed, there was also a Council of the Lord High Admiral established to assist in the execution of his admiralty duties. When unoccupied, the office was 'put into commission' and exercised by a Board of Admiralty headed by a First Lord of the Admiralty. This arrangement ran from 1709, except for two-years in 1827–1828.

The post of Lord High Admiral was finally abolished, despite a lengthy hiatus, in 1964 with the establishment of the Admiralty Board, a sub-committee (Navy) of the tri-service Defence Council of the United Kingdom. At this point, the ancient title of Lord High Admiral was resumed by Elizabeth II, who held it until 2011; she conferred the office upon her husband, Prince Philip Duke of Edinburgh, to celebrate his ninetieth birthday.

Upon Philip's death in 2021, the office holder became obscure. It is still being determined whether the office of Lord High Admiral will revert to the Crown or if it will remain vacant until Charles III, a naval officer with command experience like his father, assumes it or bestows it on someone else.

It is important to note that these Great Officers of State are separate from the Great Offices of State fulfilled by the four senior-most Secretaries of State of the government. These offices are:

- Prime Minister
- Chancellor of the Exchequer
- Foreign Secretary
- Home Secretary

Officers of the Royal Household

As well as seven Great Officers of State, there exist three Officers of the Royal Household: Lord Steward of the Household, Lord Chamberlain of the Household and Master of the Horse to His Majesty. These three officers are appointed to advise the Crown on essential issues. Although no longer politically powerful, they represent a crucial role in the organization and running of State Ceremonial. All three officers have precedence over other peers of the same rank.

There are also several units with a unique martial heritage that are more than worthy of mention due to their prominence in history and in the Royal Household.

Lord Steward of the Household

The Lord Steward of the Household, identified by a white staff, was once considered vital to running the Royal Household and held significant legal and judicial authority. Established in 1399, the Lord Steward was responsible for keeping the peace and ensuring the royal monies were spent correctly; the role of Lord Steward is now purely ceremonial, introducing the sovereign to guests at state events. There have been many interesting holders of the office, with two standing out in a very crowded field, for very different reasons. The first was Thomas Percy, Earl of Worcester (1343–1403), who held the position from 1401 to 1402 under Henry IV, although it is possible he held it for a period under Richard II. Percy was an experienced soldier, who fought in the Hundred Years' War (1337–1453) and became an ambassador and seneschal in English-controlled France. This was followed by service as the Admiral of the North between January 1384 and February 1385. Percy was very keen to make an impression as a military man, and during the 1390s built Wressle Castle in East Yorkshire. Clearly Richard felt Percy was worthy of official recognition for his past efforts and in 1397 he bestowed the title of Earl of Worcester upon him. This was followed in 1399 by Worcester's appointment as Admiral of the King's Fleet in Ireland. This appointment was most probably politically motivated by Richard, keen to secure the support of Worcester against the Lancastrian Henry Bolingbroke's rebellion. Worcester repaid Richard's gesture by siding with Henry's rebellion against Richard later that year. It is said

Dieu et mon droit

that Worcester, as a symbolic gesture of his rebellion against Richard, broke his staff of office as the Lord Steward. Within three years of Henry IV's ascension to the throne, the Percys, including Worcester, and led by Henry Percy, were rebelling against the Crown in reaction to a series of unsettled grievances, including lack of pay for defending the Scottish border.

Henry Percy, known as Harry Hotspur, a nickname given to him by the Scots on account of his aggressive leadership style in the field, was a well-liked and popular figure. In the summer of 1403, he started a campaign accusing Henry of ruling over a 'tyrannical government'. Percy's cause was supported by the last native Welshman to claim the title of Prince of Wales, Owain Glyndŵr (c. 1354–c. 1415), whose rebellion Percy had attempted to settle by negotiation as one of his demands of Henry. On 21 July Percy, accompanied by Worcester, marched to Shrewsbury, where they faced Henry and his son Henry of Monmouth (1386–1422), Prince of Wales. Upon arrival at Shrewsbury Percy's and Henry's forces now each other. Around two hours before dusk Henry raised his sword, signalling to his longbow men, forerunners to today's artillery, to unleash their first barrage. Despite the carnage that followed, Percy's Cheshire bowmen responded in kind, exacting an even more devastating toll on Henry's forces. Such was the ferocity of Percy's barrage that men fled the field, including many of those under the command of Edmund Stafford, 5th Earl of Stafford, who guarded the right flank of the royal lines. Stafford remained on the field, but his bravery was short lived, and he was slain by Archibald Douglas, 4th Earl of Douglas (1369–1424), in the ensuing mêlée. The Prince of Wales, despite being wounded in the face by a Cheshire arrow, held the left flank fast.

Percy, sensing a chance for victory, charged Henry's lines, with Douglas slaying the Royal Standard Bearer Sir Walter Blount (1348–1403), who he thought to be Henry. Percy's charge was both brave and reckless, and for his haste he paid with his life, being felled by an arrow. The cry went out 'Henry Percy King!' to which Henry responded 'Henry Percy is dead.' At this point the battle burned out, with men slowly leaving the field. Percy, now dead, had come perilously close to winning the battle, with Henry sustaining greater losses and only just retaining the Crown.

Worcester survived the battle and was accused of misrepresenting a previous offer of settlement made by Henry. It was this misrepresentation that led Percy to committing to battle and losing his life. For his act of rebellion, Worcester was publicly beheaded in Shrewsbury two days later, his head displayed on London Bridge as a warning to others.

The life of Charles John Lyttelton, 10th Viscount Cobham (1909–1977) who fulfilled the role of Lord Steward of the Household between 1967 and 1972, stands in stark contrast to that of Worcester. Educated at Eton, Lyttelton graduated from Trinity College, Cambridge, in 1932 with a degree in law. Graduation saw the start of Lyttelton's main passion: cricket, as he began to play county cricket for Worcester. This would see him selected for the England cricket team as a first-class cricketer and tour New Zealand, with which the Cobhams had an association, in 1935–1936.

In 1933 Lyttelton joined the Territorial Army, later serving with the Royal Artillery as part of the British Expeditionary Force in France in 1940. From 1943 Lyttelton commanded the 5th Maritime Regiment, Royal Regiment of Artillery at the Garrison town of Shoeburyness, Essex. The 5th Maritime Regiment was responsible for the protection of all Allied shipping in the Thames Estuary.

Post-war Lyttelton had hoped to enter the House of Commons, but the death of his father and the inheritance of his title precluded him from the Commons. Between September 1957 and September 1962, Cobham served as the ninth Governor-General of New Zealand, acting as the official representative of the monarch, then Elizabeth II. To the role he brought a sportsman's attitude with which the New Zealanders could identify, and his reputation as an outdoorsman firmly established his popularity among New Zealanders.

With the completion of his tenure Cobham was made the Lord Lieutenant of Worcestershire, serving from 1963 to 1974. In 1964 he was made a Knight Companion of the Order of the Garter. In 1967 he became the Lord Steward

Dieu et mon droit

of the Household, until 1971. Cobham's final duty to the Crown occurred in 1972 with his appointment as Chancellor of the Order of the Garter.

Cobham died peacefully at their family home in Marylebone, London, on 22 March 1977.

LORD CHAMBERLAIN OF THE HOUSEHOLD

The Lord Chamberlain of the Household is the most senior officer serving the Royal Household. The office provides support and advice to the Royal Household on various matters, and the Lord Chamberlain is the principal liaison between the sovereign and the House of Lords. The office of the Lord Chamberlain is also responsible for organizing all ceremonial activities, including the State Opening of Parliament. Other activities include the management of the Royal Mews and the Royal Travel Office.

The post of Lord Chamberlain of the Household was first recorded in 1399 by Henry IV to act as a deputy to the Lord Great Chamberlain. It was established to attend to the immediate needs of the sovereign, as well as furnish the necessary staff, including bodyguards. Other vital roles included the maintenance of property through the Office of Works and ensuring the security of the contents of the Jewel House. Over time duties were steadily replaced or removed. However, essential tasks such as managing the biennial honours list remain. A further obligation the Lord Chamberlain holds is the design and wearing of court uniforms and dress and how insignia should be worn and, by extension, the authorization of the use of Royal Arms.

While attending ceremonial events the Lord Chamberlain carries a white staff and key, both worn at the waist. These two items remain the sovereign's property throughout the Lord Chamberlain's service. They are returned upon retirement. Should the monarch die during the Lord Chamberlain's tenure, the white staff is symbolically broken by the Lord Chamberlain and placed on the sovereign's casket at the end of the state funeral. This symbolic act was last carried out by Lord Andrew Parker of Minsmere (b. 1962) at the funeral of Elizabeth II in 2022.

The role of Lord Chamberlain of the Household has been held by numerous individuals since Sir Thomas Erpingham (c. 1357–1428) was appointed in 1399, with some holding the appointment twice, or in the case of Edward Bootle-Wilbraham, 1st Earl of Lathom (1837–1898), three times. One very interesting appointee to the role was William Mansfield, 1st Viscount Sandhurst (1855–1921). Mansfield was an interesting character to say the least, serving as a Lieutenant in the Coldstream Guards, where he was regarded as being 'incurably dense' by his brother officers, and in his later political life he was considered 'almost illiterate'.

Despite these detrimental condemnations of his abilities, Mansfield did remarkably well politically, in part aided by the death of his father, General William Rose Mansfield, 1st Baron Sandhurst, an accomplished military commander, in 1876.

The Lord Chamberlain is assisted in his duties by the Comptroller of the Lord Chamberlain's Office, who is responsible for the everyday running of the Lord Chamberlain's Office. Established in 1857, the Comptroller is often a former military officer responsible for several critical roles at State Ceremonial. These include conveying the Imperial State Crown to and from the Palace of Westminster for the State Opening of Parliament, and leading the parade of the Royal Regalia, assisted by the Serjeants-at-Arms.

In Mansfield's time as Lord Chamberlain of the Household he was assisted by two very capable Comptrollers of the Lord Chamberlain's Office, which judging by previous evaluations of his capabilities, was probably just as well. Brigadier-General Sir Douglas Dawson (1854–1933) a fellow Coldstreamer, came from a distinguished military family and had joined the regiment in 1874. Dawson saw action at the Battle of Abu Klea (16–18 January 1885), followed by a period of service as a military attaché from 1895 to 1901, before a return to a command position in the United Kingdom in 1902.

In 1903 Dawson was appointed as Master of the Ceremonies, where he was responsible for receiving foreign dignitaries and presenting them to Edward VII at court. This was followed by service as Comptroller in the

Lord Chamberlain's Department under Mansfield. While Comptroller, Dawson continued to serve in the army, becoming the Assistant Director of Personal Services at the War Office from 1914 to 1915. This was followed by an appointment as Inspector of Vulnerable Points from 1916 to 1919. In 1920, he resigned his position as Comptroller and was appointed State Chamberlain, holding that office until 1924.

Dawson was replaced by another Coldstreamer, Colonel the Honourable Sir George Arthur Charles Crichton (1874–1952), who would remain in post until 1936. Crichton was commissioned in 1894 and served in the Second Anglo-Boer War (1899–1902), retiring as a Major in 1910, when he was appointed Assistant to the Comptroller of the Lord Chamberlain's Department. Returning to service during the First World War, Crichton served as commander of the Coldstream Guards Regimental District from 1917 to 1919, before being placed on the reserve list in 1920. When Crichton became Comptroller and was appointed Extra Equerry to George V, Edward VIII and George VI. Crichton would retire as Comptroller in 1936.

MASTER OF THE HORSE TO HIS MAJESTY

The appointment of Master of the Horse was established by Edward III (1312-1377) with the first appointment taking place in 1338 with King's Yeoman, John (de) Brocas (c. 1285–1365) becoming Master. Brocas was an experienced soldier who had fought at the Battle of Bannockburn, 23–24 June 1314, and had led a section of one knight, fourteen squires and twenty-four archers at the Siege of Calais (1346–1347). He had also been responsible for the upkeep of Edward II's cavalry during these conflicts, so was well versed in the need to maintain stud stocks alongside livery items. However, the stock had been run down and Brocas was dispatched to buy not only horses but spurs, saddles and halters. Given his loyalty to Edward's father, it was necessary to issue Borcas with a pardon and subsequently he was commissioned to purchase war horses and similar from Spain.

Buying horses was expensive, one of three dextrarii or destriers, destined to carry knights to war cost the Crown £120 or £114,694 today. While Brocas had free reign to buy stock from Spain, he was unable to purchase or collect stock, blood and otherwise, from counties north of the Trent, which were in the custody of Edmund de Tidmarsh.

In 1343 the Master of the Stud south of the Trent, William de Framesworth, was ordered to bring de Tidmarsh's stock to Westminster Palace. The cost of transportation would have been high given the numerous tolls demanded, especially at water crossings. Maybe it was this cost which prevented the collection of de Tidmarsh's stock, as another King's Yeoman, Roger de Normanville was appointed to replace him. Meanwhile, Brocas had returned from his adventures, which included a trip to his home province of Gascony on the French-Spanish border. The horses he returned with were later used in the campaign culminating in the English victory at the Battle of Crécy, 26 August 1346. After the Truce of Calais had been signed in 1347 Brocas returned home, where he was officially conferred with the title of Master of the Horse. For his efforts Brocas was knighted.

Now established as a member of the Royal Household, the role of the Master was to attend to all matters relating to the Royal Stables in war and peace, including the breeding and selection of horses themselves. Living as part of the Royal Household the Master of the Horse enjoyed excellent patronage, until 1854 when the role of Crown Equerry was established. After that, the Master's role became purely ceremonial, and he could be summoned for service by the Lord Chamberlain at the request of the sovereign. At the time of the change Lieutenant-General Arthur Richard Wellesley, 2nd Duke of Wellington (1807–1884), and son of the famous Field Marshal Wellesley, was the Master of the Horse.

Henry Somerset, 10th Duke of Beaufort (1900–1984), would be Master of the Horse for a staggering forty-two years between 1936 and 1978. Beaufort was a Master very much in the same vein as Brocas – a master horseman who founded the world-famous Badminton Horse Trials in 1949. It was at Badminton that horses and riders would compete in three equitation skills that were requisite for a cavalier to master: dressage, jumping and cross country.

Dieu et mon droit

Beaufort, a distant relative of the Royal Family through Plantagenet lineage, was schooled at Eton, followed by a commission into the Royal Regiment of Horse Guards (The Blues) (RHG). His was a short period of service focused on equitation and including re-establishing the International Horse Show at Olympia in 1934 after its official cessation the previous year. In 1936 Beaufort was made Master of the Horse, serving three sovereigns, Edward VIII, George VI and Elizabeth II.

Beaufort gained a reputation as a hard worker, good leader and friend to many at Court and in the wider political scene. He was friends with the actor David Niven (1910–1983) and would host Eleanor Roosevelt (1884–1962) and the exiled Emperor of Ethiopia Haile Selassie (1892–1975). Selassie stayed at Badminton House during the Italian occupation of Ethiopia in 1940. As well as his many royal duties, Beaufort remained involved with the military, the Yeomanry in particular, serving as Honorary Colonel with three regiments: the 21st (Royal Gloucestershire Hussars) Armoured Car Company, between 1969 and 1971, the Royal Wessex Yeomanry between 1971 and 1984, and the Warwickshire Yeomanry between 1971 and 1972.

Such was his renown, his nickname was simply 'Master', a nod to his involvement in field sports as much as his mastery of all matters equitation. His reputation was such that Elizabeth II, along with other members of the Royal Family, attended his funeral in 1984.

Unlike the Lord Chamberlain and Lord Steward, the Master of the Horse accompanies the sovereign at all State Ceremonial where horses are used. Working with the Crown Equerry, the Master ensures the immaculate turnout of horses, carriages, coachmen and postilions. Where horses are used, the Master accompanies on horseback; however, for some State Ceremonial events, he will often accompany the sovereign in their carriage or the carriage directly behind the sovereign and Royal Family.

When mounted as part Master for State Ceremonial, he wears a uniform designed by Edward VII. This features a scarlet tunic with gold lace on the front of the tunic, white buckskin breeches and jackboots and gold spurs.

CHAPTER TWO
SUPPORTING STATE CEREMONIAL

'Every ceremony or rite has a value if it is performed without alteration. A ceremony is a book in which a great deal is written.'
Robert Heinlein

The Royal Household is supported by a veritable army of men and women whose roles and appointments provide the tools and expertise to deliver awe-inspiring and memorable moments. A great many of these roles, such as the Yeomen, have their roots in past military glories and remain a vital part of the story of State Ceremonial and Public Duties.

CROWN EQUERRY

A relatively new role in the Royal Household, the Crown Equerry was established in 1854 as the administrative head of the Royal Mews, receiving the everyday transportation orders from Court in the place of the Master of the Horse. The Crown Equerry directs the work of the Superintendent of the Royal Mews and his staff consisting of drivers, grooms and liveried helpers. Responsible to the Master of Horse for the safe maintenance of all vehicular and air transport, the Crown Equerry also works alongside the Royal Travel Office in arranging Royal Household movements. The Royal Mews, based at Buckingham Palace, is home to the numerous Royal carriages, including six state carriages, thirty carriage horses that are either Windsor Greys or Cleveland Bays, and the automotive fleet.

Supporting State Ceremonial

Today the Crown Equerry, who enjoys a close relationship with the Royal Family, is a commissioned officer of the Household Cavalry, although that has not always been the case. One such exception was Lieutenant-Colonel Sir George Ashley Maude (1817–1894), who was born in 1817 in Enniskillen, County Fermanagh, Ireland. After going to school in Dorset, Maude was commissioned into the Royal Horse Artillery (RHA) in 1834. Maude would take part in the Crimean War (1853–1856), where he was badly wounded during the Battle of Balaklava (1854). After the war, Maude became a military assistant to the British mission led by Granville Leveson-Gower, 2nd Earl Granville (1815–1891) that attended the coronation of Tsar Alexander II of Russia (1818–1881), in 1856.

Maude became deputy-inspector to the Royal Irish Constabulary from 1858 until 1859; thereafter he was appointed Crown Equerry in 1859. This was the beginning of a long relationship with the Royal Household. In 1884 Maude received the Royal Household's Long and Faithful Service Medal for twenty-five years' service. Upon his retirement in 1894 Maude was awarded a bar for an additional ten years of service which was followed by an appointment as a Knight Commander of the Order of the Bath (KCB) in 1887.

Whenever the sovereign uses one of the horse-drawn carriages during State Ceremonial the Crown Equerry will ride alongside and is easily identified by the black chapeau bras, finished with a red-on-white feather heckle. The tunic, known as a State Tunic, is a derivative of their regimental dress and includes dark blue overalls with a scarlet seam stripe and black riding boots.

THE CONSTABLE AND GOVERNOR OF WINDSOR CASTLE

The post of Constable and Governor of Windsor Castle was established in 1086. The Constable and Governor are responsible for the castle in the sovereign's absence and act as the representative of the Lord Chamberlain. The day-to-day running is managed by the Royal Household's representative, the Superintendent. The Constable and

Governor, which has been a combined post since 1660, is in nominal charge of the Windsor Castle Garrison, provided by the Foot Guards, as well as the Military Knights of Windsor. While the post is no longer paid, the post holder enjoys free lodgings at the castle. The uniform is like that worn by general staff but features a blue tunic with scarlet collar and cuffs, although service dress is normally worn by the post holder during State Ceremonial and Public Duties.

The post of Constable and Governor of Windsor Castle has certainly seen some interesting appointees, but on two occasions the incumbent couldn't wait for his letter of appointment. William de Longchamp (d. 1197) had governed England while Richard I followed the Third Crusade (1189–1192) along with Philip II of France (1165–1223) and Frederick (Barbarossa) I of the Holy Roman Empire (1122–1190). De Longchamp's career owed a great deal to his work in Henry II's Chancery; thereafter he worked for Richard while he was Duke of Aquitaine and Chancellor to the Duchy of Aquitaine.

With Richard's ascension to the throne in 1189, de Longchamp's career took off. His first role was as Lord Chancellor of England, paying £3,000 for the honour (nearly £5 million today). De Longchamp was quick to recognize an opportunity and increased the price of having Chancery documents marked with the Great Seal, as a way of recouping his money. The same year he was raised to the Bishopric of Ely, and as a final act of sealing his authority, Richard placed the Tower of London in de Longchamp's hands, appointing him jointly with Hugh de Puiset, the Bishop of Durham (c. 1125–1195), to the office of Chief Justiciar. This allowed both men to act in his name while Richard was out of the kingdom. The relationship between de Longchamp and de Puiset was fraught, leaving Richard no choice but to split their jurisdictions. In 1190 de Puiset was given authority north of the River Humber and de Longchamp south of the river.

Within three months de Puiset was gone, eased out by de Longchamp who received a commission as a papal legate from Pope Clement III (1130–1191). De Longchamp began to assert his authority, first by restoring peace in York after the Massacre of the Jews and sending an armed force against Rhys ap Gruffydd (c. 1132–1197), a Welsh prince fighting the Marcher Lords on the Welsh borders. As a Norman, de Longchamp's belligerent nature was worsened by his insensitivities to English culture, leading to accusations of de Longchamp bringing Norman officials to replace English incumbents. Such accusations were not without evidence; in 1190 de Longchamp had besieged Lincoln Castle in the hope of deposing the Governor Gerard de Canville (d. 1214) and replacing him with the candidate of his choice. His heavy-handed approach failed, with de Canville, ably supported by his wife Nicola de la Haie (c. 1150–1230) the hereditary Constable of Lincoln Castle, seeing de Longchamp off.

In 1191 Pope Clement III died, and with him de Longchamp's legitimate papal support. By the end of the year de Longchamp had been deposed and excommunicated on account of his growing autocratic behaviour. This included two occasions of seizing the title of Constable and Governor of Windsor Castle. Now without station, de Longchamp attempted to leave England by any means necessary, including the use of disguises.

Despite his ignominious flight from the country, de Longchamp would find himself in favour once more, serving as a diplomat at the court of Henry VI, the Holy Roman Emperor (1165–1197). A brief return to England in 1194 only caused ructions between de Longchamp and Archbishop Geoffrey of York (c. 1152–1212), an illegitimate son of Henry II. The following year de Longchamp left England for a final time, returning to the court of Henry VI as a diplomat for Richard I.

The Military Knights of Windsor

Founded as the Alms Knights of St. George's Chapel and known as the Poor Knights, by Edward III in 1346. William IV renamed the Alms Knights the Military Knights of Windsor after complaints from the knights. Today the knights, who are all pensioned military officers, live at Windsor Castle. Their main duty is to escort the Knights and Ladies of the Garter and to attend the daily services in St. George's Chapel where they pray for the sovereign and Knights Companions of the Order of the Garter. Other duties include parading for state visits held at Windsor Castle, led by the Governor of the Military Knights of Windsor.

The Governor of the Military Knights of Windsor is often drawn from their ranks, with one Governor being Major General Sir Edmund Hakewill-Smith. He was born in Kimberley, South Africa, on 17 March 1896. At the start of the First World War Hakewill-Smith attended the Royal Military College, Sandhurst, commissioning as a Second Lieutenant in the Royal Scots Fusiliers (RSF). During his service on the Western Front with the 2nd (Regular) RSF, Hakewill-Smith was wounded twice. During the Hundred Days' Offensive, 8 August to 11 November 1918, he was awarded the Military Cross.

Post-war Hakewill-Smith remained in the army, serving with the British Military Mission to South Russia in 1920. In 1921 he moved to India where he became the aide-de-camp to Lawrence Dundas, 2nd Marquess of Zetland (1876–1961); he then served as the Governor of Bengal, India. Hakewill-Smith returned to the RSF, serving as Adjutant to the 2nd Battalion between 1927 and 1930. This was followed by a course at the Staff College, Quetta, from 1932 to 1933 before moving to the War Office in 1934 and leaving in 1936.

With the onset of the Second World War, Hakewill-Smith served as Commanding Officer (CO) of the 5th Battalion, Devonshire Regiment (Devons), between May and September 1940. He was then assigned as CO of 4th/5th Battalion, RSF before a promotion to temporary Brigadier on 30 March 1941. Hakewill-Smith would command the 157th Infantry Brigade, part of the 52nd (Lowland) Infantry Division, until late March 1942, when he was promoted to the acting rank of Major-General.

He then became Director of Organization at the War Office, before returning to the 52nd Division, assuming command of the 155th (South Scottish) Infantry Brigade in mid-February 1943. His command of the 155th was short lived and on 26 December 1943, with his major general rank becoming temporary, Hakewill-Smith assumed command of the 52nd (Lowland) Infantry Division. The 52nd was focused on delivering the British Army's mountain warfare capability with possible operations focusing on an invasion of Norway. Hakewill-Smith took over from Major-General Neil Ritchie (1897–1983) as the General Officer Commanding (GOC), with Ritchie commanding XII Corps until 1945.

With Allied plans changing to meet long-term strategic goals, the 52nd was no longer needed to invade Norway and Hakewill-Smith would now lead the retraining of the division from mountaineers to air assault. As part of this re-organization the 52nd was transferred to the First Allied Airborne Army. Despite a second repurposing, Operation *Market Garden* ended any future large-scale airborne operations by the Allies; after crossing the English Channel, the 52nd joined the First Canadian Army in Belgium in October 1944. Hakewill-Smith led the 52nd through several key operations, and the division took part in the Battle of Hamburg between 18 April and 3 May 1945, as part of the 21st Army Group led by Field Marshal Bernard Montgomery (1887–1976).

After the war, Hakewill-Smith became GOC Lowland District in Scotland before serving as President of the Military Court for War Crimes trial of Gneralfeldmarschall Albert Kesselring (1885–1960). Hakewill-Smith also served as the Honorary Colonel of the RSF from 1946 to 1957, before retiring in 1949.

After retirement he would serve as a Military Knight of Windsor, holding the appointment of Governor of the Military Knights of Windsor in 1951 and being appointed Lieutenant Governor of the castle from 1964 until 1972. Hakewill-Smith died in Kingston upon Thames, Surrey, in 1986.

Today the Military Knights wear the uniform of an army officer on the unattached list. This consists of black trousers with a red stripe, a red double-breasted swallow-tailed coat, gold epaulettes and brushes, a bicorn with a plume, and a sword on a white baldric.

The Gold and Silver Stick-in-Waiting

The role of Gold Stick can be traced back to the reign of Charles II after spiritual itinerant and charlatan Titus Oakes fabricated a tale that the

Catholic Church authorities in England had approved the assassination of Charles in August 1678. Alarmed by Oates's claims, Charles established the role of personal bodyguard provided by a Life Guards captain. The new post would see the incumbent follow Charles wherever he walked during his waking hours, but not in the bed chamber. As a sign of his office, the captain was given 'an ebony staff or truncheon, with a gold head, engraved with His Majesty's cypher and crown'. With the awarding of this sign of the office, the holder became known as the Gold Stick-in-Waiting or simply Gold Stick.

Given the restrictions of freedom on the incumbent the first holder of the post, Charles's illegitimate son, James Scott, 1st Duke of Monmouth, 1st Duke of Buccleuch (1645-1685), soon delegated his task to the next senior officer in his guard troop. The new role would see the incumbent accompany the Duke of Monmouth everywhere, ready to relieve the Duke as the need arose. The new role came with an ebony staff complete with a silver head, giving rise to the name Silver Stick-in-Waiting or Silver Stick. With Oates eventually brought to heel in 1681 after his claims of a plot to kill Charles were proven false, Charles retained the tradition of the Stick-in-Waiting, if only to ensure his continued safety. Through the authority of the Gold Stick, the Silver Stick can take charge of all duties should the need arise.

Today the office of Gold Stick is jointly held by the Colonels of the Life Guards (LGs) and The Blues and Royals (RHG/D). Since the reign of Victoria these officers' duties have been mainly ceremonial, with incumbents attending State Ceremonial. On such occasions, the Gold Stick conveys the Sovereign's orders to the Household Cavalry. As Colonel of The Blues and Royals, Anne, Princess Royal (b.1950), performed the duty during the coronation of her brother Charles III in place of Lieutenant General Sir Edward Smyth Osborne (b.1964), then Colonel, Life Guards. The role of Silver Stick is fulfilled by the Commander of the Household Cavalry; at the time of the coronation of Charles III that was Colonel Mark Berry. When on duty the Silver Stick is accompanied by the Silver Stick Adjutant, who fulfils the role of principal aide. This role was fulfilled by Lieutenant Colonel Ralph Griffin (b. 1963) during Charles III's coronation.

Supporting State Ceremonial

In the past, the appointments of Gold Stick and Silver Stick have been carried out by individuals who have not served with the Household Cavalry. At the Coronation of George VI in 1937, Gold Stick was Field Marshal Sir William Birdwood. Birdwood was born on 13 September 1865 in Kirkee, India. After completing his education at Clifton College in Bristol, Birdwood secured a militia commission (reserve) in the 4th Battalion Royal Scots Fusiliers (RSF) in 1883, before training at the Royal Military College, Sandhurst.

As a result of the Russian War scare of 1885, Birdwood was commissioned early as a Lieutenant in the 12th (Prince of Wales) Royal Lancers on 9 May 1885, joining the regiment in India and subsequently transferring to the Bengal Staff Corps on 20 December 1886. A year later Birdwood was transferred to the 11th Bengal Lancers in 1887, seeing action on the North-West Frontier in 1891. He then became adjutant of the Viceroy's Bodyguard in 1893, and by 1896 was a Captain, and saw action in the Tirah Campaign, or Tirah expedition, on the Indian Frontier, which ran from September 1897 to April 1898.

Birdwood then served in the Second Anglo-Boer War (1899–1902) as the Brigade Major with a mounted brigade from 10 January 1900 followed by further appointments, including the Deputy-Assistant Adjutant General on the staff of Field Marshal Horatio Kitchener, 1st Earl Kitchener (1850–1915). Birdwood returned from South Africa a Lieutenant-Colonel and followed Kitchener, who had been despatched to India as Commander-in-Chief in November, serving as his assistant military secretary and interpreter.

Birdwood was appointed military secretary to Kitchener with the rank of Colonel in 1905, followed in 1906 by an appointment as aide-de-camp to Edward VII (1844-1910) on 14 February 1906. A command appointment followed in 1908, when Birdwood was given the Kohat Brigade on the North-West Frontier as part of the Northern Army. This was followed by promotion to temporary Brigadier-General mid-1909. Birdwood's Indian adventure continued, and he was promoted to Major-General in October 1911, becoming the Quartermaster General. This was followed by appointments to the Viceroy's Legislative Council in 1912 and then Secretary of the Indian Army Department in 1913.

Within months of the start of the First World War Birdwood was establishing an army corps consisting of Australian and New Zealand troops who were training in Egypt. Given his role, Birdwood was promoted to temporary Lieutenant-General in December 1914 and given command of the Australian and New Zealand Army Corps (ANZAC). Birdwood would lead the ANZACs at Gallipoli as part of the Mediterranean Expeditionary Force tasked with capturing the Gallipoli peninsula in 1915.

Not long after Birdwood took command of the Australian Imperial Force in May 1915, while still commanding Allied troops on the ground at Gallipoli and despite his lack of success in the Dardanelles, he was given command of the newly formed Dardanelles Army in 1915. Birdwood's main accomplishment came with the uninterrupted evacuation of the Allied forces in December 1915 and January 1916. He and his troops returned to Egypt in 1916 where they were reorganized into two corps: I ANZAC Corps and II ANZAC Corps, with Birdwood taking command of II ANZAC Corps. When I ANZAC Corps departed for France in early 1916, Birdwood took command. By late 1917 Birdwood was a full General, commanding the recently formed Australian Corps and being appointed Aide-de-Camp General to George V. The following year Birdwood was in command of the British Fifth Army leading it until the end of the war where it liberated the city of Tournai, Belgium, in November 1918.

In 1920, Birdwood became General Officer Commanding the Northern Army in India and was promoted to Field Marshal in 1925 and was appointed to the Executive Council of the Governor-General of India. In August 1925 he became Commander-in-Chief, India.

Upon retirement in 1930 Birdwood made an unsuccessful bid to become Governor-General of Australia; instead, he was made Captain of Deal Castle in 1934, which benefitted from residential accommodation. In retirement Birdwood remained busy, fulfilling the role of Honorary Colonel of the 12th Royal Lancers (1920–1951), the 6th Gurkha Rifles (1926–1951), and the 75th (Home Counties) (Cinque Ports) Heavy Anti-Aircraft Regiment, Royal Regiment of Artillery (1939–1951).

In January 1936 Birdwood attended the funeral of George V, followed by his role as Gold Stick for the coronation of George VI in May 1937.

On 25 January 1938, Birdwood was raised to the peerage in recognition of his military service as Baron Birdwood, of Anzac and of Totnes, Devon. He died at Hampton Court Palace, where he lived in grace-and-favour apartments, on 17 May 1951. He was buried with full military honours, at Twickenham Cemetery, where his grave is maintained by the Australian government.

Brigadier Andrew Parker-Bowles (b. 1937) was commissioned into the Royal Regiment of Horse Guards (The Blues) (RHG) in 1960. There he climbed the ranks and served in Northern Ireland and assisted Lord James Soames (1920–1987) during the establishment of the Republic of Zimbabwe, where he received a Queen's Commendation for Bravery. Between 1981 and 1983, Parker-Bowles served as commanding officer of the Household Cavalry Mounted Regiment (HCMR). From 1987 to 1990, he served as Colonel Commanding the Household Cavalry becoming Silver Stick to Elizabeth II. In 1990 he was promoted to Brigadier, and the following year became Director of the Royal Army Veterinary Corps (RAVC), where he served until his retirement in 1994. In 2003 Parker-Bowles sat as the subject for artist Lucian Freud's portrait *The Brigadier*.

In Scotland the roles of the Gold and Silver Stick-in-Waiting are performed by the Captain General of the Royal Company of Archers, known as the Captain General of the King's Body Guard. Richard Walter John Montagu Douglas Scott, 10th Duke of Buccleuch and 12th Duke of Queensberry (b. 1954) served as the Captain General of the King's Body Guard.

THE SOVEREIGN'S BODYGUARD

The Sovereign's Bodyguard consists of four ceremonial units that sit separately from the chain of command of the Household Division yet fulfil key ceremonial roles. Except for the Royal Company of Archers, and the King's Bodyguard for Scotland, their history predates any regiment of the Household Division. All three were originally formed as personal bodyguards so their roles naturally extend to protecting the sovereign during State Ceremonial.

It is interesting to note that despite being formed later than the Yeomen of the Guard, the Honourable Corps of Gentlemen at Arms is considered more senior on account of being 'gentlemen'. In the historical context of royal service, a Yeoman is considered a servant of the Crown, while a gentleman is the lowest rank of the landed gentry. They were considered beneath esquires, knights, and barons, all of whom were not considered landed aristocracy.

HIS MAJESTY'S BODY GUARD OF THE HONOURABLE CORPS OF GENTLEMEN AT ARMS

His Majesty's Body Guard of the Honourable Corps of Gentlemen at Arms, known as the Honourable Corps, was the first officially raised royal bodyguard in 1509 by Henry VIII. Established as a mounted Troop of Gentlemen, armed with lance and spear, the Gentlemen were referred to as cadets, on account of being the younger sons of nobles. The new bodyguard was soon in action, accompanying Henry VIII at the Battle of Guinegate (Battle of the Spurs), 16 August 1513. This was followed by a diplomatic mission that ended in the events of the Field of the Cloth of Gold, in June 1520. Six years later the Troop of Gentlemen exchanged lance and spear for battleaxes, some of which continue to be used today, taking on a new dismounted role. On 24 December 1539, the Troop of Gentlemen became known as the Honourable Band of Gentlemen Pensioners. They continued to protect the sovereign as the Crown moved from the Tudor to Stuart dynasties, taking to arms once more during the Wars of the Three Kingdoms (1639–1653). At the Battle of Edgehill, 23 October 1642, Gentleman Matthews saved the Prince of Wales, who would become Charles II, from a Parliamentarian blade. This ended the period that the Troop of Gentlemen acted as the sovereign's bodyguard in the field of battle. On 17 March 1834, the Honourable Band of Gentlemen Pensioners became known as the

Supporting State Ceremonial

Honourable Corps of Gentlemen at Arms or simply the Honourable Corps. Its role became largely ceremonial as the Household Cavalry and Foot Guards took full responsibility for the safety of the sovereign at all State Ceremonial events.

Today the Honourable Corps continues to accompany the sovereign on State and Royal Household duties, including the evening reception held by the sovereign for the diplomatic corps. The Honourable Corps consists of twenty-seven Gentlemen, who have previously served as field officers. The Gentlemen are led by five officers, four of whom have served as Gentlemen before appointment. The Captain, who is the most senior appointment, is the government chief whip in the House of Lords. The Captain is assisted by the Lieutenant who is the senior permanent officer. In turn, he is assisted by the standard bearer, Clerk of the Cheque and the harbinger. Gentlemen are under 55 years of age when they are admitted to the Honourable Corps and retire at seventy.

One notable former Captain of the Honourable Corps of Gentlemen-at-Arms was Hugh Fortescue, 5th Earl Fortescue (1888–1958). In 1907 Fortescue joined the Royal Scots Greys (RSG) after completing his commissioning course at the Royal Military College, Sandhurst. During the First World War, Fortescue served as a Regimental Officer for the RSG in France, where he was wounded twice, receiving the Military Cross in 1917. After the war Fortescue went to India, serving as an instructor at the Cavalry School at Sangor. He then served as Aide-de-Camp to Henry Rawlinson, 1st Baron Rawlinson Commander-in-Chief in India (1864–1925), who commanded the Fourth Army of the British Expeditionary Force (BEF) during the war.

On his return to England in 1922 Fortescue joined the recently formed Royal Devon Yeomanry (RDY), part of the 11th (Devon) Army Brigade, (Royal Field Artillery) RFA. He was promoted Lieutenant-Colonel in command in 1924 and Colonel in 1930 becoming Colonel Commandant of the Honourable Artillery Company (HAC) in 1935. At the outbreak of the Second World War, Fortescue joined the general staff, where he remained for the duration. His only son and heir apparent, Hugh Peter Fortescue Viscount Ebrington (b. 1920), was killed in action at the first Battle of El Alamein in 1942 while serving with his father's old regiment. In 1945, under Sir Winston Churchill (1874–1965), Fortescue served as the Captain of the Honourable Corps of Gentlemen-at-Arms.

With the Conservatives' return to power, Fortescue was again appointed Captain of the Honourable Corps of Gentlemen-at-Arms, 1951–1955, where he remained under Robert Anthony Eden, 1st Earl of Avon (1897-1977) until 1957. As well as his political and military interests, Fortescue served as president of the British Horse and Royal Agricultural Societies. Fortescue died on his seventieth birthday on 14 June 1958, four days after the death of his wife, Margaret, whose funeral he was unable to attend due to illness.

The uniform of the Honourable Corps is based on the 1840s officers' pattern uniform of the Dragoon Guards, featuring a red-skirted coatee, with garter blue velvet cuffs and facings embroidered with the Tudor royal badge of the Portcullis. White gloves or gauntlets are worn when on parade, alongside the swan feather-plumed helmets that are always worn when on duty, including in church. All members carry cavalry swords and officers wear gold aiguillettes and carry sticks of office that are presented by the sovereign upon appointment. The headquarters for the Honourable Corps remains at St. James's Palace, traditionally the closest location to the residence of the sovereign.

Colonel-in-Chief: His Majesty the King
March: *The Nearest Guard*

Battle Honours
1513   Guinegate
1520   Field of Cloth of Gold – Despite not being a battle it remains listed on the Corps Standard
1544   Siege of Boulogne
2009   Riband Honour 'The Nearest Guard 1509–2009'. Presented by Elizabeth II on the quincentenary of the Honourable Corps

King's Body Guard of the Yeomen of the Guard

By far the most visually recognizable and best known of the bodies that make up the Sovereign's Bodyguard are the Tudor-dressed Yeomen of the Guard, also known as 'Beefeaters'. Founded by Henry VII in 1485 as a dismounted bodyguard, after the Battle of Bosworth Field, it is the oldest British military corps. As Henry celebrated his victory, Sir Reginald Bray (c. 1440–1503) appeared with Richard III's gold diadem, found in a thorn bush close to where Richard had fallen. This moment was monumental, for it not only marked the death of the last English king in battle but the start of the use of the symbol of a hawthorn bush topped by a crown, that can be seen today on the Standard of the Body Guard.

Since 1485 the Yeomen of the Guard, currently numbering seventy-three officers and Yeomen, has provided unbroken service to the Crown; a legacy reinforced by the words of Henry VII who claimed the guard had been established for the 'holding of the dignity and grandeur of the English Crown in perpetuity, his successors, the Kings and Queens of England, for all time'.

From this moment the Yeomen of the Guard took on three distinct and important roles. They became the only royal bodyguard, they were the first permanent armed body in the country, and they became the 'Nearest Guard' giving them the right to stand closest to the sovereign on state occasions.

Within two years of their founding, the Yeomen of the Guard found themselves in combat, at the Battle of East Stoke in Nottinghamshire. Today the battlefield, cleaved in two by the Roman Fosse Way, is given over to crops that take advantage of the early-morning sun, and is interspersed with copses of oak and ash. On 16 June 1487 the area was little different when it played host to the final battle between the Tudor House of Lancaster and the Plantagenet House of York.

The battlefield was ideally sited for both parties: for Henry it left him close to Nottingham, some seventeen miles to the southwest, while the Yorkists could access the strategic market town of Newark-on-Trent, a mere four miles to the northeast. The main battlefield sat between the Fosse Way and the cliff side of the Trent Valley. At East Stoke, the cliff drops sharply leaving an exposed, almost sheer-sided, heavy red clay soil which forms a ravine, known as the Red Gutter leading to floodplains and the River Trent. Here the river surrounds the site on three sides, with the village of Fiskerton at its furthest point on the opposite bank of the river. To the east of the site is the village of Elston, home of the famous Darwin dynasty, but then a small hamlet through which ran a dumble, a small beck lined mostly by willows, a geographic feature peculiar to Nottinghamshire.

For the Yorkists, this was an opportunity to unseat Henry and replace him with a 10-year-old pretender, Lambert Simnel (c. 1477–1534). The Yorkists, led by John de la Pole Earl of Lincoln (c. 1460–1487) had crowned Simnel Edward VI at a service in Dublin on 24 May. Lincoln, Richard III's nephew, who had been declared heir apparent by the late king, saw an opportunity to use the child as a political pawn, especially as the boy's acumen had been declared safe by a priest.

The emboldened Lincoln left England for Europe in March 1487 to visit his aunt, the Dowager Margaret Duchess of Burgundy (1446–1503) at the Burgundian Court of Mechelen (Malines). Margaret was a keen supporter of Lincoln's cause, giving him financial aid and funding 2,000 German and Swiss mercenaries led by German mercenary Martin Schwartz (d. 1487), who was described as an able yet somewhat arrogant commander. While in Europe, Lincoln gathered support from several English Lords and military figures sympathetic to his cause including Francis Lovell, 9th Baron Lovell, 6th Baron Holand (1459–1487), and Thomas David, a Captain of the English garrison at Calais.

By late spring the Yorkists had gathered themselves and their forces, arriving in Ireland in early May, subsequently crowning Simnel. Supported by local nobles including Sir Thomas FitzGerald of Laccagh (c. 1458–1487), Lincoln recruited 4,500 Irish mercenaries, mostly Kerns, who fulfilled a light infantry role, adding them to his German and Swiss mercenaries. A month later, on 4 June, Lincoln arrived in England where he picked up more support from nobles loyal to his cause, and another 8,000 soldiers.

The first clash of arms occurred at Tadcaster, Yorkshire, with the destruction of a Lancastrian camp on 10 June. From there Lincoln pressed southward outmanoeuvring Henry's northern army before ordering a diversionary attack on Bootham Bar, York, on 12 June. This covered Lincoln's continued march south, increasingly engaging with Lancastrian cavalry. These skirmishes, while doing little harm, slowed his advance enough for the Lancastrian main force to arrive and assemble in Nottingham. Reinforced from across England and Wales, Henry was able to field a stronger, better-equipped and better-led army; on 15 June he moved towards Newark-on-Trent after hearing news that Lincoln had forced a crossing of the chest-deep River Trent at various points around Fiskerton.

By the morning of 16 June, the Yorkists had moved to a point known as Rampire Hill, just south of East Stoke village, giving Lincoln's force a commanding position on the forward slope. Here his left flank was parallel to the Trent and the right flank, crossing the Fosse Way, nudged the parish boundary of Elston. Lincoln now placed his pistol-armed German and Swiss mercenaries and the Irish Kerns, some 8,000 men, in two blocks facing Henry.

The Lancastrian force, some 12,000 strong, was split into three. The vanguard, containing some 6,000 men, was led by John de Vere, 13th Earl of Oxford (1442–1513), an experienced commander. Henry trusted Oxford implicitly and Oxford arranged his forces accordingly, placing cavalry on either side of his main force, all facing south with the crossroads of East Stoke, with its small leper colony, behind him. No matter how experienced he and his men were, Oxford still faced the prospect of advancing uphill.

He wasted no time, and ordered his archers to fire into the Yorkist ranks at around 9:00 am. The ensuing barrage slammed into the Yorkists, the lightly armoured Kerns were killed en masse and Schwartz's mercenaries too far away to use their firearms effectively. The Yorkists, perhaps sensing they were in a killing ground, moved forward to attack Oxford's main force, in the hope of breaking it. With the surviving mercenaries on their side, it looked as though the predominantly infantry-based Yorkist force would break Oxford's force.

For almost three hours the two sides slashed, gouged, shot and struck one another, the red Trent clay became slick as the bloodiest battle in English history raged upon it. Meanwhile, the two Lancastrian flanking 'battles' remained on the edge of the mêlée as Henry, accompanied by his Yeoman Guard considered the situation. Oxford's vanguard was continuously fed with replacements directed by Henry's uncle Jasper Tudor (1431–1495). Despite the close-combat nature of the engagement, the archers continued to pour volley after volley into the Yorkist mass, sapping its strength as much as the sword and halberd, in what had become an infantry battle.

Eventually, the tide of battle began to turn, and Oxford was able to wheel his forces to push the Yorkists on the soft floodplain that lay between East Stoke and the River Trent. The retreating Yorkists were now split, with most falling down the cliff face, desperate to escape across the Trent, now almost a mile away in places. The Lancastrians fell like wild dogs upon the retreating Yorkists, especially around the Red Gutter, showing little mercy to the retreating Yorkists, later stripping and hanging 300 Irish prisoners. Soon stories of the river turning red from spilt blood were making their way from the battlefield, shared, no doubt by survivors for pity, or by victors to prevent further rebellion. Among the many dead were Lincoln, Fitzgerald and Schwartz.

Henry was again victorious, and the Yorkist plot was put to bed. He remained the shrewd politician and rather than wreak an awful vengeance in blood from rebellious nobles, he hit them where it hurt most, their purses and pride. Simnel was spared punishment, Henry fully aware of the child's manipulation by the Yorkists. After working in the royal kitchens as a spit turner Simnel would become an austringer. The Yeomen left the field, no doubt some having taken part in the mêlée, with their first battle honour.

The Yeomen continued to fulfil a range of tasks in the Royal Household, and by the time of Henry VIII, who introduced the now-familiar dress, over 600 Yeomen were serving the Royal Household. Henry established the Gentleman Spears in 1509 to further his protection, a force made up of cadets from noble families, whose rank elevated them in social status over the Yeomen. It also had the effect of usurping the Yeomen from their position as the Nearest Guards, despite the Yeomen belonging to an experienced military organization. Today the Gentleman Spears are known as the Honourable Corps of Gentlemen at Arms and after an intervention by Queen Victoria, the matter of who would be the Nearest Guard was settled. The Yeomen would act as the de facto Guards, supporting the Honourable Corps of Gentlemen at Arms at State Ceremonial.

Regardless of Henry's establishment of the Gentleman Spears, the Yeomen of the Guard remained an organization of great renown, and during the Tudor reign it was not uncommon for members to buy their appointments. Not all appointments were bought, and the role of Captain attracted famous names of the Tudor period, including that of Sir Walter Raleigh (1552–1618). Raleigh's appointment in 1586 by Elizabeth I was made in part to keep him by her side. However, Raleigh's lascivious behaviour would lead to his imprisonment in the Tower not long after for an affair with a maid-in-waiting. His subsequent release would see Raleigh fall out of favour. Following several adventures overseas he was reinstalled as Captain once more in 1597. In 1603, following Elizabeth's death Raleigh was once again interned in the Tower, accused of an attempt to instal a pretender on James I's throne. Raleigh was not released until 1616, when ordered by James to search for gold. Raleigh's failure to find gold saw him sent to the Tower for a third and final time, and he was executed on 19 October 1618.

On James's enthronement the Yeomen of the Guard was not as large as it had been some seventy-five years before. Elizabeth had made huge cuts to the 600-plus Yeomen that served her father and James made further refinements and banned the purchase of commissions and positions, with men recruited on merit alone. In 1605 Yeomen, alerted by William Parker, 4th Baron Monteagle (1575–1622) who'd received a warning letter, discovered Guy Fawkes (1570–1606), in the early hours of 5 November during a search under the old House of Lords. Fawkes was found with thirty-six barrels of poorly hidden explosive, his aim to assassinate James. This event led not only to the establishment of Bonfire Night, held every 5 November, but also to the instigation of The Search, a tradition that has been carried out by the Yeomen of the Guard on the eve of every State Opening of Parliament since.

Following the defeat of Charles I after the Wars of the Three Kingdoms, the Yeomen of the Guard was exiled with Charles II. The establishment of the Standing Army in the post-Restoration monarchy saw changes to the introduction of the Troops of the Royal Guards, who would later became the Life Guards. They replaced the Gentleman Spears, then known as the Gentleman Pensioners and Yeomen of the Guard as mounted escorts.

Despite these changes the Yeomen of the Guard were still employed in being the Nearest Guard to the Sovereign and during the reign of William III they prevented four assassinations. Despite their effectiveness the changes continued, and in 1834 the Metropolitan Police took on most of the responsibilities for the protection of the Royal Household. Despite this the Yeomen continued to serve the Crown and during the 1848 Chartist Riots they were summoned to protect the Royal Palaces with muskets and bayonets.

By the mid-nineteenth century the role of the Yeomen of the Guard had become refined with the purchase of commissions once again abolished, and the instigation of separate uniforms for officers and Yeomen. From this period the Yeomen of the Guard began to refine their duties, splitting them between State Ceremonial such as Coronations and the twice-yearly State Visits, held every spring and autumn. Other duties include escorting the sovereign at the Maundy Service and during investitures.

The Yeomen of the Guard was initially led by three officers including a Captain, who would also undertake the more delicate diplomatic missions on behalf of the sovereign. He was assisted by a Lieutenant, a dedicated standard bearer and the Clerk of the Cheque, who fulfilled the adjutant's role and is identified by a silver topped ebony cane. These three posts are followed by the Ensign, traditionally charged with carrying the standard and the Exons, the most junior of the officers of the Yeomen of the Guard. The Yeomen of the Guard draws officers and Yeomen from the three Great British military services, and is organized into four divisions, each led by a Sergeant Major. Candidates must have completed at least 22 years of service, be aged between 42 and 55, and have attained the rank of Sergeant or Petty Officer. Potential Yeomen must also have been awarded the Long Service and Good Conduct Medal. All Yeomen retire at 70 years of age. Finally, there were the Yeoman Ushers, a role that is now known as the Yeoman Usher of the Black Rod. This is a Crown-appointed role and the incumbent acts as the deputy to the Lady or Gentleman Usher of the Black Rod. Black Rod also attends to the Lord Speaker in carrying the mace in and out of the House of Lords chamber.

The uniform of the Yeomen of the Guard has changed several times over the past 500 years. The original flamboyant Tudor uniform introduced by Henry VIII is now refined to include ruffs and the familiar round velvet bonnet. While the Yeoman's uniform features many of the original aspects of the Tudor design, the officers owe its appearance more to recent tastes. As officers are former military officers their uniform reflects the martial aspect of their past, a factor William IV was keen to promote.

The current officer's uniform bears a striking resemblance to the uniform of the Foot Guards of the 1830s, but the bearskin is replaced by a bicorn topped with feathers. The officers also carry a sword along with their silver-topped ebony wand of office which is personally presented to them by the sovereign upon their appointment. Should the officer retire or be promoted their wand is returned or a new one is issued. Sergeant Majors, one per division, are also issued with an ebony wand of office

The Yeoman's uniform now features a scarlet doublet with blue velvet over gold lace trim, which is accompanied by scarlet breeches and scarlet merino stockings or tights. Monk shoes, featuring a prominent red, white and blue rosette are also worn. A lined Inverness blue cloak is also issued, but only worn in inclement weather and at Royal funerals.

Unlike Yeomen Warders, all Yeomen of The Guard carry a sword, with a Baldric passing over their *left* shoulder to support the weight of the sword on their belt. The Yeomen are often seen carrying the partisan polearm. This fearsome-looking weapon is topped with a steel blade featuring a blue and gilt finish, upon which is laid the Royal Arms and Royal Cypher and Crown. The head is fitted into a long gilt socket, below which is a large yellow and crimson tassel. The blade is attached to a 185-cm (6ft 2-in) lance which is fitted with a brass shoe. The Yeomen of the Guard parade as the Sovereign's Bodyguard at most State Ceremonial occasions.

Colonel-in-chief: His Majesty the King
Motto: *Dieu et mon droit (God and my right)*
March: *Men of Harlech*

Battle Honours
1487   Field of Stoke
1492   Boulogne
1497   Blackheath
1513   Tournai*
1544   Boulogne*
1690   Boyne
1743   Dettingen

* These honours are displayed on the Corps Standard

Yeomen Warders of His Majesty's Royal Palace and Fortress the Tower of London, and Members of the Sovereign's Bodyguard of the Yeoman Guard Extraordinary

The history of the Yeomen Warders of His Majesty's Royal Palace and Fortress the Tower of London, and Members of the Sovereign's Bodyguard of the Yeoman Guard Extraordinary, or Yeomen Warders, can be traced back to 1078. Established to guard over state prisoners, the role has developed, seeing many changes, including the appointment in 2007 of the first woman warden, Moira Cameron (b. 1964).

Yeomen are often referred to as Beefeaters, a nickname that may be seen as well meaning but is far from highly regarded by either group. Its

Supporting State Ceremonial

roots are subject to myth and uncertainty. One possible origin lies in the French word *buffetiers*, or buffet servers; however, as with all things the simplest answer is often the most likely. In recounting a trip to England Cosimo III de' Medici (1642–1723) recalled seeing the Yeomen of the Guard consume a 'reasonable portion [of beef, that] is allowed daily by Court' during his state visit in 1669. This was true at the time and remained so almost 150 years later when ten kilograms a day was shared among the thirty Yeomen on duty as St James's Palace. This ration was supplemented by eight kilograms of mutton and seven kilograms of veal. All of which was washed down by no less than 168 litres of beer.

When gathered for specific occasions, such as royal birthdays, where the entire guard, eighty-one strong, would turn out, the food rations swelled. Yeomen were treated to ninety-eight kilograms of meat and 144 loaves. To help consume this large amount of food the Yeomen were issued with 473 litres of beer and 273 litres of wine. Further to these impressive rations the Yeomen were given royal venison twice a year and three plum puddings every Sunday. The Yeomen were also given five geese a year. The benevolence ended in 1813 and Yeomen were given 3s 9d a day for food in lieu.

The final possibility behind the origins of the nickname lies in the occasional impish behaviour of a younger Henry VIII, who disguised himself as a Yeoman to visit Reading Abbey, incognito. The Abbot, possibly Thomas Worcester, invited the Yeoman in and he was fed a substantial meal, which featured a large joint of beef. The Abbot, who observed the king's feasting, raised a glass to his guest proclaiming he was unable to partake due to a sickly stomach, adding he wished he had 'an [sic] hundred pounds if I could eat as heartily of beef as you'.

A few weeks after the incognito visit, the Abbot was arrested and placed in the Tower, without reason. There he was fed nothing but the customary diet of bread and water, for several weeks. One day he was presented with a large joint of beef, which he ate with vim and vigour. Midway through his feast Henry appeared, demanding his £100 for curing the Abbot's loss of appetite. True to his word, the grateful Abbot paid the £100, a not inconsiderable amount at the time, around £72,000 in today's prices, and was promptly released.

The Abbot clearly took his imprisonment in good spirits, for he would regale the story to any Yeomen of the Guard upon seeing them, doing so that often it became accepted that all Yeomen were Beefeaters. Allied to numerous accounts of the Yeomen's love of beef from the seventeenth century onwards this is most probably the likely story behind their famous nickname.

Today the role of the Yeomen Wardens in any State Ceremonial event is restricted to attending coronations, where they form a Guard of Honour inside the Annex of Westminster. More recently, the Yeomen Wardens have been involved in guarding the casket of Elizabeth II at her Lying in State in Westminster Hall. On both occasions the Yeomen Wardens are attired in their traditional Tudor style state dress, which is like that worn by the Yeomen Guard with the exception that ruffs are worn at all times and the red and gold baldric is omitted.

Colonel-in-chief: His Majesty the King
Motto: *Dieu et mon droit (God and my right)*

THE ROYAL COMPANY OF ARCHERS, THE KING'S BODYGUARD FOR SCOTLAND

Whilst rarely seen during State Ceremonial, the Royal Company of Archers, known as the Royal Company was founded in 1676 as the Edinburgh Archers, then a private members' club. Today they play a key role during certain key State Ceremonial events. Most recently in 2022 when the Royal Company provided a Guard of Vigil for Elizabeth II's lying in state.

The first recordings of the use of the long bow were made in the twelfth century, during the reign of William I of Scotland (c.1142–1214). For those men without a horse practice was mandatory, and led to several unpopular enforcement laws, including the banning of football and golf by James II of Scotland (1430–1460), to ensure archery was practised. The Royal Company was founded in 1676 as the Edinburgh Archers, following

Supporting State Ceremonial

a long tradition of the use of archery, and sought to reignite interest in the art, considered by the founders to be a useful recreation. Shortly after founding there followed a turbulent history of Scottish and English history, which would see the Protestant William III take the throne from the Catholic James II in 1688. The subsequent return of a Stuart monarch, Queen Anne, in 1702 saw the archers petition Her Majesty for a Royal Charter 'to establish the liberty and prestige of the Company once and for all'. This was granted in 1704, and the newly named The Royal Company of Archers was given public access for practices in public places legally allotted for the shooting of arrows. A reddendo, a unique Scottish legal clause which specifies the services to be rendered by a vassal, in this case The Royal Company to his superior, formed part of the Royal Charter. This reddendo stipulated The Royal Company could be called upon to render yearly to Her Majesty and her successors, if so requested, 'one pair of barbed arrows'. The next century, Jacobite Rebellion aside, was one of steady growth and establishment.

When George IV visited Edinburgh in 1822, the Royal Company offered to act as the official bodyguard for the Sovereign while he and his successors were in Scotland. George, a keen archer agreed to this request. George V's visit in 1911 saw The Royal Company develop its ceremonial escort duties.

Today the Royal Company of Archers, known as The Royal Company, function as the Sovereign's 'Body Guard in Scotland'. In this instance it performs its duties at the request of the monarch at any State Ceremonial and key event taking place in Scotland, including the annual Royal Garden Party at the Palace of Holyroodhouse. Other duties supported by The Royal Company include investitures, and the presentation of new colours for Scottish regiments which are presented at a parade at Holyrood Park. Another duty is the attendance outside St Giles' Cathedral, Edinburgh, at the service of installation of the Knights of the Most Ancient and Most Noble Order of the Thistle, the greatest order of chivalry in Scotland. Subsequent coronations at Westminster Abbey will witness the presence of the Royal Company's Captain General in his role as Gold Stick for Scotland.

Walter Montagu Douglas Scott, 5th Duke of Buccleuch, 7th Duke of Queensberry (1806–1884) served as Captain General from 1838 to 1884. Three years later in 1822 George IV stayed at Montagu Douglas Scott's during the first visit of a reigning Hanoverian monarch to Scotland. The visit would cement Montagu Douglas Scott's place in royal circles and he would be invited to the coronations of William IV and Queen Victoria, with the Duke acting as Gold Stick for Scotland during Queen Victoria's coronation on 28 June 1838. Queen Victoria, like her predecessor, would later visit the Montagu Douglas Scotts.

After studying at St John's College, Cambridge Montagu Douglas Scott returned to Scotland to manage the family estate in 1827, and became involved in politics, representing the Conservatives. The following year he was appointed Lord Lieutenant of Midlothian (Edinburgh), a post he held until his death in 1884.

Montagu Douglas Scott was appointed a Knight of the Garter in 1835 and a Privy Counsellor in 1842, serving as Lord Privy Seal from 1842 to 1846. The beginning of 1842 also saw the start of his involvement with the militia when he was appointed Colonel of the Edinburgh Militia, which had been raised in 1798 by his grandfather Henry Scott, 3rd Duke of Buccleuch and 5th Duke of Queensberry (1746–1812), who had held the title of Captain General from 1778 to 1812.

Montagu Douglas Scott's political career continued to grow and he was appointed Lord President of the Council from January to July 1846 in Sir Robert Peel, 2nd Baronet's (1788–1850) government. While in government Montagu Douglas Scott reluctantly supported Peel's decision to repeal the Corn Laws, which had imposed tariffs on imported corn and other foodstuffs between 1815 and 1846.

With the ending of Peel's political career Montagu Douglas Scott directed his energies elsewhere joining the Canterbury Association two years later. The Canterbury Association was formed to establish a colony in New Zealand and part of that plan was to build a town called Buccleuch, in his honour, near Alford Forest in the Ashburton District, Canterbury, New Zealand, but aside from the name and location the project failed to materialize.

Supporting State Ceremonial

Montagu Douglas Scott had maintained his association with the Edinburgh Militia which became the Queen's Edinburgh Light Infantry Militia in 1852. The new name was a gift after the regiment had lined the streets from Edinburgh railway station to Holyrood Palace when Queen Victoria visited Edinburgh on her way to Balmoral Castle. In March 1857 Montagu Douglas Scott was appointed an aide-de-camp to Queen Victoria, a post he held until he resigned his command in May 1879. Subsequently he was appointed the first Honorary Colonel of the Queen's Edinburgh Light Infantry Militia.

In 1879 the Historical Manuscripts Commission (HMC), which had been founded a decade earlier to document the location of records and papers in private hands, discovered a box amongst the Duke of Buccleuch's papers at Dalkeith. Within the box was a contract proving Charles II had married Lucy Walter (1630–1658), which meant that Montagu Douglas Scott was the rightful king of the United Kingdom, being the eldest agnatic descendant of James Scott, 1st Duke of Monmouth. On being shown the deed, Montagu Douglas Scott threw it on the nearest fire, remarking, 'That might cause a lot of trouble.'

Montagu Douglas Scott died on 16 April 1884, aged 77, and was buried in the family crypt of the Buccleuch Memorial Chapel in St. Mary's Episcopal Church, Dalkeith, Midlothian. Today a statue of Montagu Douglas Scott can be found on the Parliament Square in Edinburgh, Scotland.

Members of the Royal Company must be Scots or have strong Scottish connections, with membership by election. The structure of the organization is divided between officers and members. The officer corps is led by a Captain General, who in turn is assisted by four Captains, four Lieutenants, four Ensigns and twelve Brigadiers, who are part of 520-strong Royal Company. When on parade the band is supported by their band of pipes and drums.

Members of the Royal Company of Archers wear a dark green tunic with black facings, sash and belt. This is worn with dark green overalls featuring a black and crimson seam stripe. Archers also wear a Balmoral bonnet which sports the Royal Company of Archers badge behind which is fixed an eagle feather.

Apart from its role as the Sovereign's Bodyguard, the Royal Company of Archers still functions as an archery club with members vying for any of the thirteen annual prizes available, including the Musselburgh Arrow. This challenge, which was first started in 1603, making the competition the oldest archery competition, seeing The Royal Company archers compete for the Musselburgh Silver Arrow, awarded to the best shot of the event.

Motto: *Dal gloria vires, Nemo me impune lacessit, Dulce pro patria periculum*
March: *Archers March*

Chapter Three
Royal Service

'I declare before you all that my whole life whether it be long or short shall be devoted to your service.'

Elizabeth II

The age of the chivalry saw many changes in how fighting was conducted on the battlefield, especially by knights. Whilst some of the behaviours would be scoffed at in contemporary western society, they were very much of their time. For example, should a knight fall from his mount, as they occasionally did in the heat of battle, or were disarmed, to maintain personal honour they could only surrender to a social equal, that is another knight. If this occurred, the captured knight could expect to be hosted by his captor whilst a suitable ransom was raised by his family. There were the occasional exceptions, with Welsh archers making a name for themselves by killing fallen knights and robbing the corpses.

Knights, as members of an Order of Chivalry were able to ask for, and receive hospitality, even in an adversary's country, given they were operating in a feudal society. The soldiery were below knights socially so were often killed out of hand as prisoners, or on occasion killed by the knights of their own side, especially if their performance was believed to be below par. The peasants' lot on the battlefield was far from a happy one either way, and more than likely influenced the Welsh archers' behaviour and world views. Interestingly the Saracens gained a reputation of being better hosts to knightly captives than their crusader rivals. Other aspects of the codes allowed for pauses in fighting for removal of the dead and wounded, and occasional safe passage for third parties caught up in the fighting, though this was rare. The chivalrous codes of conduct developed over time and their nearest expressions are the treaties and protocols that can be found in the Geneva Conventions.

The age of chivalry also gave rise to a great many military and social developments, including the art of heraldry. This was added to the mystique that already surrounded the process of becoming a knight which involved sacred life guiding oaths, which ensured loyalty, courage and self-sacrifice. Perhaps it was the sombre tone of these oaths that led many adherents to believe they were above their fellows.

By the eleventh century heraldry had become a remarkably complex art, and despite its ability to identify one as a noble within certain social circles, it was not seen on the battlefield. This inevitably caused issues, and with armour becoming more sophisticated it became increasingly difficult to tell friend from foe. In July 1087 an event occurred that would change this situation during a clash between William the Conqueror and his son Robert II of Normandy (1051–1134). The pair had a volatile relationship at best, which led to Robert rebelling against his father. During one of the skirmishes the two met on the field, with the result of William being unseated from his mount. Robert, now positioned himself to deliver the coup de grace, heard the voice of the fallen knight calling for aid and realized it was his father. This moment spurred both parties to adopt identifying symbols on their shields, a practice which soon proliferated.

Soon the custom had extended to a knight's retinue, who adopted key elements or whole sections of their leader's arms, who had also adopted a crest to indicate rank. An example of this was the House of Plantagenet (1154–1485) that adopted a sprig of broom, or *planta genista*. Not only did this help identify the living, it also made the herald's role of identifying the dead far easier. By now heralds were able to remember numerous coats of arms, and many found themselves in the employ of royalty and senior noblemen, their service becoming an invaluable asset. The term herald itself, in this instance, meant 'strength of an army'.

Royal heralds in particular were used by newly elevated knights to see if their chosen coat of arms was available and designs became more complex as noble families married. The process was also driven by the feudal social systems of whether the bearer was a 'gentle' man, who held tenure to land, or a serf, who included traders. If one was lucky enough to have a few acres in deepest Suffolk, then you were considered a 'gentleman' and the laws of chivalry applied to you. Good manners and a decent bearing wouldn't grant you the same rights if you were a wool trader in Herefordshire. Feudalism was literally everything. This of course led to some unscrupulous social climbing and claims of noble heritage taking place. Despite the best efforts of the early heralds, a cottage industry producing false coats of arms, that shrewdly avoided all reference to the crown, was soon established.

THE COLLEGE OF ARMS

> Henry V: *Well then I know thee: what shall I know of thee?*
> Montjoy (French herald): *My master's mind.*
> *Henry V*, William Shakespeare

The College of Arms is a part of the Royal Household with members accompanying the monarch as heralds on various state occasions. The organization and planning of all State Ceremonial falls within the privilege of the Earl Marshal, the College's chief. This results in the heralds having roles to perform at every significant royal ceremony. However, and for the wearer, thankfully, the herald's full dress uniforms are only worn twice a year at the State Opening of Parliament and Garter Service held at Windsor Castle.

On State Ceremonials, the ordinary and extraordinary officers lead the Royal Procession, preceding the Sovereign and other Great Officers of State. In the occasion of the State Opening of Parliament the heralds accompany and remain with the monarch during the speech, before leaving with the monarch and making their way to the bounds of the Palace. Garter Service or Garter Day is held every June on the Monday of Royal Ascot week with the annual service taking place at St. George's Chapel, Windsor Castle.

On this day new Companions of the Order of the Garter are personally invested with their insignia at the throne Room of Windsor Castle by the Sovereign. After lunch the members proceed to St. George's Chapel led by members of the College of Arms in their tabards, the Military Knights of Windsor and contingents of the Sovereign's Bodyguard. This ceremony is especially significant for the Garter King of Arms, the senior officer of the College, who is an officer of the Order.

The College is also responsible for organizing some of the most important and complex ceremonies concerning the life of the monarch. After the death of a sovereign the Accession Council assembles at St. James's Palace to make a formal proclamation of the accession of the next sovereign. The traditional method of publishing the council's proclamation recognizing the new monarch remains unchanged, and it continues to be read out by various members of the College assigned by the Earl Marshal, who receives the text of the proclamation from the council in person. The proclamation is then read throughout London, with the first reading made from Proclamation Gallery by the Garter King of Arms which overlooks Friary Court at St. James's Palace, to announce the new monarch.

This is followed by a further reading with a ceremony held at the Temple Bar, the principal ceremonial entrance to the boundary between the City of London and the City of Westminster. From there a detachment of heralds, accompanied by troopers of the Royal Horse Guards, formally demand admission to the precinct of the City of London from the City Marshall and City Remembrancer. The boundary indicated by a silken rope is removed and the detachment marches to meet the Lord Mayor and City Sheriffs, where the proclamation is read. Other readings by members of the College take place at the corner of Chancery Lane, and at the Royal Exchange, which was originally built as a centre of commerce for the City of London. Today the Royal Exchange is home to a Fortnum & Mason department store.

At State Funerals, the heralds lead the Royal Procession as it enters the place of worship. Historically during the procession of Royal Funerals (usually of the sovereign) the heralds would carry a piece of armour, including helmet, spurs and gauntlets, representing the various marks of chivalry. During a Royal Funeral a herald will read the full list of the styles and titles of the deceased.

For the Coronation Ceremony, members of the College form part of the Royal Procession as it enters Westminster Abbey. The members of the College walk in the procession in virtue of them being His Majesty's 'Kings, Heralds and Pursuivants of Arms of England'. They are accompanied by Scottish contemporaries, the Lord Lyon, and the Heralds and Pursuivants of Arms of the Lyon Court.

For the Coronation Procession the Garter King of Arms is usually placed next to the Lord Great Chamberlain and his role in the Coronation is to guide, but not perform the ceremony. The Coronation is the only ceremony that the Kings of Arms are allowed to wear their distinctive crowns, making them the only group of individuals, apart from the King and Queen, authorized to do so.

OFFICER OF ARMS

An Officer of Arms, also known as a herald, has been a Crown appointment since 1484. They assist in the arrangement of State Ceremonial, as well as controlling and initiating armorial matters. The latter role has its roots in the early medieval period where the proclamation and organization of tournaments was the herald's primary function. Once the tournament had begun the herald was responsible for the marshalling and introductions of contestants, as well as score keeping; just think the excitable Geoffrey Chaucer in the 2001 film, *A Knight's Tale*.

The knights taking part in tournaments were recognized by the coats of arms on their shields as well as their helmet crests. This led to heralds rapidly acquiring an expert knowledge of the arms purposes, and whom they belonged to, leading to the responsibility of recording, and then later, controlling their use by bearers such as knights. Given coats of arms were also hereditary, heralds soon became experts in genealogy.

Despite the slow decline of the use of arms during jousting, civilian, social and antiquarian uses of heraldry grew, ensuring heralds kept their unique skills and knowledge. Heralds would also act as messengers, sent by monarchs or noblemen, in a role that saw them acting as the predecessors to that of the modern diplomat, although their messages were often far from diplomatic with heralds often sent to convey challenges between adversaries.

During battles the heralds of differing sides would often watch the proceedings together from a nearby vantage point. One such observation took place at the Battle of Agincourt (1415) where both heralds agreed that the English were the victors, with the French herald Montjoie proclaiming Henry V the victor. Such an act gave Henry the right to name the battle, which in this case was named after the local Château de Azincourt, now long since disappeared.

In the medieval period, heralds served both the monarch and certain noblemen, with heralds being a key part of the Royal Household from as early as the twelfth century. From 1420 the Royal Heralds began to use a common seal, and in 1484 they were granted a charter of incorporation by Richard III. At the same time as their incorporation, they were gifted a house in Coldharbour in Upper Thames Street, London, to store their records. Henry VII confiscated Coldharbour from the heralds and the property was given to his mother Lady Margaret Beaufort (1443–1509), as her London home.

A new charter was awarded to the Royal Heralds by Queen Mary in 1555, together with the site of the present College of Arms on which then stood Derby Place. The original building was lost to the Great Fire of London in 1666, and the building of the present College was started in 1670 by Francis Sandford, Rouge Dragon Pursuivant, and Morris Emmett, the King's bricklayer.

Queen Mary's charter laid the way for the organization of heralds in England. This granted the authority of the thirteen Officers of Arms in Ordinary, to form a corporation made up of the Kings, Heralds and Pursuivants of Arms (College of Arms). Officers of Arms whose appointments are of a permanent nature are referred to as Officers of Arms in Ordinary. The Officers of Arms in Ordinary form the College of Arms and as members of the Royal Household receive a nominal salary.

Royal Service

Those individuals who are given temporary or occasional appointments are referred to as Officers of Arms Extraordinary.

When attending ceremonial events all heralds wear a heavily decorated surcoat, also known as a tabard, an item of clothing long associated with heralds, which features the Royal Arms of the Royal Household. They also carry a wand indicating their status while English and Scottish Kings of Arms wear a distinctive coronet of office, used for ceremonial purposes such as at coronations. The Officers of Arms consist of three ranks: Kings of Arms, Heralds of Arms, and Pursuivants of Arms.

The King of Arms is the senior rank of an Officer of Arms holding the authority to grant armorial bearings and occasionally certify genealogies and noble titles. Today the English Kings of Arms consist of the Garter Principal King of Arms, known as Garter, who acts as the senior of the three English Kings of Arms, whose office was established in 1415 by Henry V.

Sir Alexander Colin Cole (1922–2001) fulfilled the role of Garter Principal King of Arms from 1978 until his retirement in 1992. After schooling at Dulwich College, London, Cole left London for Cambridge, then Oxford, where he read law. The Second World War interrupted his studies and Cole joined the Coldstream Guards, reaching the rank of Captain and marrying in 1944. After the war Cole returned to his studies and in 1949 was called to the bar at The Honourable Society of the Inner Temple, one of the four Inns of Court, allowing him to practise law. Around this time his interest in becoming an Officer of Arms was kindled, and in 1952 Cole was Fitzalan Pursuivant Extraordinary at the Coronation of Elizabeth II. After the coronation Cole moved from law to the College of Arms, after the 1954 revival of the High Court of Chivalry. The High Court was revived to deal with the matter of the Manchester Corporation versus Manchester Palace of Varieties for wrongfully displaying the city's coat of arms. Cole found himself defending the Palace of Varieties, losing the case.

After a short term as Fitzalan Pursuivant Extraordinary, Cole became a full member of the College of Arms, fulfilling the role as an Officer in Ordinary as Portcullis Pursuivant of Arms in Ordinary in 1957.

He remained in this post for nine years until his appointment as the Windsor Herald of Arms in Ordinary in 1966. The following year Cole also served as the college's registrar and librarian, roles he held until 1974. Four years later, in 1978, Cole was appointed Garter Principal King of Arms, a position he held until 1992. As Garter, Cole modernized the rules surrounding who could become an Officer of the College, which required appointees to be university graduates as well as having served a heraldic apprenticeship. Cole removed these rules opening the door to a more inclusive recruitment and appointment process. As Garter, Cole continued to change and challenge the status quo, seeking to make the College a desirable establishment to aspire to joining and belong as a herald. To help boost the College's public image Cole recognized the importance of the physical and oversaw substantial restoration work at the fabric of the College building at Victoria Street, London.

Whilst he made a great many changes, many of which were broadly welcomed, he faced criticism for not preventing the establishment of the Canadian Heraldic Authority (CHA) which received its letters patent in 1988. As a result of its establishment the CHA became the first Commonwealth realm outside the United Kingdom to have its own heraldic authority.

As well as Garter Principal King of Arms Cole was a member of the Court of Common Council, the primary decision-making body of the City of London Corporation from 1964. Cole would become Sheriff in 1977 but had to turn down the opportunity to take the post of Lord Mayor of London as the roles of this appointment would have clashed with those Cole fulfilled as Garter.

The Garter Principal King of Arms is followed by the Clarenceux King of Arms, who represents the southern part of England, southward from the River Trent that runs from Staffordshire to the Humber Estuary, since the sixteenth century. As such the Clarenceux King of Arms is the senior of the two provincial kings. The junior of the two provincial Kings is the Norroy and Ulster King of Arms. This is a combined post which covers the six counties of Northern Ireland as well as counties north of the Trent. Formed by the merging of the Ulster King of Arms that had been vacant since the death of Sir Neville Wilkinson (b. 1869) in 1940 and the region Norroy in 1943, the king has jurisdiction over the six counties of Northern Ireland as well as those of English counties north of the River Trent.

THE ENGLISH HERALDS OF ARMS IN ORDINARY

Strictly speaking a Herald of Arms is an Officer of Arms, ranking between King of Arms and Pursuivant, though the title is often inaccurately applied to all Officers of Arms. An Officer of Arms is appointed by the Sovereign with the authority to control and initiate armorial matters, arrange and participate in ceremonies of state and conserve and interpret heraldic and genealogical records.

Over time heralds became associated with the regulation of the many coats of arms that they encountered at sporting events. This led to the science of heraldry becoming increasingly important and regulated over the years with the herald becoming an expert in coats of arms. Another heraldic task, especially in the United Kingdom, is the public declaration of proclamations, although in some circumstances this will fall to the Lord Lieutenancy of each county in the United Kingdom.

Today the six Herald of Arms in Ordinary Officers are:

The Chester Herald of Arms in Ordinary
Chester is said to have been instituted by Edward III as herald of Edward of Woodstock (1330–1356), also known as the Black Prince, the Prince of Wales. The title was in abeyance for a period during the reign of Henry VIII, until 1525, when the Chester herald became one of the Heralds in Ordinary. In 1911, when the future Edward VIII was created Prince of Wales, the Chester Herald became a member of his entourage.

Lancaster Herald of Arms in Ordinary
Originally Lancaster, whether as Herald of Arms or as King of Arms, was a title reserved for the Earls and Dukes of Lancaster. Its first recorded

use was in 1347 when Henry of Grosmont (1310–1361), then the Earl of Lancaster and founder member of the Order of the Garter, made a proclamation at the siege of Calais (1346–1347). On Henry IV's accession the Earl was placed into the Crown establishment and was given palatinate powers over the county of Lancashire. That arrangement was continued under Henry V and VI, ending in 1464. Thereafter the Earl reverted to his rank of herald. Since the reign of Henry VII Lancaster has been one of the six Heralds in Ordinary.

Richmond Herald of Arms in Ordinary

Richmond occurs from 1421 to 1485 as herald of John, Duke of Bedford, George, Duke of Clarence, and Henry, Earl of Richmond, all of whom held the Honour of Richmond. Henry on his accession to the throne as Henry VII in 1485 made Roger Machado, the then Richmond, a King of Arms, since whose death in 1510 Richmond has been one of the six Heralds in Ordinary.

Somerset Herald of Arms in Ordinary

This title has been successively private, royal, at once private and extraordinary, and again royal. In 1448/9 Somerset was herald of Edmund Beaufort, Duke of Somerset, but he must have been a Royal Officer in 1485, when he was the only herald to receive coronation liveries. In 1525, when Henry Fitzroy was made Duke of Richmond and Somerset, the then Somerset herald was transferred to the duke's household and as such he must be counted a private officer, although he was appointed by the King and shared the heralds' fees as a herald extraordinary. On Fitzroy's death in 1536 the then incumbent returned to the Crown establishment, and since then Somerset has been one of the Heralds in Ordinary.

Windsor Herald of Arms in Ordinary

The office of Windsor is said to have been instituted by Edward III. Windsor has been one of the six heralds in ordinary since 1419. The first post holder was Thomas More, who served under Henry VI. Interestingly it's said the Windsor Herald was established by Edward III, although there appears to be little proof to confirm this, aside from the heraldic badge. This features Edward III's (Edward of Windsor) sunburst, represented by sun rays shooting up from a white cloud, which is royally crowned.

York Herald of Arms in Ordinary
It has been suggested that York herald was originally the officer of Edmund of Langley, created Duke of York in 1385, but the first reliable reference to York is in a patent of 1484 granting to John Water alias Yorke, herald, as fee of his office and for services to Richard III, his predecessors and ancestors, the manor of Bayhall in Pembury, Kent, and £8 6s. 8d. a year from the Lordship of Huntingfield, Kent.

As of 2024 of the six Herald of Arms in Ordinary, the Heralds of Lancaster and Somerset remain vacant.

ENGLISH HERALDS OF ARMS EXTRAORDINARY

English Heralds Extraordinary is a supernumerary Officer of Arms in England, who are not members of the College, but who process with the other heralds on ceremonial occasions. At present there are seven English Heralds of Arms Extraordinary:

The Arundel Herald of Arms Extraordinary
Though a Royal Herald, the Arundel Herald of Arms Extraordinary is not a member of the College of Arms and was originally a private herald in the household of Thomas Fitzalan, 5th Earl of Arundel, 10th Earl of Surrey (1381–1415). The first herald, John Cosoun, is known to have served the Earl in Portugal in 1413 and later in France, where he attended his dying master in October 1415. The title was revived in 1727 as Herald Extraordinary with Charles Green taking up the post on 9 October that year. He retained the role until 1735 with eight subsequent appointments being made, with historian Professor Anne Curry (b. 1954) appointed in May 2022.

A badge was assigned to Arundel in 1958, which was derived from the Fitzalan earls of the fourteenth century, featuring a galloping horse carrying a sprig of oak in its mouth.

The Beaumont Herald of Arms Extraordinary

The office was created in 1982 and named after the barony of Beaumont, one of the subsidiary titles of the Earl Marshal, Francis Sedley Andrus the Duke of Norfolk 1915–2009). The office has remained vacant after the death of Andrus in 2009.

The Maltravers Herald of Arms Extraordinary

Maltravers Herald of Arms Extraordinary is a royal herald, but not a member of the College of Arms. The present office was created in 1887 by the Earl Marshal, Henry Fitzalan-Howard, 15th Duke of Norfolk (1847–1917), a renowned philanthropist. The office is known to have been held by a pursuivant to John Maltravers, 1st Baron Maltravers (c. 1290–1364). The unique heraldic badge, officially assigned in 1973, is blazoned as *A Fret Or*. It derives from the coat of arms of Maltravers *Sable a Fret Or and a Label of the points Ermine*, and was the badge of the Fitzalan Earls of Arundel, passing to the Howard Dukes of Norfolk with the onset of the third creation of the title in 1580.

The New Zealand Herald of Arms Extraordinary

On 6 February 1978, Phillip Patrick O'Shea (b. 1947) was appointed as the first New Zealand Herald of Arms Extraordinary to Elizabeth II with letters. As the New Zealand Herald of Arms Extraordinary O'Shea, a librarian and long-term government advisor, works in New Zealand. He fulfils the role of Officer of Arms responsible for the regulation of all heraldry in New Zealand. His appointment was made by Royal Warrant of Elizabeth II as Queen of New Zealand and addressed to the Earl Marshal of England. By establishing the New Zealand Herald's appointment in this manner, the role is more akin to that of Officers of Arms in Ordinary than Extraordinary Heralds. This also means that any armorial ensigns in New Zealand continue to be granted exclusively by the Kings of Arms of the College of Arms in London.

Although affiliated with the College of Arms in London, as New Zealand Herald O'Shea is not a member of the College Chapter.

As New Zealand Herald of Arms Extraordinary O'Shea advises the New Zealand Government on heraldic matters. He also represents the College of Arms in New Zealand, and as such acts as the deputy to Garter Principal King of Arms and is *ex officio* a member of the Royal Household. This allows the New Zealand Herald of Arms Extraordinary to attend the Governor-General, or the sovereign, if present, at ceremonial occasions. These include the swearing-in of a new Governor-General, the ceremonial opening of Parliament and making announcements such as the recent proclamation of Charles III on 11 September 2022. Since 2002 the New Zealand Herald of Arms Extraordinary has been appointed by the Governor-General to proclaim the dissolution of Parliament.

When performing duties the New Zealand Herald of Arms Extraordinary wears more appropriate attire consisting of morning dress, his badge of office and herald's baton. The badge of office features a Māori Koru, representing the rafters of Māori meeting houses, coloured in the traditional manner proper and ensigned by a representation of the Royal Crown also proper. The traditional tabard of the Royal Arms is only worn at ceremonial occasions when assembled in England together with the other heralds.

The appointment of New Zealand Herald of Arms Extraordinary does not affect the jurisdiction of the Lord Lyon, King of Arms to grant coats of arms to citizens of New Zealand of Scottish descent or, to matriculate a coat of arms in favour of a New Zealand petitioner where they have a right of succession to those arms or a differenced version of that coat of arms.

The Norfolk Herald of Arms Extraordinary
From 1539 the Norfolk Herald of Arms Extraordinary was a herald to the Dukes of Norfolk, though the first holder, John James, was paid a salary by King Henry VIII. Subsequent Norfolk heralds have been officers extraordinary, though the office has not always been filled but rather revived when required. In 1958 the badge of office was assigned appearing as *Two Ostrich Feathers saltirewise each charged with a Gold Chain*

laid along the quill. The badge derives from the ostrich feather badge awarded to Thomas Mowbray, Duke of Norfolk, and the first Marshal of England by Richard II around 1387.

The Surrey Herald of Arms Extraordinary
In 1856 Edward Dendy became the first Surrey Herald of Arms Extraordinary, an English Officer of the Crown, though he was not a member of the corporation of the College of Arms in London. The Surrey Herald of Arms Extraordinary badge of office was not assigned until 1981 and features *Within a representation of a Herald's Collar of SS Argent a Tabard chequy Or and Azure*. These were the arms of John de Warenne, Earl of Surrey, who had fought in the Second Barons' War which took place between 1264–1267.

This war, led by Simon de Montfort, 6th Earl of Leicester (c. 1208 – 1265), had sought to replace Henry III's selected courtiers with a more formalized court of barons. It also targeted England's Jewish community, which had been lending considerable sums of money to de Montfort, to seize and destroy any and all evidence of outstanding baronial debts.

Initially de Montfort's forces did well, but on 4 August 1265 Prince Edward, later Edward I, defeated the rebellious de Montfort at the Battle of Evesham. Such was the ferocity of the battle that the contemporary historian Robert of Gloucester (c. 1260– c. 1300) described the battle as the 'murder of Evesham, for battle it was none'. De Montfort was to lose his life on the field, his body desecrated and torn asunder by the vengeful Edward. Within two years the last of the remaining rebels had surrendered at the Isle of Ely, Cambridgeshire, closing a war that had claimed 15,000 souls.

It is through de Warenne the earldom descended through the Fitzalans to the Howard Dukes of Norfolk and Earls Marshal.

The Wales Herald of Arms Extraordinary
The history of the Wales Herald of Arms Extraordinary can be traced back to the short-lived Wales Herald of the late fourteenth century. As an Officer of Arms Extraordinary the Wales Herald of Arms Extraordinary (*Herodr Arbennig Cymru*), falls under the Courts of England and Wales's

Royal Service

jurisdiction as a Royal Herald, and therefore a member of the Royal Household. Despite not being a member of chapter of the College of Arms, the Wales Herald of Arms Extraordinary processes with the other heralds at ceremonial occasions.

The post was formally re-established in 1963 as an Officer of Arms Extraordinary, with its first appointee being Francis Jones. Jones, a writer, archivist and historian, had initially started working as a teacher before moving on to his work as an archivist in the early 1930s. With the onset of the Second World War Jones was commissioned into 4th Battalion, the Welch Regiment (Welch), now the Royal Regiment of Wales (RRW), prior to being transferred to the Pembroke Yeomanry, now the 224 (Pembroke Yeomanry) Transport Squadron, Royal Logistic Corps (RLC).

Jones would later land in North African as part of 102nd (Pembroke & Cardiganshire) Field Regiment and took part in Battle of Sidi Nsir, Tunisia on 26 February 1943. His actions during the battle were mentioned in despatches. Jones, like most of the British Army in North Africa fought in the Sicilian and Italian campaigns. Once in Italy Jones, as second-in-command of the 102nd, would take part in Battle of Monte Cassino (January–May 1944). Thereafter, he was posted as a General Staff Officer to the War Cabinet Offices, Historical Section, where he would write the Official War Record for the Sicilian and Italian campaigns. He was later appointed battery commander in the Surrey Yeomanry (Queen Mary's Regiment) whose lineage is continued by 2 (Surrey Yeomanry) Field Troop, 579 Field Squadron (EOD), part of 101 (London) Engineer Regiment (Explosive Ordnance Disposal) (Volunteers).

Today the Wales Herald is part of the procession during the official opening of a session of Senedd Cymru (Welsh Parliament). The badge of the Wales Herald of Arms Extraordinary was awarded in 1967 and depicts the *Croes Naid* (Cross of Neith) which is said to contain a fragment of the True Cross of Jesus Christ and is blazoned *Issuant from an open Royal Crown of the 13th century*.

A Pursuivant of Arms, also known as a Pursuivant, is the junior Officer of Arms, whose role dates to the mediaeval era when nobles employed their own Officers of Arms. Today many Pursuivants are attached to official heraldic authorities, including the College of Arms or the Court of the Lord Lyon in Edinburgh. The Lord Lyon King of Arms and the Lyon Clerk and Keeper of the Records are charged with controlling all armorial matters within a strict legal framework that is unique to Scotland.

This court, which is part of Scotland's criminal jurisdiction, has its own prosecutor, the Procurator Fiscal, who is not an officer of arms, to maintain neutrality in all matters. The Lord Lyon and the Lyon Clerk are Crown appointments and as such carry the Crown's authority, with the Lord Lyon appointing the other Scottish officers. As in England, the Officers of Arms in Scotland are members of the Royal Household.

There still exist some private pursuivants who are not employed by a government authority, such as those pursuivants of arms appointed by clan chiefs in Scotland. These pursuivants of arms look after matters of heraldic and genealogical importance for clan members.

As with other Heralds there are Pursuivants of Arms in Ordinary and Extraordinary with sixteen Heralds allied to the four nations of the United Kingdom.

Today many of the ceremonial duties of heralds have disappeared; however, they still carry out and organize duties under the direction of the Earl Marshal, who has powers of supervision over the heralds and the College of Arms.

Such duties include the annual service of the Sovereign and Knights Companion of the Order of the Garter, held in June at Windsor Castle as well as the State Opening of Parliament. Whilst attending these ceremonies the heralds wear their ornate tabard, which is embroidered front, back and sleeves with the Royal Arms.

Two key State Ceremonial duties that fall under the authority of the Earl Marshal are the arrangement of State Funerals and the monarch's coronation in Westminster Abbey, which the heralds assist in organizing.

THE HONOURABLE THE KING'S (OR QUEEN'S) CHAMPION

The Honourable The King's (or Queen's) Champion is a hereditary office within the Royal Household. The Champion's role takes place

Royal Service

at the monarch's coronation and is intended to challenge anyone who contests the new monarch's entitlement to the throne to trial by combat. Indeed, one of the first accounts of the King's Champion was made in 1328 when, at Tamworth Castle the King's Champion 'appearing armed in the Royal Arms and mounted on the King's best charger to make proof for the King against any who opposed his Coronation'.

The first King's Champion was believed to be Robert Marmion (died c. 1129), 1st Baron Marmion of Tamworth, who served as King's Champion to William the Conqueror, possibly whilst still in Normandy. Marmion's military prowess was proven in his defence of the castle of Stephen of Blois at Falaise in 1140 against Geoffrey of Anjou (1113–1151), later Geoffrey V. This could infer that the title of King's Champion originally had more than symbolic meaning.

The title continued to be carried by subsequent Barons Marmion of Tamworth passing ultimately to Philip Marmion (d. 1291). Philip began the use of the '3 Swords' badge, which was later adopted by the Dymokes to denote being hereditary Champions of England, from around 1265. Philip became the Sheriff of Warwickshire and Leicestershire, as well as fighting with the Royalists in the Second Barons' War (1264–1267). He died without a legitimate male heir, so the office of King's Champion of England and Manor of Scrivelsby passed to the Dymoke descendants through Philip's granddaughter Margaret Ludlow. Margaret was the daughter of Sir Thomas Ludlow and Johanna Marmion, Philip's daughter, and was married to John Dymoke, who was the King's Champion at the Coronation of Richard II in 1377. Since then, the role of Champion has been carried out continuously by the Dymoke family.

As the monarch could not fight in single combat against anyone except an equal, the trial by combat remains purely ceremonial and holds a central place in the Coronation banquet. One of the more interesting elements of the Champion's role was the requirement to ride into Westminster Hall during the Coronation banquet in full armour, complete with colourful helmet plumes. The mounted champion would be escorted by the Earl Marshal and the Lord High Constable, who would attend in full dress, robes and coronets, and await the challenge to all comers.

As with all traditions and ceremonies, especially those of a regal matter, embellishment, even beyond the armour-wearing Dymoke riding into Westminster Hall, continued, the most memorable one being a challenge read out by the Garter King of Arms.

The words of the challenge have varied over the years, but those used for the coronation banquet of George IV, held in Westminster Hall in 1821 are recorded as being:

> If any person, of whatever degree soever, high or low, shall deny or gainsay our Sovereign Lord George, King of the United Kingdom of Great Britain and Ireland, Defender of the Faith, son and next heir unto our Sovereign Lord the last King deceased, to be the right heir to the imperial Crown of this realm of Great Britain and Ireland, or that he ought not to enjoy the same; here is his Champion, who saith that he lieth, and is a false traitor, being ready in person to combat with him, and in this quarrel will adventure his life against him on what day soever he shall be appointed.

To add further theatre to the occasion, in case riding a horse in armour across a tiled floor wasn't enough, the champion would literally throw down the metal gauntlet as he progressed into Westminster Hall. The gauntlet would be thrown first at the entrance, then in the middle of the hall, and finally at the foot of the throne. Prior to each throw the Garter King of Arms would repeat the challenge, with the clatter of metal on stone indicating the challenge was set. It was also a subtle indication for the inquisitive or slightly tipsy to not to even think about picking up the fallen gauntlet and focus on the task in hand. The dropped gauntlet would then be recovered by the Garter on each occasion and returned to the Champion, who would finally be rewarded with a gilt-covered cup, the monarch having first drunk to the Champion from it.

The tradition continued to be carried out by successive Dymokes, until the coronation of George IV when the holder of the post at that time was Reverend John Dymoke. As a clergyman, John could not act as champion, so the honour passed to his 20-year-old son Henry.

As Henry did not possess a horse, he resorted to hiring a mount from the colourful Astley's Circus then based in London. Given the extravagance of George IV's coronation banquet, which cost around £250,000, almost £20 million in today's money, perhaps the theatre of tradition was well placed; it was also the last time the act of throwing down the gauntlet was performed.

On this occasion the banquet menu was prepared in no less than twenty-three kitchens, which produced 160 tureens of soup, as well as courses of fish, roasted meat and vegetables, all accompanied with sauce from 480 gravy boats. Attendees to this grand epicurean event drank a staggering 9,840 bottles of wine and 100 gallons of cold punch. Should anyone remain unfilled by this veritable bacchian feast they could simply help themselves to any one of the 3,721 cold dishes provided, which included pasties and jellies.

Ten years later at the coronation of William IV, significant cuts to expenditure were made; these included eschewing the traditional coronation banquet, thus negating the requirement for the presence of the King's Champion. Henry would return once more at the Coronation of Victoria in 1838; however, it was decided not to include the traditional ride and challenge of the Champion, and a possibly relieved Henry was made a Baronet in recompense.

At the 1902 coronation of Edward VII, the Dymoke family's claim to undertake a historic role in the coronation was admitted by the Court of Claims, and he was allowed to be Standard Bearer of England. In 1953 Lieutenant-Colonel John Dymoke, Royal Lincolnshire Regiment (RLR), now Royal Anglians (RA), had his claim admitted at the coronation of Elizabeth II and acted as Standard Bearer of the Royal Standard. At the coronation of Charles III in 2023, John's son Francis (1955–2023), carried the Royal Standard after his claim was upheld by the Coronation Claims Office.

The Champion's armour which was used for the coronations of James I to George IV can be seen in St. George's Hall at Windsor Castle. Of note the ride and challenge has not yet been revived since its cancellation in 1831.

THE LORD-LIEUTENANCY

Today a Lord-Lieutenant acts as the monarch's personal representative in each of the ninety-nine Lieutenancy areas of the United Kingdom. Historically, each Lieutenant was responsible for organizing the county's militia. Lieutenants were first appointed to several English counties by Henry VIII in the 1540s, with the military functions and powers of the Sheriffs allocated to them. This left each of the Lieutenants responsible for the establishment and efficiency of the militia in his county, a role which continued with the yeomanry and volunteers. As well as managing his newly established militia the Lieutenant was also their commander, responsible for selecting the men and commissioning those he felt were suitable to lead as officers. The commissions were purely temporary and covered the period for when the militia was called to arms, often as a response to invasion, possible or otherwise, by Scotland or France.

As the Lieutenancy model of managing the militias settled and gained structure, they were proven to be a success and in 1550 their long-term establishment was approved by parliament. Widespread adoption of the Lieutenancies did not come until 1585, with the threat of invasion by Spain, when Lieutenants were appointed to all counties and counties corporate, such as the County of the Town of Nottingham. It was at this point that their role became permanent with appointments remaining filled until the War of the Three Kingdoms (1639-1653). At the conclusion of the war the Lieutenancies were abolished under the new Commonwealth government. With the return of Charles II and the restoration, the appointment was re-established under the City of London Militia Act 1662. The act saw Lieutenants appointed to 'counties at large', which now included the counties corporate within the parent county. The adoption of the new title of Lord-Lieutenant was also introduced, as most of the post holders were peers of the realm.

There continued to be the odd exception, included Haverfordwest, Pembrokeshire, Wales that continued to appoint its own Lord-Lieutenant until 1974. Other exceptions include the City of London, which was given a Commission of Lieutenancy, while the Constable of the Tower of London and the Warden of the Cinque Ports were *ex officio* Lieutenants for the Tower Hamlets and the Cinque Ports respectively. This unique position arose as both were treated as counties in legislation regarding Lieutenancy and militia affairs.

The Militia Act of 1802 provided for the continued appointment of Lieutenants, giving them command of their respective county's militia. In the case of counties corporate the authority to appoint Deputy Lieutenants (DLs) in the absence of a Crown-appointed Lieutenant fell upon the Chief Magistrate or similar civic leader. In 1871 as part of the Cardwell Reforms, led by Secretary of State for War Edward Cardwell, 1st Viscount Cardwell (1813–1886), the Regulation of the Forces Act removed the Lieutenancy as de facto head of county militia, with their powers reverting to the Crown. Clearly this did not go down well in some quarters for little over a decade later in 1882 the Militia Act, part of the Childers Reforms made by Secretary of State for War Hugh Childers (1827–1896) saw the jurisdiction of the Lieutenants in the Crown reinstated. The act also saw that the Lieutenancies were re-structured allowing for future Crown appointment. Now the office of Lieutenant was honorary and held during the Royal Pleasure, but virtually for life with their appointment made by letters patent under the Great Seal. The period also saw further responsibilities given to the appointed Lieutenant, who would often become their counties Keeper of the Rolls, recommending appointments to the county's bench of magistrates. As part of the Haldane Reforms by Secretary of State for War Richard Haldane (1856–1928), the Territorial and Reserve Forces Act 1907 established county territorial force associations. In 1921 under the Territorial Army and Militia Act, the Lieutenancies formally lost the right to raise a county militia.

In 1995 forty-eight ceremonial counties were created in England, each receiving a Lord-Lieutenant; these ceremonial counties were further defined in the Lieutenancies Act of 1997. In Wales from 1996 Lord-Lieutenants were appointed to one of the eight preserved counties. Interestingly the City of London has been unaffected by changes since 1882, as it has a Commission of Lieutenancy rather than a single Lord Lieutenant with the Lord Mayor of the City of London acting as head of the commission.

IRELAND AND NORTHERN IRELAND

In Ireland, the appointment was slightly different with the Officer in Charge of the county militia traditionally called Lieutenant until James II; thereafter, they became known as Governor. In 1832 the Custos Rotulorum (Ireland) Act cancelled the commissions of the Governors and transferred the militia and county magistrate functions to the office of Lord-Lieutenant who had been appointed by letters patent. The new Lord-Lieutenant acted as Viceroy and as such was empowered to appoint Deputy Lieutenants.

With the foundation of the Irish Free State in 1922, the role of Lord-Lieutenant of Ireland, then held by Edmund Bernard FitzAlan-Howard, 1st Viscount FitzAlan of Derwent, the first Roman Catholic to be appointed to the post since 1685, became redundant. Subsequently the post holder's powers were transferred to the Governor of Northern Ireland.

With the establishment of Northern Ireland in 1921 the Lord-Lieutenants continued to be appointed through the Governor of Northern Ireland to the six counties of Ulster and the two county boroughs of Derry and Belfast. Interestingly, in 1973 the counties and county boroughs, along with the post of Governor of Northern Ireland, were abolished as local government units, with Lord-Lieutenants appointed directly by the crown to 'counties and county boroughs ... as defined for local government purposes immediately before 1 October 1973'.

SCOTLAND

The first recorded appointment of a Lord-Lieutenant was Colin Lindsay, 3rd Earl of Balcarres. Lindsay was a strong supporter of James II and was appointed Lord Lieutenant of Fife in 1688. From 1715 Lieutenants were appointed to only a few counties, though by 1794 permanent Lieutenancies were finally established by Royal Warrant. Three years later the Militia Act of 1797 saw Lieutenants appointed 'for the Counties, Stewartries, Cities, and Places', and consequently given the powers to raise and command county militia units like their English counterparts. Interestingly, the Lord Provosts of Edinburgh, Glasgow, Aberdeen and Dundee as the convenor or chair of their local authority, and the civic head of their respective cities were also the Lord-Lieutenants. When the Local Government (Scotland) Act of 1973 replaced the counties with regions, each region was permitted to have one or more Lord-Lieutenants appointed. This allowed each region to create areas approximated to the previous counties with Lord-Lieutenants appointed accordingly. Further changes in 1996 saw further local government reorganization, with Lord-Lieutenants appointed to 'Lieutenancy areas', districts that are roughly equivalent to the historic Scottish counties.

While in their Lieutenancies, Scottish Lord-Lieutenants are officially permitted to fly the banner of the Royal Arms of Scotland, or The Lion Rampant, as it is more commonly known.

★

Today the Lord-Lieutenant is now an honorary titular position which is held until the post holder's seventy-fifth birthday and remains a sovereign's appointment. As a Lord-Lieutenant, the individual is the monarch's county representative tasked with the duty of upholding the dignity of the Crown. While acting as the Crown's representative the civic responsibilities of Lord-Lieutenants are many, including the delivery of proclamations that remain a key part of their role. Lord-Lieutenants, supported by their county's administration services, will be tasked with arranging visits of members of the Royal Family and escorting royalty. Other duties include overseeing citizenship ceremonies, the presentation of medals and awards on behalf of the Crown and advising on honours nominations. There are also the key national ceremonial duties to attend which can include attending Remembrance parades and celebrations of key regal milestones such as Jubilees.

As well as civic duties, Lord-Lieutenants participate in various voluntary and social activities within their county. Such activities can include building community connections, attending county fairs and supporting charitable causes through promotion or sharing their professional expertise. Their links to the armed forces remain steadfast maintaining links to their country's Reserve Forces' and Cadets' Association (RFCA).

As well as these roles the Lord-Lieutenant is responsible for the selection of the High Sheriff through the Privy Council as well as leading the local magistracy as chairman of the Advisory Committee on Justices of the Peace. Given the range of tasks, each Lord-Lieutenant is supported by a Vice Lord-Lieutenant and Deputy Lieutenants, all of whom they appoint. As the Sovereign's representative the Lord-Lieutenant remains non-political and may not hold office in any political party.

The Vice Lord-Lieutenant is the immediate proxy, taking over when the Lord-Lieutenant is unavailable, while the Deputy Lieutenants assist where required. In England and Wales Deputy Lieutenants receive their commission of appointment through the appropriate government minister, who is normally the Lord Chancellor, or in Scotland by the Scottish Minister, by command of the Sovereign. Unlike the office of Lord-Lieutenant, which is an appointment in the gift of the Sovereign, the position of Deputy Lieutenant is an appointment of the Sovereign's appointee, and therefore not strictly speaking a direct appointment of the Sovereign.

Deputy Lieutenants are chosen from the ceremonial county's population, and have either served the local community, or have a record of wider public service. Deputy Lieutenants will represent the Lord-Lieutenant at a range of local ceremonies. One of the serving Deputy Lieutenants will also be appointed to be Vice-Lieutenant. The appointment as Vice Lord-Lieutenant does, however, expire on the retirement of the Lord-Lieutenant who made the choice, with the Vice Lord-Lieutenant reverting to Deputy Lieutenant status.

Whilst undertaking formal events Lord-Lieutenants and their deputies, wear a dark blue uniform similar in the style of a General Officer's Army

No. 1 dress. This is similar in appearance to a Lieutenant General's uniform, but with silver buttons, epaulettes, sash and details rather than the usual gold. A cap, with the appropriate national symbol is also worn, and a sword with a steel scabbard is carried if appropriate. The national symbols used on the uniform vary depending on the country location of the lieutenant's county, with a rose worn in England, shamrock in Northern Ireland, a thistle in Scotland and Prince of Wales' feathers in Wales.

The uniform for a Vice Lord-Lieutenant is similar in appearance to a brigadier's uniform while the Deputy Lieutenant's resembles that of a field officer such as a Lieutenant Colonel.

Other differences include the absence of the crown above the national symbol on shoulder boards with Deputy Lieutenants wearing narrower shoulder boards. For the collar Vice Lord-Lieutenants wear blue cord instead of silver on the red collar patches with Deputy Lieutenants having a simple grey stripe. Another difference is caps, with a Vice Lord-Lieutenant's peak decorated with a single row of silver braid stylized as oak leaf around the peak of the cap. Some Deputy Lieutenants may be seen with no oak leaf but simple gold tape, like that of a field officer, although the Vice Lord-Lieutenant's style hat is occasionally worn by Deputy Lieutenants. Of note, for some Deputy Lieutenants a blue band appears in the middle of their red cap band, like the cap band of the Honourable Artillery Company. The Deputy Lieutenant's uniform omits the shoulder boards, with the relevant national symbol worn on the jacket's epaulettes.

In 1975 a badge was provided for female Lord-Lieutenants to wear as an optional alternative to the uniform. The badge consists of an enamel version of the uniform cap badge topped by a jewelled crown, suspended from a ribbon of the same colour as the uniform sash.

HIGH SHERIFF

The Office of High Sheriff is an independent non-political royal appointment for a single year and remains the oldest secular office in the

United Kingdom after the Crown, dating from the Saxon era (410–1066). It is this period which gifts the post its name, when the 'Shire Reeve', or the Anglo-Saxon *Scir-gerefa* was responsible to the Crown for the maintenance of law and order within the shire, or county, as well as collecting and returning taxes. On top of maintaining local order some shire reeves are recorded as leading contingents at the Battle of Hastings in 1066.

The Normans chose to continue the Office, adding to its powers so that by the twelfth century the High Sheriff, a name change instigated in 1254, was empowered as a representative and agent of the Crown. Alongside tax collection, legal cases were judged in the monthly court of the hundred (a sub-unit of the shire), with the High Sheriff granted law enforcement powers. These included the power to raise the 'hue and cry', a process by which bystanders are summoned to assist in the apprehension of a criminal witnessed committing a crime. For the wider pursuit of criminals within their shire High Sheriffs could summon and command the *posse comitatus*, Latin for 'power of the county'.

After the signing of the Magna Carta in 1215, the Sheriffs' and subsequently the High Sheriffs' powers were gradually restricted over succeeding centuries. Under Henry I the Exchequer took over the Sheriff's tax collection powers and began to audit the Sheriff's accounts. Henry II then introduced the system of Itinerant Justices from which evolved the trial by jury assizes system and the current system of High Court Judges going out on circuit.

Regardless of the changes the Sheriff remained responsible for issuing writs, preparing the Court, prisoners and juries, and executing any pronounced sentences, including death sentence. It was also the Sheriff's responsibility to ensure the safety and comfort of the judges, a task which continues to this day, with High Sheriffs responsible for the care and well-being of High Court judges. By the middle of the thirteenth century, more powers were transferred to the newly created offices of Coroners and Justices of the Peace. By the late 1800s the Sheriffs' powers concerning police and prisons had passed to the Prison Commissioners and local constabulary and the care of Crown property was transferred to the Crown Commissioners.

The Sheriffs Act of 1887 consolidated the law relating to the Office of High Sheriff and remains the key act by which Sheriffs are selected and carry out their roles. The Act confirms that the Office of Sheriff should be held for one year only and a Sheriff who is also a magistrate should not sit as such during their year of office. The Act also confirmed the historic process of nomination and selection by the Sovereign whereby the incumbent High Sheriff appoints a suitable successor to serve in their county in three years' time. Upon taking their appointment, usually in April, the incumbent serves voluntarily and without cost to the public purse, for the next twelve months.

Every year the Presiding Judge of the Circuit and the Privy Council consider all nominations to the Office of High Sheriff in England and Wales prior to being presented to the Sovereign in Council. The nominations, which consist of three prospective High Sheriffs for each county, are presented in a meeting of the Lords of the Council in the King's Bench Division of the High Court of Justice. This is presided over by the Lord Chief Justice annually on 12 November. Subsequently, the selection of new High Sheriffs is made in a meeting of the Privy Council by the sovereign the following March. It is at this meeting that the custom of 'pricking' the appointee's name with a bodkin takes place. Excluded from nomination and appointment under the Sheriffs Act of 1887 are Peers of Parliament and Members of the House of Commons, and, by extension, Members of the Welsh Assembly. Other exclusions include those who are serving as full-time members of the Judiciary, Inland Revenue, as well as Officers of the Post Office, and Commissioned Officers of His Majesty's Armed Forces receiving full pay. These exclusions reflect the essential requirement that the Office of High Sheriff remains a non-political appointment.

Today's duties of the fifty-five High Sheriffs in England and Wales are far more amenable than their shire reeve ancestors. They continue supporting the Crown and the judiciary as well as initiatives that encourage crime reduction and social cohesion. Today the High Sheriff's principal formal duties include attendance at royal visits such as Maundy services in the county and provide support to the Lord Lieutenant as appropriate.

The Office remains independent and non-political, allowing High Sheriffs to bring together the community they serve without accusations of bias. The ceremonial uniform, known as Court Dress, remains fundamentally unchanged since the late seventeenth century, with ladies wearing an adapted style of Court Dress. Both Court Dresses consist of a black or dark blue velvet coat fitted with steel buttons and finished with a lace neck jabot. Also worn are breeches, skirt or dresses with buckled shoes and a cocked hat; a sword may also be carried. Some High Sheriffs may wear their military uniform instead of Court Dress if they are retired. When Court Dress is not worn, a High Sheriff will wear their badge of Office as a necklet.

Chapter Four
Preparing for Parade

'Up, Guards, and at them again.'
Arthur Wellesley,
1st Duke of Wellington

Perfecting the Art

The Sovereign's Birthday Parade is the culmination of weeks of practice and inspections. For the Household Cavalry Mounted Regiment (HCMR), the work starts with the return of their mounts from their winter break at the Defence Animal Training Regiment, based in Melton Mowbray, Leicestershire. Understandably, a good break, winter feed and wet conditions will see the mounts returned Thelwellesque, in appearance, and welcomed by experienced hands. The turnaround from muddied and rough-looking field horse to stabled cavalry mount is remarkable and a testimony to the professionalism of all. Despite looking smart, the horse and riders of the cavalry must undertake a series of inspections. The Riding Master takes the first inspection. Here, the beauty is truly in the eye of the beholder for the Riding Master, as mounts and riders are inspected in their ceremonial dress known as the Mounted Review Order, with the regimental troopers and musicians fully inspected. There follows further inspection by the HCMR's Adjutant, Commanding Officer and finally, the Major General Commanding the Household Division known as the Major General's Review. Today, this role is carried out by the General

Officer Commanding the London District, a tradition that can be traced back to the first appointment of Prince Adolphus, Duke of Cambridge (1744–1850) and Colonel-in-chief of the Coldstream Regiment of Foot Guards as Commanding Home District in 1804.

The Major General Commanding the Household Division's springtime parade, a significant event that mirrors much of what will occur later in the early summer at the Trooping of the Colour, includes an Advance in Review Order. The inspections are also made in the barracks, with every member of the HCMR quizzed by the Brigade Major on their technical knowledge and practical skills, from riding proficiency to turnout scrutinized. The King's Troop are likewise inspected by the Major General, with every rider, mount, and QF 13-pounder gun inspected in preparation for State Ceremonial, Public Duties and the inevitable public appearances. This inspection takes place at the spiritual home of the Artillery, Woolwich, which is also home to the King's Troop's King George VI Lines. Away from State Ceremonial and Public Duties, public appearances, with their musical rides, provide excellent promotional opportunities for the HCMR and King's Troop, showcasing the skill and precision of all involved and acting as ambassadors for the wider British military equitation community. The musical ride always attracts great interest as it entertains and enthrals the viewer with horses and guns performing manoeuvres that increase in tempo and dash as the music speeds up. Interestingly, it's not uncommon for the soldiers and officers of the HCMR and King's Troop to maintain two sets of ceremonial dress, as the tunic, in particular, will often attract all types of dirt, especially when crossing boggy ground. Indeed, such is the prowess of the King's Troops Musical Ride that it forms part of their formal inspection by the Major General, complete with musical accompaniment.

For the troopers of the HCMR, there is one final accolade they can vie for: the Princess Elizabeth Cup also referred to as the Richmond Cup. This cup, an idea of the late Elizabeth II when she was a young princess, is a testament to the troopers' dedication and skill. Every February, the top eight finishers of the early spring inspections of an individual's Mounted Review Order are put forward for one final inspection at Hyde Park.

Preparing for Parade

Here, the inspection is carried out in the presence of a senior member of the Royal Family, with the appearance of horse and rider intensely scrutinized. The competing Troopers will have recently completed their Phase 2 training, including a twelve-week riding course at the Household Cavalry Training Wing (HCTW) at Combermere Barracks, Windsor. This course is followed by a four-week Kit Ride at Knightsbridge Barracks, a place most likely to be their home. Here Troopers are shown how to clean and maintain their ceremonial equipment and, most importantly, how to ride effectively and safely when wearing it. Successful completion of this course confers upon the graduating Trooper the status of Mounted Dutyman and the all-important diploma in Equine Management. As their careers progress, Mounted Dutymen can choose to develop and qualify in specialist trades such as farrier, saddler and tailor.

Despite the attention the HCMR and King's Troop attract from the Major General, it is with greater scrutiny, as the dismounted Major General, that the Foot Guards are inspected. As a fellow Guard, any inspection will be hawklike, and knowledge of the standards will undoubtedly demand the excellence from all. Today, the Major General's Review focuses on the regiment trooping their colour and those who have returned to Public Duties. These reviews, like those experienced by the HCMR and King's Troop, focus on all aspects of life in the parading regiment, from the day-to-day administration to inspections of those in dress uniform at London or Windsor. The first troops to be inspected are the bandsmen and women of the accompanying band so they can play whilst the Major General tours the parading regiment's ranks. This is followed by an inspection of the headquarters company that involves technical inspections to ensure that staff members can support the regiment to the highest standards. Finally, the fighting elements of the regiment are inspected. During his inspections, the Major General is accompanied by the Brigade Major, the Garrison Sergeant Major (GSM) and the Regimental Tailor, complete with chalk, to manage any changes required of the parading regiment's uniforms. After that, the Subaltern's regimental knowledge is scrutinized by the Brigade Major. Regimental knowledge focuses on various topics and replicates what the sweating Subalterns would have encountered during their training at Royal Military Academy Sandhurst (RMAS), such as identifying key regimental, battles and core values.

WALKING THE WALK

'Drill is a pill that should be taken twice daily!'
                    Words of wisdom from the Drill Square.

'For troops who march in an irregular and disorderly manner are always in great danger of being defeated.'
                    Flavius Vegetius Renatus (d. after 383CE)

The history of foot drill movements can be traced back to the days of the Roman Empire when the need to move significant numbers of men by foot meant that simply ambling along wouldn't do. The discipline of military movement guaranteed a great many things:

- Unit cohesion as a battle tactic
- Prevention of physical fatigue and psychological stress
- A regular pace of marching twenty miles in five hours
- The navigation of obstacles

The various formations were practised almost incessantly except for crossing water, by fording or by a bridge. Disciplined troops could rapidly change these formations without breaking step and in response to hand signals or voice commands. The former was helpful in a tactical advance into battle, while the latter was for training, parades or the simple movement of a body of troops between two points. With the fall of the Roman Empire and its legions, the use of drill seemingly fell away.

The general anarchy of military movement continued for over 1,000 years as kingdoms slugged it out in Europe and the Middle East. Mounted knights were keen to show off their prowess rather than their battle space management skills, and the accompanying troops, dragged

Preparing for Parade

from their homes and operating in appalling conditions, simply followed. With the development of warfare and the introduction of gunpowder in particular, allied to the expansion of organized bands of soldiers into mercenary corps, best exemplified by the famed Swiss Mercenaries, known as *Reisläufer*, drill slowly returned both on and off the battlefield. It wasn't until the sixteenth century that drill made a noticeable return as Maurice of Orange (1567–1625) sought to regulate the movements of his soldiers as they handled their firearms. This led to adopting forty-two separate movements, from taking up arms to firing. The developments continued as the professionalization of European armies was increased by seventeenth-century leaders such as Sweden's Gustavus Adolphus (1594–1632). Adolphus was already finessing the martial sciences by developing combined arms whilst simultaneously looking at how the battle space management of his standing army, one of the largest in Europe, could be refined.

This period of military history often called the Pike and Shot period, highlighted the need for a well-drilled military, be it organizing a defensive anti-cavalry phalanx or advancing onto enemy infantry. The pike phalanx, for example, would also be employed to protect the valuable musketeers firing their muskets or earlier arquebus, a weapon that was Chinese in origin and had begun appearing on the European battlefield as early as 1411. Both were of immense strategic and tactical importance, and their slow operation and weight exposed the musketeer to fire from enemy musketeers, archers or raids by determined infantry. Thus, their protection was vital, and the pike was the ideal weapon to provide that protection. These technological developments led to complex drill movements of both weapons and soldiers. By the time of the Wars of the Three Kingdoms, these drill movements were at their peak.

With the growing use of firearms, the introduction of the bayonet and the steady professionalism of the military in the late sixteenth century, the battle space was further transformed by the introduction of line infantry. The Line Infantry were the acme of seventeenth-century military science, and European armies rapidly embraced the concept. Its simple formation of two to four ranks of soldiers drawn up side by side in rigid alignment allowed them to maximize the effect of their forward firepower. Line infantry would use three key formations in battles: the line, the square and the column, formations of which can be seen during the Sovereign's Birthday Parade. Using and being part of line infantry required almost draconian discipline with the simple movements of manoeuvre, practised to the point where they became second nature. In the British Army, the regular regiments that used these new line tactics were now called regiments 'of the line' or line regiments; battles could be won or lost depending on the standard of a regiment's drill that acted as a force multiplier.

The Prussians' perfection of drills would inspire the high standards of drills later expected of the British line regiments. The Prussians were automatic in their movements, with their soldiers subjected to the harshest routines and conditions to mould them into unthinking yet highly competent soldiers, quick to respond to orders. Such was the quality of instruction that soldiers could soon focus simply on their commands rather than the haze of battle, utilizing the psychological advantage of belonging to a mass that moved and fought as one. This behaviour would prove to be a distinct advantage as countries expanded their colonies, able to outfight local forces that often outnumbered their own. The drill of movement ensured that the mass retained its discipline, especially when attacked by cavalry. For the British, the Crimean War would be the climax of their use of drill as a force multiplier. With rapidly developing technologies, the line, column and square as key tactical formations would become redundant, and by the time the First World War had settled down into trench warfare, it was obsolete. That is not to say the basis of drill as a disciplined manner of moving and controlling troops was over; far from it. Its advantages for movement by foot have never been bettered, and it remains a crucial tool to introduce recruits to the importance of teamwork, coordination and discipline.

With the New Year's inspections ending, preparations for upcoming State Ceremonial and Public Duties events begin earnestly, and the Guards start their Spring Drills. This two-week cycle of battalion-sized drills is carried out by the Regimental Sergeant Major and the many

Drill Sergeants (DSgt), with the efforts of all battalion members under eagle-eyed scrutiny. The process starts from scratch with slow and quick time marching practised, and pace length retained at 30 inches (762 mm). This distance is ensured by the diligent use of the infamous pace stick, the visual badge of office for those instructing drill and under whom all are drilled. This set pace also allows the RSM and, for State Ceremonial, the Garrison Sergeant Major to design and coordinate the movements of all involved properly. Interestingly, for the 2023 Coronation of Charles III, the GSM Andrew 'Vern' Stokes (Coldstream) used an earpiece system to relay a metronome beat of the correct pace to ensure the 6,000-odd personnel of the visiting units remained at the proper pace throughout the movement phases. This kept the long thread of personnel moving and ensured everyone was at the right place and time.

Once the physical movement of the drill has been perfected to the RSM's satisfaction and is in line with the ordinances of the Army School of Ceremonial (ASC), attention is turned to the arms drill. Rifles are used for the rank and file; sword drills are polished for the officers, and for the Ensigns, Colour Drill. This is followed by practising the various formations the battalion is expected to perform during State Ceremonial. The Household Cavalry is also prepared for their involvement. While their daily Public Duties will see smaller groups of members of the HCMR in Mounted Review Order, for the entire HCMR to rehearse requires a different approach to that taken by the Foot Guards.

Given that upward of 150 horses will be involved in State Ceremonial, any mass movement of HCMR is performed in the early morning hours, generally around 1:30 am. The primary purpose is to ensure every aspect of the horse and rider's safety is met. At this point, the commanding officer or his appointed deputy, usually the Adjutant or Second-in-Command (2IC) accompanied by a riding instructor or saddler, perform their checks. Girth belts are often tightened as some horses have a mischievous habit of expanding their barrel (chest) during initial fitting. Other tasks include checking of bits, the wear of shoes and any areas of grooming that need addressing. All defects are noted by the Orderly Corporal and addressed as soon as practicable. Like their Foot Guard brethren, all rehearsals are conducted in Service Dress Mounted instead of Mounted Review Order to preserve the condition of their dress uniforms and accoutrements. There will always be exceptions to the rule, and new routes are proofed by riding in Mounted Review Order, which makes the rider wider than they are in Service Dress Mounted, ensuring a route can be navigated safely. Any rehearsal is always done under strict timings, and any area used is prepared and laid out with key personalities fully aware of their responsibilities beforehand. Plans are also shared electronically and studied, with attention paid to Hyde Park, where their inspection by the Major General Commanding the Household Division occurs.

The Massed Bands of the Household Division are the last to be checked. Like their mounted and foot peers, the Guard-like bearing of the musicians, all members of the Royal Corps of Army Music (RCAM), is scrutinized from wind to percussionists. From the state of their range of attire to their drill and equitation, no stone is left unturned in the pursuit of excellence. The Massed Bands of the Household Division comprise all the bands, Corps of Drums and Pipes and Drums of the Foot Guards regiments taking part in the Sovereign's Birthday parade. They are joined by their mounted contemporaries from the Household Cavalry, who have been playing or massing together since 1971.

The work-up of the massed bands to the Trooping the Colour ceremony is understandably different from that of the other participants. In January, once the announcement of which Foot Guards Regiment is to be awarded the honour of Trooping its Colour, the Senior Director of Music (SDOM) will begin their work. The selection of suitable music, from regimental quick and slow marches to incidental themes, is presented at an initial meeting featuring the key senior personalities of the parade. The SDOM will include the Regimental Headquarters of the regiment who will be trooping their colour, and the Field Officer in Brigade Waiting all discussing the score to be used. This ensures the music played is relevant and recognizes the anniversaries of any battle honours or important dates such as VE Day, and most importantly, ensures the score has not been used in previous parades. Headquarters Household Division occasionally will intervene by requesting new music or musical arrangements. This information will be gathered in a draft programme, in which the SDOM and the key parade personalities will work together until February when a date in March for the music audition is chosen. The SDOM is also responsible for drawing up a list of alternative pieces, quite a task given the sheer library of martial music they have at their disposal and the chances any suggestions may have been played in the past or, worse still, be deemed wholly inappropriate.

The audition brings together the Major General Commanding the Household Division, the Brigade Major, the GSM and representation from the parading regiment. A single Foot Guards band is charged with presenting the music that not only faces the scrutiny of this well-versed panel of marital and musical expertise but also faces the television cameras, as their audition is recorded for later reference. On top of this, a previous parade, with the sound muted, is played at the same time. This allows the band to play the music selection to the sequences of the earlier parade, ensuring that the timing matches precisely. This gives the gathered panel an opportunity to identify any issues, recommend any suitable changes to the SDOM's musical arrangements and then arrange a second or even third audition to ensure the musical score flows smoothly with the physical sequence of the parade. A critical aspect of any chosen piece of music is that the parading troops must hear its tempo and beat across the expanse of Horse Guards Parade. The soldiers on parade will be listening to the beat of the bass drum, as this is used to indicate timing and halts. It is here that the GSM's experience is priceless. Once the panel is satisfied the score is suitable, the musical programme is agreed upon. The final musical list is issued to the Foot Guards Central Music Library, allowing each musician to begin their practice in preparation.

Horse Guards Parade

Horse Guards Parade is the venue for Trooping the Colour and its precursor, Beating the Retreat. Separated by Horse Guards Road, Horse Guards Parade faces the twenty-three-hectare (fifty-seven-acre) St. James's Park, one of the five royal parks found in Central London.

Once the restricted hunting grounds and recreation centre of the Royal Household, these parks were opened to the public in 1871 by the Crown Lands Act 1851. Horse Guards Road becomes a holding area for troops and horses during Trooping the Colour and other events. It also becomes home to makeshift stables, complete with farriers. Behind its famous façade lies Whitehall, home to the British civil service, leading to Westminster Abbey. To the north is the famous red asphalt surface of the Mall running alongside St. James's Park and leading to Buckingham Palace. On the opposite side is Birdcage Walk, where Wellington Barracks is located. Wellington Barracks is home to Massed Bands of the Foot Guards and the State Ceremonial and Public Duties companies of the Grenadier, Coldstream and Scots Guards. It opened in 1863 and was designed by Sir Francis Smith and Philip Hardwick, who also designed the riding school and stables for Hyde Park Barracks, the London home of the Household Cavalry. Wellington Barracks is also home to the famous Guards Chapel, which had been rebuilt after its destruction by a V1 on 18 June 1944 with the loss of 121 souls.

Horse Guards' connection with military celebrations can be traced back to its use as a tiltyard, an area where tournaments were held. It was Henry VIII who, in 1530, requisitioned the Palace of Whitehall, which had been the home of English governance since 1049 and had been used by various church figures. Cardinal Thomas Wolsey (1473–1530) was to be the last religious occupier, having extended what was known as York Place to such a size it rivalled Lambeth Palace in grandeur. Henry quickly moved into York Place from the fire-damaged Westminster Palace shortly after Wolsey's death. The first recorded use of the term 'Whitehall' was in 1532 and was made in reference to the building's white stone. Over the next 160 years, the palace grew to such a size that by the time of its destruction by fire in 1698, it had a staggering 1,500 rooms. The destruction was not wholesale, with the Banqueting House remaining alongside other elements of the building that survived and later incorporated into neigbouring buildings as the Palace of Whitehall grew in political importance.

Today, the main building at the centre of Horse Guards Parade is known simply as Horse Guards, serving as a stables and barracks for the

Household Cavalry. The site has been in use as a cavalry stable since 1663, when Charles II built the stables and barracks on the site of the tiltyard of the Palace of Whitehall. The new building also served as an entrance to the Palace of Whitehall and later St. James's Palace, the most senior of the Royal Households' London residencies and home of the Accession Council. It is for these reasons that Whitehall retains the King's Life Guard. During its use as a guard to St. James's Park beyond, the main entrance, which is only used by the sovereign to this day, was flanked by two sentry boxes large enough to accommodate mounted troopers. A little over a century later, the world was a different place: Horse Guards had grown in importance and was now a hub of military planning for Britain's growing army. Wear and tear were taking their toll, and in 1745, George II commissioned architect William Kent (1685–1748), the father of the English Palladian style, to redesign Horse Guards. Kent worked wonders with his new design that would utilize the existing area occupied by the rapidly deteriorating Horse Guards to give George a large building that did not encroach on its surroundings. Kent would die in 1748, two years before the old Horse Guards was consigned to architectural history. His idea would be realized with the assistance of John Vardy (1718–1765), who in turn was assisted by William Robinson (1720–1775), who would later become the Clerk of Works at several Royal palaces, including Buckingham Palace. The build would take ten years to complete, and by its end, there was stabling for sixty-two horses (today, seventeen are stabled at Whitehall).

The new Horse Guards remained the Headquarters of the British Army and was home to several key personalities, including Field Marshal Arthur Wellesley, 1st Duke of Wellington when he served as Commander-in-Chief of the British Army. Before his State Funeral, the office he once occupied, known as the Levee Room, would be his final resting place. Today, it remains in use as the office of the Major General Commanding London District; the living quarters are now office space, but the Duke's desk remains in use.

The completed building retained several previous features, including the Baroque clock tower at its centre. On the Whitehall side of the clock tower, a distinctive black mark can be seen above the Roman number two on the clock face, supposedly marking the time of the execution of Charles I that occurred close by. This clock and its bells begin the Trooping of the Colour at 11:00 am. The clock also indicates the start of the dismounted inspection of the guards and horses, which occurs daily at 4:00 pm. This routine began in 1894 when Queen Victoria found the guards drinking and gambling in the afternoon instead of tending to their duty. Infuriated by this decidedly unbecoming behaviour, Victoria decreed that every day, at 4:00 pm, there was to be an inspection of guard for the next 100 years. It remains a key part of life at Horse Guards, despite the 100 years expiring in 1994, at the request of Elizabeth II, out of respect for the tradition.

Against this historical backdrop, the members of the Royal Family will gather in the Levee Room to watch the Trooping of the Colour. The sovereign either mounted or on the king's saluting dias will overlook the parade ground and gaze upon the Guards Division memorial, designed by architect Harold Chalton Bradshaw (1893–1943) and the sculptor Gilbert Ledward (1888–1960). The monument features bronze figures representing each of the five Guards regiments standing easy and was cast from the metal of captured German guns. The inscription upon the monument that commemorates the fallen from the Guards Division and related units during the First World War and of the Household Division in the Second World War and other conflicts since 1918 was written by Rudyard Kipling (1865–1936) and reads:

> To the Glory of God and in the memory of the Officers, Warrant Officers, Non Commissioned Officers and Guardsmen of His Majesty's Regiments of Foot Guards who gave their lives for their King and Country during the Great War 1914–1918 and of the Officers, Warrant Officers, Non-Commissioned Officers and Men of the Household Cavalry, Royal Regiment of Artillery, Corps of Royal Engineers, Royal Army Service Corps, Royal Medical Corps and other units who while serving the Guards Division in France and Belgium 1915–1918 fell with them in the fight for the World's Freedom.

Beating the Retreat

Before Trooping the Colour, the Massed Bands will perform the Beating Retreat on Horse Guards Parade. Beating Retreat can trace its roots back to a sixteenth-century ceremony used to recall nearby patrols to their quarters. This heralded the end of the patrol and was also used on the battlefield to disengage from contact with an adversary. It would be cavalryman Lieutenant General Humphrey Bland (1686–1763), who in his 1727 publication *Treatise of Military Discipline*, would lay out a more rational approach to the use of drums to sound a recall or Retreat, stating drummers were to mount the castle ramparts at the setting of the sun giving notice of the closure of the camps or castle gates in thirty minutes. The use of drum beat as a recall or notice method was further refined by Prince William Augustus, Duke of Cumberland (1721–1765), who distinguished between a Retreat and a Tattoo. The Duke stated the Retreat was to be beaten at sunset and the Tattoo to be beaten at a later hour as decided by the commanders of individual encampments.

Today, Beating Retreat is a vibrant event held on the Wednesday and Thursday evenings before the Trooping of the Colour. It is often accompanied by visiting military bands. The modern practice of Beating Retreats and Tattoos, introduced after the Second World War, features Guards in their colourful State Dress providing lively entertainment. The audience is treated to a spectacular Saturday night display that includes musical rides from the King's Troop and Household Cavalry, accompanied by the Massed Bands, including the Pipe and Drums of the Household Division.

The current format was introduced in 1996, and after several changes, it has now become a colourful evening event featuring fireworks, big screen accompaniment and visiting troops, all in the shadow of the Horse Guards.

Trooping the Colour

It is the choreographed splendour of the Trooping the Colour that is truly synonymous with all the State Ceremonials and Public Duties carried out by the Guards and supported by the Royal Household, the London Division and countless others. It is an immutable show of soft power symbolizing global Britain. It is the culmination of the art of soldierly discipline and martial excellence, the likes of which remain unsurpassed. Its background as a ceremony is easily traced to the days of the House of Hanover. Still, its background as an essential military act is arguably more important in understanding its significance, especially in today's world of smart technology. Since the early days of conflict, military leaders have needed to gather their troops in battle quickly.

Given that the chaos of battle often drowned out drums and trumpet calls, a flag or 'colour' was quickly adopted to aid the assembly of a commander's troops. By the eighteenth century, this recognition system had been simplified, and using a single regimental or battalion colour, or guidon for cavalry units, became the norm. In battle, the colour could be found in the centre of the line, allowing for its quick identification in the heat of battle.

The term 'Trooping the Colour' has its roots in the Restoration period (1660–1700) in which every garrison town would witness the daily guard mount that was started by the main guard parading through the town's main streets. By the mid-eighteenth century, whenever the sovereign was in residence in the garrison's district, a Captain's guard would be posted to help protect the sovereign and a daily parade was made that included 'Trooping the Colour', a ceremony more likely to be seen in London than the provinces.

In 1747, George II set forth regulations governing the use of colours, partly due to the recent Jacobite Rebellion of 1745, that was part of a broader standardization of the British Army. First and foremost, George was intent on reining in the loyalties of officers and men to their regimental Colonels and ensuring their loyalty was first and foremost to the Crown. Other changes related to uniforms, drill and tactics; it was in these changes that the role of colours would become formalized. By Royal Warrant, it was declared that each infantry regiment battalion would now carry two colours to identify it on the battlefield: a King's, Queen's or Royal colour of the Union Flag and a regimental colour of the same colour as the regiment's facings. As the colours had become an essential part of command and control every soldier needed to be able to recognize their battalion's colour. This led to the colour being carried or 'trooped' down the assembled ranks of the battalion at the end of the day's march before the colours were lodged safely for the night in a ceremony known as 'Lodging the Colour'. The following morning, the colour would again take its place in the battalion's ranks. The act of Trooping the Colour in London by the Brigade of Guards took place as early as 1755.

The battalion's colours were now regarded with a reverence accorded to the most sacred of relics; indeed, it was common for colours to be consecrated by an Anglican priest, and by 1825, colours would be consecrated when being formally presented to the battalion. The colour attracted a great deal of mystique and respect, so it was considered a stain on the regimental honour should their colours be lost. To prevent such loss, the colours were always protected in the field by a colour party consisting of Ensigns and experienced Sergeants, around which the battalion would rally when needed.

The nineteenth century saw warfare become increasingly fast paced, to the point that some regiments eschewed carrying their colours for fear of losing valuable experience and the colours themselves. It was due to the events at the Battle of Isandlwana, South Africa, on 22 January 1879 and the loss of two colours of the 24th (The 2nd Warwickshire) Regiment of Foot that Parliament acted on the matter. Debates raged about whether colours should still be carried on the battlefield. As if to push Parliament into a decision, heavy casualties among the colour party of the 58th (Rutlandshire) Regiment of Foot at the Battle of Laing's Nek, South Africa, on 28 January 1881, led to a ban on colours being carried in battle. Indeed, then Adjutant-General to the Forces Garnet Wolseley (1833–1913) remarked that after this engagement, any Colonel who ordered the colours to be carried into action should be tried for the murders of the men lost carrying them. Wolseley's remarks, no matter how blunt, were reinforced when the Secretary of State for War Hugh Childers (1827–1896) instructed on 29 July 1881 that colours would no longer be taken into the field. The military hierarchy fully supported the edict, and on 2 March 1882, the Commander-in-Chief of the Forces, Prince George, the Duke of Cambridge (1819–1904), ordered that regiments posted on active service must leave their colours behind. This made the colours of the 58th (Rutlandshire) Regiment of Foot the last to be carried into battle, and those of the 1st Battalion of the South Staffordshire Regiment became the last to be taken on active service when they were at Alexandria in 1882.

While the rest of the British army's infantry regiments were content to field the King's and regimental colours, the regiments and battalions of the Guards sport colours of a differing pattern. Given the unique tasks carried out by the Guards regiments in protecting the sovereign and Royal Household, their colours are unique. The King's Colour is scarlet with the regimental insignia, arms and battle honours with the Union Flag canton on the colours of any additional battalions. The individual Regimental Colours appear as the Union Flag with regimental insignia and the regimental battle honours listed; unlike other infantry regiments, all five Guards regiments carry their battle honours on both colours. Until the 1820s, the Guards infantry also paraded company colours alongside the regimental battalion colours. A third colour, the Guards State Colour, is unique to the Grenadier, Coldstream and Scots Guards and is only used when the monarch is present. This design is scarlet with the regimental insignia and arms at the centre, with the Royal Cypher at the corners. No battle honours are present on these colours.

Interestingly, only the Grenadier Guards lost their colours in battle, on 8 March 1814 when the 2nd Battalion, 1st Regiment of Foot Guards, lost theirs during the Siege of Bergen op Zoom, Netherlands. Historically, the guidons carried by the cavalry remained lodged behind regimental lines during battle to prevent damage and loss. Today, the Household Cavalry are presented with a new guidon by the sovereign every decade. In contrast to the Household Cavalry and Guards Division, the King's Troop, Royal Horse Artillery, like all artillery units, is not represented by colours or guidons. Instead, they are represented by Troops Ordnance QF 13–pounders that have been involved in Trooping the Colour since 1997.

The Sovereign's Birthday Parade

The best way to describe The Sovereign's Birthday Parade is as an elaborate and often complex dance with the Trooping the Colour forming the centrepiece. The Field Officer in Brigade Waiting supervises the entire parade, with the Brigade Major and the Adjutant's assistance, all on horseback. They are joined by the Garrison Sergeant Major, who coordinates the ceremony proceedings.

Before the actual ceremony itself, there are the inevitable rehearsals, a fact of military life on the parade square and in the field that is often overlooked by observers, to ensure excellence is maintained. The first of the formal Trooping the Colour public rehearsals is the Major General's Review that usually takes place two weeks before the official Sovereign's Birthday Parade. This is held to ensure that the months of drill and work by all, from the GSM to the Master Tailor, is of the highest possible standard, with any snags identified before The Colonel of the Regiment's review. This is followed a week later by another public rehearsal, the Colonel of the Regiment's review, held a week before the official Sovereign's Birthday Parade. The Colonel's Review, reviewed by the member of the Royal Family whose regiment is parading on the Sovereign's Birthday Parade a week later, is held to guarantee the excellence of all involved.

As the Household Cavalry Mounted Regiment will form the Sovereign's Escort, the rehearsals are slightly different, especially as most taking part are in their first two years of service as Troopers, and half again are parading for the first time. Unlike the Foot Guards, the HCMR only has one chance to rehearse its route on the day and assemble and rehearse its manoeuvres in Hyde Park before the Major General's Review. This parade is given the unusual name of 'the String Band' because Guardsmen simulate the presence of Foot Guards Massed Bands with lengths of string. The rehearsals are slowly built up until a division of twenty-five mounted troopers can accurately and safely wheel and maintain their line and position, or dressing, in the ranks. Meanwhile, the Divisional Officer will maintain the pace to keep the space between divisions equal, not easily done when riding a creature that can be as temperamental as it can be compliant. Once the divisions are confident, they move onto Horse Guards Parade proper. Once gathered, the right-hand marker, whose role is to provide a visual anchor for the rest of the division and the division's officer, identifies previously used markers, such as statues and other landmarks that remain suitable for visual reference points. These will aid the right-hand marker in judging the straightness of the advancing line. The final piece of this equine-powered juggernaut is the Centre Man, who ensures the officer remains central to his division. While the divisions move, the Adjutant and Riding Master can check that their moving plans are accurate, preventing needless manoeuvring of horses and ensuring that everything is in the right place at the right time. Notes are made so any adjustments are made prior to the HCMR's appearance before the Major General's Review.

On the day of the Sovereign's Birthday Parade a strict timetable is followed. After an early start, all involved participate in a physical training activity to awaken their bodies, men and mounts. Once gathered, they are marched to their necessary forming-up points. Those Foot Guards not on parade are formed into half-companies of Guards, whose task is to line The Mall from Buckingham Palace to Horse Guards Parade in preparation to secure the passage of the Sovereign and Royal Family. This Foot Guard is far from merely ceremonial or symbolic, and alongside civilian police officers, forms a secure net against any attempts to endanger any member of the Royal Family. On more than one occasion, this unique security arrangement has prevented harm from coming to parading troops and the Royal Family.

The parade's start is indicated by the entrance of Guardsmen bearing marker flags, known as Keepers of the Ground, onto Horse Guards Parade. The Keepers of the Ground mark the positions for No.1 to No.6 Guards with marker flags representing the respective company colours of each regiment on parade. Led by the massed bands of the Massed Bands of the Foot Guards, the six companies of Foot Guards then march on to Horse Guards Parade via The Mall. Once assembled, the six companies of Foot

Preparing for Parade

Guards form up along two sides of the perimeter of Horse Guards Parade in an extended L that echoes the defensive formation known as the hollow square. The Massed Bands have now taken up position on the south side of the parade ground. Once the Guards are formed, members of the Royal Family arrive at Horse Guards Parade in two barouche coaches, with the No. 3 Guard opening ranks to allow the carriages to pass. The carriages then proceed to Horse Guards building, where occupants will view the ceremony from the Major General's office.

At this point, the Royal Procession makes its way down The Mall on horseback along with the HCMR, who provide the Sovereign's Escort, with two divisions riding before Charles III who is mounted on horseback, with two more divisions and the Massed Mounted Bands following. The Life Guards and The Blues and Royals alternate the leading and following every year. On arrival the Sovereign's Escort, the Massed Mounted Bands and the King's Troop form up behind No. 1 to No. 5 Guards on either side of the Guards Memorial on the edge of St. James's Park. At 11 o'clock, the King arrives, crossing Horse Guards Parade followed by the mounted Royal Colonels, who salute the colour as they pass. The Guards present arms whilst the Massed Bands play the National Anthem.

The King begins his 'Inspection of the Line' whilst the Massed Bands of the Household Division start their programme. At this stage, the King, led by the Brigade Major and is followed by the mounted Royal Colonels: Princess Anne, The Princess Royal (b. 1950), Gold Stick in Waiting and Colonel of the Blues and Royals, and HRH Prince William of Wales (b. 1982), Colonel of the Welsh Guards. The Master of the Horse, the Crown Equerry, the Equerries in Waiting and The General Officer Commanding London District are also in the King's procession, which turns before No. 6 Guard to the left of the line. Charles and the Royal Colonels acknowledge the colour in salute; the Royal Colonels then pass behind No. 6 Guard as Charles moves towards the Sovereign's Escort of the Household Cavalry, the Massed Mounted Bands, and the King's Troop. From there, Charles will move to the dais, taking his place for the remainder of the ceremony. For the King's Inspection phase of the parade, the musical accompaniment will consist of quick- and slow-time music performed by the stationary massed bands. During the parade, the Massed Bands, when at a standstill, will use the opportunity to flex their musical muscles and showcase their talent, performing the most demanding pieces of music. Of the traditional themes that have become firm favourites, the Senior Drum Major orders the slow march performance of Giacomo Meyerbeer's (1791–1864) *Les Huguenots* that sees the Massed Bands at their most guard-like and has been used at this point in the parade since the end of the last century.

As the Massed Bands move aside, a lone drummer breaks away to take up a position two paces to the right of the Escort For the Colour' where he will give the Drummer's Call to troop the colour through the ranks. The regiment trooping its Colour for the parade forms No. 1 Guard and is referred to as 'Escort *for* the Colour'. Once they have collected their colour, they are referred to as 'Escort *to* the Colour'. From the start of the parade, the colour is held by the Colour Party consisting of a Colour Sergeant and two other guardsmen, the tallest of the parading regiment, of No. 1 Guard, standing well spaced on the northern side of Horse Guards Parade. The three mounted officers drawn from No. 1 Guard will issue the 113 drill commands during the parade. The most senior of the three is the Field Officer in Brigade Waiting (rank of Lieutenant Colonel), who maintains the central position on the parade ground and is assisted by the Major of the Parade. The final mounted officer is the Adjutant. The dismounted GSM coordinates the entire event on Horse Guards Parade and The Mall.

As the trooping parade commences, an orderly approaches the Regimental Sergeant Major (RSM), taking his pace stick, allowing the RSM to draw his sword. During peacetime, the RSM will only draw his sword during a parade where a colour is trooped. The Escort marks time whilst the Massed Bands clear the line of march; the Ensign looks for a white stone, fifteen paces from the Colour Party, that indicates where he will halt the Escort. The RSM now marches from the rear of the Escort, sword drawn in symbolic protection of the colour. He is followed forward by the Ensign *for* the Colour who will carry the colour through

Preparing for Parade

the ranks of Nos. 2–6 Guards. The RSM salutes the colour, takes a pace forward, and receives the colour in his left hand from the Sergeant of the Colour Party. The Escort *for* the Colour marches off in quick time to the *British Grenadiers*, a march introduced into England as a military march during the reign of William III. The Royal Artillery first adopted it as its quick march in 1716, followed by the Grenadier Guards in 1763. No matter which regiment's colour is being trooped, the *British Grenadiers* is always played, a nod to the historical use of the right flank company of every battalion once being a grenadier company.

The Ensign now salutes the colour, sheathes his sword, receives the colour and places it in his colour belt. He then turns and shows the colour that will be trooped. The Escort has become the 'Escort *to* the Colour' at this stage. The Ensign, selected from one of the regiment's four Second Lieutenants, becomes the parade's focus. The selection is made by rehearsing all four hopefuls, who are drilled by the Regimental Drill Sergeant while being keenly observed by the Commanding Officer, who will have the final say over who is best suited to the role. There follows six weeks of instruction for the Ensign; with every movement, from slow march to sword drill, becoming slick and second nature. The most important move the Ensign will execute during the parade will be the Flourish of the Colour. This is the moment the Ensign lowers the colour before His Majesty the King, who acknowledges the Flourish along with the Royal Colonels before the Sovereign's Birthday Parade; the Ensign will have received a letter of encouragement from the previous year's Ensign that will hopefully assuage his nerves.

The entire parade presents arms while the National Anthem is played. The Escort moves through the assembled guards' ranks in slow time while the Massed Bands play *Escort to The Colour* and the *Grenadiers Slow March*. The latter was once used to march Grenadiers back to barracks after changing the guard and was adopted by the Grenadier Guards in 1815.

On command, the Massed Bands slowly move from the centre of Horse Guards Parade and perform the Spin Wheel drill manoeuvre. The Spin Wheel is a complex drill manoeuvre that has its roots in the 1920s when the Irish and Welsh Guards bands were incorporated into the Massed

Bands. With their addition Horse Guards Parade lacked the necessary space to wheel the Massed Bands, so the Spin Wheel was developed. It is coordinated by the non-commissioned officers within the ranks of musicians, resulting in the entire formation pivoting on its centre. The massed bands then halt in the centre of the parade ground and precisely positioned, they march off in quick time.

The Escort to the Colour, having cleared No. 2 Guard and resuming its place on the right of the line, now presents arms; the rest of the parade is ordered to slope arms, and all officers are ordered to take posts. The colour moves to the rear of the Escort, and Nos. 1 to 5 Guards are ordered to turn about by the mounted Adjutant of the Parade. Nos. 2 to 5 Guard right form at the halt to music from the drums, followed by Nos. 1 to 5 guards performing a turnabout. All six Guards companies then march past in line abreast in slow time. The Field Officer in Brigade Waiting and Major of the Parade move to take their places at the head of the parade for the salute. The Colour is Flourished, or lowered in salute, as it passes the King at the saluting dais; the subsequent raising of the Colour is known as the Recover. The Massed Bands play each of the Guard's Regimental Slow Marches while each company passes the dais. The Adjutant brings up the rear of the march past, and as he clears the dais, the Field Officer rides out ten yards from behind the dais, turns his horse and salutes the King. The bands pause momentarily as the Field Officer orders the Quick March before riding across to the head of the parade to lead the parade once more in a quick-time march past. This time, the Massed Bands Guards play the Guards' Regimental Quick Marches as each company passes the dais. Once more, the Adjutant follows the parade, and the Field Officer rides out to salute the King.

The Massed Bands of the Household Division now make way for the Massed Mounted Bands of the Household Cavalry led by the kettle drum horses. These horses have always been Heavy Horse breeds, either part-bred Shire or Clydesdale and have traditionally been geldings. In 2023, there was a break with tradition when 10-year-old mare and former Welsh Shire cart horse Willa Rose was accepted as a Drum Horse

Preparing for Parade

and given the name Juno by Queen Camilla (b. 1947) after two years of training. Interestingly, the Drum Horses hold the rank of Major, the only animals in British Army service to have a commissioned rank. The Massed Mounted Bands play *The March of the Preobrazhensky Life-Guard Regiment*, a Russian piece dated to the time of Peter I (1672–1725), as they pass the dais. This particular match was a favourite piece of Lord Louis Mountbatten (1900–1979), Gold Stick of the Life Guards, and is now included as a mark of respect.

With the Mounted Bands now positioned opposite the dais, the King's Troop are first to take the salute as they take precedence over all other units when on parade with their guns. As the King's Troop passes the dais, the King acknowledges the leading gun as the colour on account of artillery regiments' guns being their colour and, as such, are granted the same respect as the embroidered colours and guidons of other regiments. The Kings' Troop walk-past is accompanied by the Royal Artillery Slow March, *The Duchess of Kent*. Surprisingly, Princess Victoria, Duchess of Kent (1786–1861), mother of Victoria, circa 1836, wrote the piece that was first played in 1843. As the Life Guards contingent of the Sovereign's Escort, who all ride black horses, walk past the dais, the music changes once more to the Life Guards' Slow March followed by The Blues and Royals walk past which is accompanied by the *Blues and Royals* Slow March. Finally, the regimental farriers, carrying their distinctive axes, once used to dispatch injured horses in battle pass. Farriers of the Blues and Royals have the distinction of wearing a black horsehair plume on their Albert helmets. At this stage, the parade takes on a more vibrant phase of movement and musicality as a mounted trumpeter signals 'The Trot' and the Sovereign's Escort trots past the dais once more to the tune *The Keel Row*.

The mounted band's director of music, who is waiting until the last division of the Sovereign's Escort has stopped, turns inwards as a signal to the Field Officer. This is followed by the assembled troops presenting arms, and *The Royal Salute* is again played. The Field Officer now reports to the King that his Guards are ready to march off. The GSM salutes, indicating that the carriages transporting members of the Royal Family have passed the end of the approach road where the mounted troops are assembled and are returning to Buckingham Palace. The King then leads his troops back down The Mall to Buckingham Palace, led by the Massed Bands of the Household Division. The Keepers of the Ground now return to Wellington Barracks. The King stops at the gates of Buckingham Palace, and the entire parade once again marches past in salute, watched by members of the Royal Family from the famous balcony. At this point, those guards performing Public Duties at the Palace take their places while the remaining Guards return to Wellington Barracks, and the Sovereign's Escort returns to Hyde Park Barracks.

Trooping the Colour is now ending, with The Kings' Troop moving to Green Park, adjacent to Buckingham Palace, in readiness for firing a forty-one-gun salute at 12:52 pm, based on a twenty-one-gun salute, a salute reserved for Heads of State. The additional twenty rounds are fired as the gun position is within a Royal Park. At 1:00 pm, A Battery, the Honourable Artillery Company fires a sixty-two-gun salute at the Tower of London. As a finale, the Royal Air Force lends its voice to splendour by performing a flypast of modern aircraft from its operational squadrons and vintage types from the Battle of Britain Memorial Flight (BBMF).

The Gun's Salute: the Artillery gives voice

> 'Renown awaits the commander who first restores artillery to its prime importance on the battlefield.'
>
> Winston Churchill

Cannon fire has a unique charm and satisfaction that adds a touch of martial grandeur to any event. London District is privileged to have two distinct batteries: The Honourable Artillery Company and The King's Troop Royal Horse Artillery. Each has its unique operating style, with The Honourable Artillery Company using the modern 105-mm light gun and the King's Troop relying on traditional horsepower to pull their six QF 13-pounder guns.

A Battery, The Honourable Artillery Company (HAC)

Today, The Honourable Artillery Company (HAC) maintains a ceremonial role in providing a saluting battery at the Tower of London for state occasions, such as the Trooping the Colour. The HAC took over the role from the Royal Artillery when the latter's small Tower of London detachment was disbanded, and the decision made to pass any gunnery tasks to the artillery component of the HAC. The first HAC salute was fired on 6 May 1924. Since 1931, the senior appointed HAC artillery officer has been known as the Master Gunner within the Tower. Sir Douglas Morpeth (1924–2014) was a previous incumbent in this role. He served with the Royal Artillery in India, Burma and Malaya between 1942 and 1947 when he was demobbed as a Captain. Returning to college, Morpeth studied business and moved to London in 1951. Morpeth joined the HAC the same year, commanding the 1st Regiment HAC from 1964 to 1966. Lieutenant-Colonel Morpeth was appointed Master Gunner in the Tower of London in 1967, a position he held until 1968.

Outside of the HAC, Morpeth had become a Chartered Accountant and campaigned for the simplification of Tax Laws and accountancy standards and was instrumental in the founding of the International Accounting Standards Committee (IASC) in 1973 alongside Sir Henry Benson (1909–1995). Benson had served with the Grenadier Guards during the Second World War, during which he guarded Windsor Castle and, while there, wrote a report on improving military communications. In 1942, Benson was promoted to Major and transferred to the Special Operations Executive, where he remained until 1944 when he was promoted to Colonel and moved to the Ministry of Supply to help reorganize munitions factories. Benson became Director of Operations (Accounts), placing him in charge of 100,000 people. Upon leaving the army in 1945, Benson was an acting Brigadier. Morpeth's interests in the traditions of the City of London continued outside of the HAC, and he helped found the Worshipful Company of Chartered Accountants in England and Wales, which was created with full livery status in 1976.

In 1981, at 57, Morpeth was knighted for his services to the accounting profession.

Since 2018, the Salutes have been a regular feature carried out by A Battery, HAC. Positioned alongside the River Thames, in full view of the iconic Tower Bridge, they fire three 105-mm light guns. These guns, with their thunderous voice, are the heart of the famous salutes. These salutes, a visual and auditory spectacle, are not only fired on the Sovereign's Birthday Parade but also on significant days like the King's Ascension Day, the King's Birthday, and the Queen's Birthday, marking these events with a resounding salute that echoes through the city.

The King's Troop, Royal Horse Artillery (RHA)

Each Troop (the term Battery was not used at the time) of RHA had six QF 13-pounder guns, 180 personnel, and horses. The Troop was then broken down into sub-divisions or 'Subs', a term still used with the King's Troop. The Sub consists of a gun and limber; six horses are hitched in pairs to the limber shafts. An ammunition wagon is also included in the Sub. The near-side horses are ridden by drivers, who control the off-side horses with whip and rein. Two gunners rode the limber and were responsible for the Sub's equipment. A further eight gunners followed them. The Sub was led by a Number One, usually a sergeant. Today, each Sub is mounted on horses whose coats get progressively darker: A Sub mounts are a chestnut colour while F Sub mounts have a rich black coat. F Sub mounts were recently used to transport Elizabeth II to her final resting place at Windsor Castle in 2022.

Together, two Subs made a division commanded by a Subaltern, with three divisions making a troop, traditionally commanded by a Captain, who in turn was assisted by a 'Second Captain'. This organization gave a Troop considerable flexibility in the field. Divisions could operate independently of the Troop, giving commanders on the ground much-needed support when required. The Troops were supported by a formidable logistical backup, including baggage and a blacksmith's forge wagon. Another wagon also carried spare wheels, which was wise given

Preparing for Parade

the speed at which the ton-and-a-half guns could be moved cross-country. The King's Troop maintains a healthy stock of wheels to this day. Also included were farriers, wheelwrights, saddlers and a surgeon.

To tow the heavy guns and limbers, the Troop stables an impressive 120 horses and is the only ceremonial unit to be commanded by a Major instead of a Lieutenant-Colonel. The Troop's horses are selected annually from two breeders in Ireland and are chosen to be either Troop Chargers or the smaller Lines Horses, used to drive the guns and limbers, and officially described as 'Light Irish Draught'. The Lines Horses are sized according to the role they will play. Leaders usually stand around 16 hands, centres 15.3 and the wheelers 15.2 hands or smaller. Once the horses have been checked by the Royal Army Veterinary Corps (RAVC), the Lines Horses have their manes hogged, and all mounts are given a number stamped onto their hoofs. This tradition stems from when the hoof was removed to prove the horse had died in battle and had not been lost or sold.

Initially, the Troop were equipped with the larger Ordnance Quick Firing 18-pounder Mark I. This gun featured the unique wire-wound barrel that produced a lighter, more robust, cheaper-to-manufacture barrel than a fully built-up one. Its recuperator, which returns the gun barrel to its firing position after recoil, is protected from damage by a thick rope. The 18-pounder was replaced by the QF 13-pounder field gun of First World War vintage, and at least one gun in use today saw service during that period. The King's Troop guns are finished in bronze-green with the recuperator rope painted white and highly polished bright work. The King's Troop has access to nine 13-pounders, of which six are used for ceremonial purposes, and all are kept in perfect order in the Troop's covered Gun Park. These are looked after by members of the Troop and Royal Electrical and Mechanical Engineers (REME).

Unlike the Infantry and Cavalry, the Artillery doesn't have colours or guidons, and it uses guns as its colours. When on ceremonial duties, these guns are accorded the same dignity and respect as the colours or guidons of the other member regiments and units of the army. This tradition can be traced back to the Artillery's early history when a team carried its colour on the largest piece in its artillery train. This gun was designated the 'Flag Gun'. The Flag Gun was used until the end of the eighteenth century. After this, the guns themselves came to be regarded as the colours of the Artillery.

Training of horse and rider remains a crucial part of life in King's Troop, with riders often undertaking equitation instruction in full ceremonial dress.

The Bands of the Household Division

> 'Music expresses that which cannot be put into words and that which cannot remain silent.'
>
> Victor Hugo

Music has played an essential role in military formations since ancient times. Horns and drums have heralded defeat and victory alike; they have entertained and helped provide communication in battle and acted as psychological instruments of war. Despite changes in technology, with radio-based communications taking over from trumpet and drum, there remains a need for military bands to continue playing, especially in ceremonial and public relations exercises.

Today, State Ceremonial is led by the Bands of the Household Division who make up seven of the fourteen regular Army State Bands. The Musicians, Drum Majors and Directors of Music come together to provide suitable musical accompaniment to events like the King's Birthday Parade. Although they wear the uniforms of the Household Division, the men and women of the State Bands of the Household Division are now part of the wider Royal Corps of Army Music (RCAM). This allows musicians to develop their art and move around the fourteen bands, gaining valuable experience as they do so.

The RCAM was founded in 2021 as a result of changes brought about after the ending of the Cold War and the moving of the Corps of Army Music from its home at Kneller Hall to be split with the Corps

Preparing for Parade

Headquarters moving to Gibraltar Barracks, Hampshire, with the Royal Military School of Music relocated to HMS *Nelson,* Portsmouth. With the forming of the RCAM came a mass reorganization, and a corps that could field sixty regimental and corps bands thirty years previously had shrunk to a mere fourteen, including the six bands of the Household Division.

The Band of the Household Cavalry was formed in 2014 by merging the Life Guards and Blues and Royals (RHG/D) bands that play both mounted and dismounted. The Bands of the Foot Guards have maintained their individual status as regimental bands, but, like the Mounted Band of the Household Cavalry, they are members of the RACM and remain under its command and control. State Trumpeters stay under the command of the Royal Household.

When not providing musical accompaniment to State Ceremonial and Public Duties, bands provide music around the globe, with many musicians proficient in at least two instruments. In addition to these skills, the musicians of the Mounted Band of the Household Cavalry are also skilled equestrians, riding some of the largest horses in the British Army.

One key music event for the Bands of the Household Division, including Pipes and Drums, is the Beating Retreat, now played on the Wednesday and Thursday evenings preceding Trooping the Colour. This ceremony was first recorded in 1589, when 'ye Drumme Major will advertise those required for watch'. This ceremony was further developed so that by 1727, it became customary 'half an hour before the setting of the sun the drummers and Port-Guards are to go upon the ramparts and beat a retreat to give notice to those without that the gates are to be shut'. The drummers were expected to play continuously for fifteen minutes for this act.

Over the centuries, every regiment and corps in the British Army has adopted their own quick and slow marches, and the Household Division is no different, with the Bands of the Household Division playing Regimental marches with clarity during State Ceremonial.

Despite the many social and military changes over the past four centuries, State Bands of the Household Division still maintain ties with their traditional homes. The Mounted Band of the Household Cavalry is based at Combermere Barracks, Windsor, and Hyde Park Barracks, London, while Wellington Barracks, London, is the home of the Bands of the Foot Guards.

Like all musicians, members of the Bands of the Household Division have secondary roles, including drivers and medics. The one exception is that of Pipers, who form the regimental sustained-fire machine-gun platoons used for infantry battalion fire support.

THE MOUNTED BAND OF THE HOUSEHOLD CAVALRY

The Life Guards (LG) were the first band in the new Standing Army to parade with kettledrums, bringing them from the Netherlands on their return to England in 1660. By 1822, the band, although small, also included trumpeters, French horns and hautbois (oboes). These were augmented by the gift of a set of silver kettledrums by William IV in 1831, to the then 2nd Life Guards band, led by Herr Froenherdt, on 4 May. Another set was gifted to 1st Life Guards on 23 July of the same year. These drums remain in use and are often seen at State Ceremonial. When in use, the drums carry the Royal Coat of Arms.

The Blues and Royals (RHG/D) musical history replicates the regimental history, and the current band was formed in 1805 when RHG/D was still the Royal Regiment of Horse Guards (The Blues) (RHG). On 23 April, George III presented the band with a set of silver kettledrums, led by a Herr Stowasser, who was appointed as the first bandmaster of the Regiment. A further amalgamation with the 1st Royal Dragoons (The Royals) in 1969 saw the band become the Band of the Blues and Royals.

The Mounted Band of the Household Cavalry, part of the Household Cavalry Mounted Regiment (HCMR), like its parent regiments, has a long and illustrious history. The band's role extends beyond ceremonial duties. In times of war, they would accompany the cavalry on the battlefield, providing crucial signals and communication through their music. The mounted band ride black horses, a habit that may stem from attending to Charles II at his coronation. The exception to this rule is

Preparing for Parade

the trumpeters who are mounted on greys. This tradition, which was cavalry-wide, stems from the need for commanders to readily identify these essential musicians on a crowded battlefield. Trumpeters' horses will also be seen wearing a scarlet and black horsehair plume attached to the harness beneath the throat. The larger Drum horses are normally Clydesdale or Shire, chosen for their strength in carrying the solid silver drums and either piebald or skewbald. These magnificent horses lead the Mounted Band at the State Ceremony. At the same time, trumpeters can also be seen leading a change of the guard. Horses used by musicians are often guided by reins attached to the rider's arms or stirrups, as well as the usual subtle saddle and leg pressure gestures. The horses used by the Mounted Band are loaned to them form the HCMR stables and are specifically chosen for their placid nature and experience.

The Mounted Band of the Household Cavalry wears similar dress based on the uniforms worn by the Household Cavalry Mounted Regiment (HCMR). The Mounted Band also wears the eye-catching golden State Dress. This is unchanged since it was originally purchased by The Lord Mayor of London to celebrate the restoration of Charles in 1660 and is worn in the presence of either senior royalty or the Lord Mayor of London. The crimson velvet coat is overlaid with gold lace and carries the Royal Cipher predominantly on its front and rear. State Dress also includes white buckskin breeches and jackboots, or in the case of kettle drummers' knee boots, to prevent fouling the large kettle drums. This is topped with a dark blue velvet jockey cap, adopted during Victoria's reign. A crimson cloak, edged in gold lace, is worn in inclement weather.

Tack for all riders is black leather, with black sheepskin saddle covers for both Life Guards and Blue and Royal musicians. The Directors of Music have a shabraque or saddle cloth. This is dark blue for the Life Guards and scarlet for the Blues and Royals, featuring the regimental cypher and battle honours in each corner.

State Dress Mounted Band musicians will also appear in Full Mounted Review Order dress, like the dress worn by troopers and officers in the HCMR, but in all cases omitting the cuirass to enable easier breathing.

In Full Dismounted Review Order, the musicians exchange their white buckskin and jackboots for dark blue trousers, also known as overalls.

Regimental Music
The Mounted Band of the Household Cavalry maintains many of the traditions of its antecedent bands and historical regimental traditions, including the music that was unique to the original bands.

Marches of the Life Guards
Quick   *Millanollo*
Slow   *Life Guards Slow March*
Trot Past   *Keel Row*

Marches of the Blues and Royals
Quick   *Quick March of the Blues and Royals*
Slow   *Slow March of the Blues and Royals*
Trot Past   *Keel Row*

THE BANDS OF THE FOOT GUARDS

Like their mounted compatriots, each of the five regiments of Foot Guards has its own Corps of Drums led by a Drum Major. In the case of the Scots and Irish Guards, a Pipe band is also fielded and led by a Pipe Major.

All Bands of the Foot Guards musicians have secondary roles, traditionally stretch bearers. In the first Elizabethan era, drummers, often boys, were expected to be able to speak another language. This would enable them to use a second language to help communicate with enemy forces to discuss terms and communicate with the local population. As they played a key role in court, they were also expected to act with complete discretion, lest they disclose secrets or scandals.

The uniforms of the Corps of Drums members remain firmly based on the regiments that they represent with minor alternations. The back of the bearskins worn by the Corps of Drums is trimmed to a point, while the collars of the tunics are edged with blue. This, in turn, is overlaid with ribbons of blue fleur-de-Lys on a white lace background, a throwback to the courts of medieval England. The ribbon is repeated on the front, arms of the tunics, and their shoulder-mounted Musicians' Wings. Other members of the bands will wear the standard scarlet tunic of the guard's regiments, which they represent, with the embellishment of Musicians' Wings.

Drum Majors wear a similar tunic style, though their lace is gold braid, and four inverted chevrons indicate their rank on their lower right sleeve. The Drum Major wears the appropriate regimental sash and mace, protected by white gloves, and carries a sword. Trousers for members of the Corps of Drums and regimental band are dark blue with a scarlet welt running down the outer seam.

Regimental Drum Majors of the Foot Guards on State Ceremonial will wear State Dress with a jockey cap and white buckskin gaiters over black boots. They will also wear a crimson apron edged with a gold fringe and held in place with a clasp bearing the respective regimental cypher. The final detail is the Regimental Drum Major sash, which displays the regimental cypher and associated battle honours.

The Directors of Music wear the same uniform as their fellow officers in the Guards Division but with slight alterations. These include a white piped dark blue tunic collar edged with gold, top and bottom, and a slightly taller bearskin. The tunic features white piped edges, and the shoulder straps are edged in gold braid. Like the Drum Major, the Director of Music carries a sword slung in white leather for regular duties and gold with red leather backing for State Ceremonial. Finally, a crimson sash is usually worn, though this is changed to a crimson and gold sash for State Ceremonial. Like all members of the Guards Division, the Director of Music wears the same dark blue trousers but with a broad scarlet welt running down the outer seam.

When playing as Massed Bands of the Foot Guards, which will number over 200 musicians, the Senior Director of Music (SDOM) will select and arrange suitable music. The process is mostly undertaken for the Trooping of the Colour and can involve several meetings and auditions before the final pieces are agreed upon by the Major General, Brigade

Major, and Garrison Sergeant Major. Once agreed upon, the process of ensuring each musician knows their playlist begins.

Band of the Grenadier Guards

In 1685, Charles II authorized the engagement of 12 Hautbois (Oboe players) to serve as the band of the Grenadier Guards. Over the next 90 years, the band grew to include three more Hautbois, two French horns, and bugle horns. By 1794, the band consisted of sixteen musicians, including the regimental Timebeater, who, until the Second World War, wore a band of mourning for Charles II's passing.

The band's reputation was such that it caught the attention of the Baroque composer George Fredric Handel (1685-1759). In a testament to their musical prowess, Handel gifted the march from the opera *Scipio* to the regiment before its first performance in 1726. This was just the beginning of their association, as the famous composer was later commissioned by George II to score *Music for the Royal Fireworks*, to be played by the musicians of the Royal Household, which included wind players from the Foot Guards.

Today the band consists of around forty-eight musicians and fields a range of ensembles, including the Marching Band, an eighteenth-century Ensemble, Dinner Trios and Quartets, and a Fanfare Trumpet Team.

Regimental Music
Quick	*The British Grenadiers*
	The Grenadier March
Slow	*Scipio*
	The Duke of York

Band of the Coldstream Guards

The first band of the Coldstream Guards was formed in 1742 by eight civilian musicians. The regimental officers paid them every month to accompany the changing of the guard at St. James's Palace, then the chief Royal Residence. This arrangement suited both parties until a clash of dates led to the officers approaching the Colonel of the Regiment, Frederick Augustus, Duke of York (1763–1827) and second son of George III, for an attested band. The Duke agreed that under the direction of Music Major C. F. Eley, a band of twelve German musicians was to be assembled and subsequently formed on 16 May 1785. The band consisted of two Hautbois, four clarinets, two bassoons, two horns, a trumpet and a Serpent.

Over the next 100 years, the band grew, gaining wind and brass instruments and mustering fifty-one musicians by 1900. The band also grew in the public eye, courtesy of a wax and cylinder disc recording made in 1898, the first band to do so. The recording of martial music would continue into the twentieth century. The band of the Coldstream Guards would also become prolific performers, touring North America in 1903.

During the Second World War, the band continued to support the war effort by touring the United Kingdom and delivering performances to military and civilian audiences. However, they were not to escape the horror of the war, and on 18 June 1944, whilst performing at the Guards Chapel, Wellington Barracks, a VI flying bomb struck, killing 120, including the Director of Music and five musicians.

Today, the band continues its performance legacy, leading key public music displays, including opening the 1985 Live Aid concert at Wembley Stadium. It also performed *The Star-Spangled Banner* at Buckingham Palace, London, during the daily ceremonial Changing of the Guard on 12 September 2001. The national anthem of the United States of America was performed with the permission of Elizabeth II as an act of solidarity in the immediate aftermath of the 9/11 terrorist attacks. The band of the Coldstream Guards also played the end credit theme tune *Who Do You Think You Are Kidding, Mr Hitler?* for the famous BBC television series *Dad's Army*.

Regimental Music
Quick   *Millanollo*
Slow   *Figaro*

BAND OF THE SCOTS GUARDS

The history of the Band of the Scots Guards is a little more obscure, although it was recorded in 1716 that the regiment had a small number of Hautbois in its service. By 1888, the band had grown to forty-four musicians, including the Pipe Major and five pipers, who joined the regiment in 1856.

Since 1920, the Pipes and Drums of the Scots Guards have worn the now familiar feathered black Highland Bonnet, which features a red, white and blue diced headband. Further adornment is provided by a blue-over-red hackle worn on the left of the bonnet and held in place with a silver regimental badge. Before this, pipers wore the Glengarry Bonnet, adorned with a Blackcock feather plume. Musicians wear a traditional dark blue doublet with white piping and lace details, over which the waist belt and the now redundant shoulder belt, once used to carry a sword, sit. Pipers continue with the Highland tradition of carrying a dirk, which hangs from right-hand side of the waist belt, and the *sgiandhu*, tucked into the top of the right hose.

The kilt and associated plaid, held in place by a large silver regimental brooch, are of Royal Stuart pattern, with trews worn when not employed on State Ceremonial. The sporran is made of horsehair, and the hose is of dark red and scarlet crossed diamonds partially covered by white spats. The pipes are a three drone set with a royal blue bag garnished with Royal Stuart, cords, tassels and ribbons.

Pipe Major's uniform is like that of the musicians of the Pipes and Drums but with a few differences, including silver rather than white details. The Pipe Major rank is indicated by four inverted chevrons on the right sleeve, topped by a crown and a crimson sash worn underneath the Royal Scot sash. A Broadsword, attached to a warrant officer's belt, is carried on all occasions, with scarlet and gold pipe banners carried during State Ceremonial.

The Pipe Major can also be called upon to fulfil the role of Piper to the Sovereign. While fulfilling this role, the Pipe Major is deemed to be on secondment and part of the Royal Household. For the duration of the secondment, he retains his regimental rank.

All members of the Pipes and Drums complete their basic training at the Infantry Training Camp, Catterick Garrison, North Yorkshire. After that, they develop their art at the Army School of Bagpipe Music and Highland Drumming in Edinburgh, Scotland. As trained infantiers, the Guardsmen of the Pipes and Drums form part of the Commanding Officer's tactical group and have seen action in the 1982 Falklands Conflict and the 1991 Gulf War.

The Scots Guards also have regimental dancers who appear at global shows accompanied by the Pipes and Drums, performing their own Scottish country dance, the *The Scots Guards*.

Regimental Music
Quick   *Hi'lan Laddie*
Slow   *Garb of Old Gaul*

BAND OF THE IRISH GUARDS

The Band of the Irish Guards was formed on 21 November 1900, fielding a band of thirty-five musicians led by Bandmaster Warrant Officer Charles Hassell. The following year the band joined their fellow musicians of the Band of the Grenadier Guards in the Trooping of the Colour on 9 May 1901. On 24 May they joined with the other bands of The Brigade of Guards as part of the Massed Bands to celebrate Edward VII's King's Birthday Parade. This was also the first time that the Sovereign took the salute on Horse Guards Parade. This momentous occasion was followed by a South African War medal presentation on 12 June, where the band supported an Irish Guards Guard of Honour. The band was quick to establish their quality. As a result of its 1905 tour of Canada, it was presented with an ornate silver cup from the citizens of Toronto.

The First World War saw the band deploy to Europe as part of the British Expeditionary Force and as guests of the French and Italian governments. The band provided morale-boosting music to those serving overseas. Post-war, the band continued to entertain, and on 23 January 1923, it is believed they became the first military band to play live on the British radio station 2LO, which would later become the British Broadcasting Corporation (BBC).

The Irish Guards Drums and Pipes were formed in 1916 when John Redmond MP, a prominent Irish nationalist, presented the regiment with several sets of Irish War Pipes. Initially, men of the then 3rd (Reserve) Battalion were trained in the use of the pipes by the Pipe Major of the London Irish Rifles, with the Pipes financed by the regiment's officers. In 1918, the Pipes were officially placed on the establishment table.

Members of the Drums and Pipes wear the distinctive saffron kilt, also worn by pipers of the Royal Irish Regiment (RIR). Initially, they played the distinctive two-drone Irish War Pipe, which delivers a slightly higher and more distinctive pitch than its three-drone Scottish counterpart. In 1960, the pipers exchanged their Irish War Pipes for the standard three-drone Scottish bagpipe. Like their Scots Guards counterparts, the men of the Drums and Pipes are fully trained infantry soldiers, with four losing their lives on active service in Iraq.

The band continued supporting the army during the Second World War, touring the North Africa and Mediterranean theatres between October 1943 and May 1944 and supporting the regiment in Palestine in 1948. Later, band members were deployed to the Gulf (Operation *Granby*) in 1991 and deployed as a band as part of the NATO peacekeeping force (Operation *Agricola*) in Kosovo in 1999.

Along with their ceremonial duties, the band continues to provide music for entertainment and touring. One accolade accorded to the band was the honour of being the first foreign band to play in the Tokyo Imperial Palace in the presence of the Empress Consort Nagako and two of the five Crown Princesses. The band also performed on several film soundtracks, including *Oh! What a Lovely War* and the whistling *Colonel Bogey* for the soundtrack of *The Bridge on the River Kwai*.

In 2000, the band celebrated the regimental centenary by performing at Dublin's National Concert Hall alongside the Irish Defence Force's (IDF) Number One Band. This was also the first visit to the Republic of Ireland by a British Army band since 1922.

Regimental Music
Quick   *St. Patrick's Day*
Slow   *Let Erin Remember*

BAND OF THE WELSH GUARDS

The Band of the Welsh Guards, the youngest of all the Guards Division bands, was formed on 9 October 1915, with forty-four musicians playing instruments gifted to them by the City of Cardiff. A significant milestone in the band's history was their first King's Guard Mounting on St. David's Day, 1 March 1916. This event not only demonstrated the band's musical proficiency, it also marked the beginning of a series of events that would help establish their reputation. The following year, the band embarked on morale-boosting tours that continue to this day. The pinnacle of the band's career occurred on 1 July 1969 at the investiture of Charles, Prince of Wales, which took place at Caernarfon Castle, North Wales. The band's dress for the State Ceremonial remains the same as the regimental dress, with drummers attired accordingly.

    The band's wartime role is as Chemical Decontamination Assistants and outside of State Ceremonial and events across the globe, the band also fields a dance band and salon orchestra.

Regimental Music
Quick   *Rising of the Lark*
Slow   *Men of Harlech*

THE COUNTESS OF WESSEX'S STRING ORCHESTRA

The Countess of Wessex's String Orchestra (CWSO) has its roots in the string sections of the Royal Artillery Band, the first official British military band, formed in 1557. After its demise as a Regular Army State Band in 2014, it was felt that a State String Orchestra would best fill the gap left behind. The twenty-four-piece CWSO was founded on 1 April 2014, named after Sophie, Countess of Wessex (b.1965), then daughter-in-law of Elizabeth II, who is also the Colonel-in-chief of RCAM.

Its inclusion in the Bands of the Household Division gives the organization an orchestra that can perform at Royal Household events, entertaining listeners with non-traditional instruments. The CWSO also enjoys an excellent working relationship with string ensembles from the other armed services, including the string orchestra of the Royal Marines Band Service and the RAF Salon Orchestra.

Honourable Artillery Corps of Drums and Regimental Band

As with all units, the Honourable Artillery Company can field two musical sections, the Corps of Drums and the Regimental Band, both staffed by reservists. One of the first mentions of musicians was in an article of *The Tatler* dated 12 July 1709, where an Exercise of Arms of the Artillery Company was accompanied by 'Beat to Arms and march around the Hall ... and makes a show as if for a battle'. To help fund such activities, an allowance of £4 was made to provide, among other things, drums and music.

Today, the Honourable Artillery Corps of Drums are part of the Headquarters Squadron. They provide trained personnel for A (1st City of London) Battery and maintain their ceremonial drumming role. The Corps of Drums is the last remaining sub-unit from the old infantry battalions of the Honourable Artillery Company. They wear the silver grenade beret badge with the Household Division scarlet stripe over the navy-blue beret patch. They also wear the Foot Guards stable belt, beret and tactical recognition flash. The Corps of Drums and the Band wear a forage cap with silver grenade, and a navy-blue stripe is placed over the scarlet headband. The Pikemen and Musketeers are accompanied by drummers, who wear period costumes during ceremonial events.

The Regimental Band of the Honourable Artillery Company is primarily made of musicians who wear the standard scarlet tunic and traditional fleur-de-lys lacing of the Grenadier Guards musicians, with silver musician wings, instead of the gold of their regular counterparts. The Regimental Band is made up of highly experienced musicians who perform at State Ceremonial, Public Duties and special events, often playing wind and string instrumentation alongside their regular counterparts as well as choirs from the world of music. Indeed, many former regular musicians go on to play with the Regimental Band as reservists.

Regimental Music
Quick	*The British Grenadiers*
Slow	*The Duke of York*
Canter	*Bonnie Dundee*
Trot	*The Keel Row*
Walk	*The Duchess of Kent*

A VERY PUBLIC FACE

THE CHANGING OF THE GUARD

Every member of the Household Division and the Royal Household is uniquely positioned within the British Army; they operate under near-constant public scrutiny. From worldwide broadcasts of State Ceremonial to the social media circuses of influencer poses, public ignorance and faux intimidation that often ends in a police charge for the offender, today's Guards are under constant watch. Errors that would have gone unnoticed thirty years ago are tomorrow's headlines and talking points. Yet, for all these occasionally negative, often funny and regularly heart-warming moments, the men and women of the Household Division and the Royal Household continue to fulfil their roles of protecting the Royal Palaces and residences with the utmost diligence.

The fundamental everyday public duty carried out by the Household Division remains the Changing of the Guard. This duty stems from the reign of Henry VII when the Body Guard of the Yeomen of the Guards were charged with protecting the Royal Body. In 1509, with the ascension of Henry VII to the throne, a Troop of Gentlemen was formed, armed with spear and lance to protect the sovereign, in battle or elsewhere. They served with several sovereigns at home and on the field of battle, later becoming known as the Honourable Band of Gentleman Pensioners, until 1834, when they became known as the Sovereign's Bodyguard of the Honourable Corps of Gentleman-at-Arms. With the conclusion of the Wars of the Three Kingdoms and Charles II's subsequent exile, the bodyguard continued to serve the sovereign, joining Charles in exile in France, taking the title the Life Guards. With the restoration of the monarchy in 1660 and the return of Charles and his entourage, including Life Guards, the task of protecting Charles remained as the risk of harm from political and religious opponents remained high. Now protected by the mounted regiment of Life Guards and three regiments of Foot Guards, Charles set a precedent that remains in place almost 500 years later. Given the vast geographical spread of Royal Palaces and residences, mounting guards at every location would be impractical. Today, the HCMR and Foot Guards provide a guard at the London palaces and Windsor and Edinburgh Castles; occasionally, these are replaced by visiting units from British or Commonwealth militaries.

Today, the King's Guard is comprised of two detachments: the Buckingham Palace Detachment, where Changing the Guard takes place every Monday, Wednesday, Friday and Sunday at 11:00, and the St. James's Palace Detachment. The Duty or Old Guard will form up in front of the Palace in preparation for their relief by the New Guard that has marched from Wellington Barracks. The ceremony of the Changing of the Guard reflects 600 years of tradition, representing a formal handover of responsibilities. A Band or Corps of Drums accompany it, playing a medley of martial and popular music. The King's Life Guard are the mounted troopers of HCMR responsible for providing the guard at the official entrance to St. James's Palace and Buckingham Palace outside Horse Guards Parade at the Palace of Whitehall. At Windsor, the Windsor Castle Guard takes place on Tuesdays, Thursdays and Saturdays at 11:00 am and consists of the New Guard marching from Victoria Barracks, Windsor, led by a Band or Corps of Drums. Once at the castle, the Guard conduct a ceremonial handover of responsibilities before the Old Guard marches back to Victoria Barracks. The Household Cavalry changes guard on Horse Guards Parade daily at 11:00 am and 10:00 am on Sundays. On days of rehearsals, such as those needed for the Sovereign's Birthday Parade or other events taking place on Horse Guards, the Guard Change can move to 4:00 pm.

The use of St. James's Palace as part of the daily life of the Royal Household started in 1698, during the reign of William III, when it became the sovereign's official residence after Whitehall Palace was destroyed by fire. St. James's Palace that gives its name to the Court of St. James's, serves as the official royal court for the Sovereign of the United Kingdom, and is home to His Majesty's Marshal of the Diplomatic Corps, who is a senior member of the Royal Household, acting as the King's link to the diplomatic community in London. The Marshal's duties include arranging the annual diplomatic corps reception by the Sovereign and the presentation of credentials ceremonies for ambassadors and high commissioners, as well as formally accrediting British ambassadors. The Marshal is also responsible for supervising the attendance of diplomats at state events and liaising with foreign diplomatic missions on behalf of the monarch. Previous incumbents of His Majesty's Marshal of the Diplomatic Corps have included Lieutenant General Sir George Sidney Clive, Grenadier Guards, serving as Marshal from 1934 to 1946. Clive would see service in Sudan (1898), the Second Anglo-Boer War and as Head of the British Mission at the French Army headquarters from 1915 to 1918. As St. James's Palace remains the official residence of the court, it is here that the Colour is lodged, and the Captain of the Guard establishes his headquarters.

The Guard at Buckingham Palace is perhaps the most iconic of London Districts Guard responsibilities. Buckingham Palace, with its commanding views of The Mall and Constitution Hill, was built as Buckingham House in 1703 for John Sheffield, 1st Duke of Buckingham and Normanby (1648-1721) and Lord Lieutenant of the North Riding of Yorkshire. Given its size and proximity to St. James's Palace, the Palace of Whitehall and the Royal Parks of St. James and The Green Park, George III purchased the property for Queen Charlotte (1744–1818) in

1762. Initially known as Queen House, George IV began reconstruction work in 1821. Upon completion in 1825, it became known as Buckingham Palace. It would be William IV's successor, Victoria, the last monarch from the House of Hanover, who would become the first monarch to choose Buckingham Palace as her permanent residence on her accession to the throne in 1837. Since then, Buckingham Palace has become synonymous with the Royal Family, Public Duties and State Ceremonial with its vast red-granite gravel forecourt. Today, it forms the main stage for the culmination of the Changing of Guard that is heralded by the arrival of the Corps of Drums of the Regiment mounting the King's Guard, and in the case of the Irish Guards, led by the regimental Irish Wolfhound. The St. James's Palace detachment, including the Ensign and Colour and the Buckingham Palace detachment, follow the Corps of Drums. The size of the detachment will vary as to whether his majesty is in residence, indicated by the presence of the Royal Standard of the United Kingdom. When the King is in residence, the guard will consist of three officers and forty other ranks, which is reduced to three officers and thirty-three other ranks when the King is away from the Palace.

The regiment that provides the King's Guard will also provide the Guard for His Majesty's Palace and Fortress, the Tower of London, built by William the Conqueror, where sentries are posted outside the Jewel House and The King's House. Known as the Tower Guard, the duty regiment provides a single officer, six non-commissioned officers (SNCOs), fifteen guards and one drummer for the task. The Tower Guards work alongside the Yeomen Warders, the Resident Governor of the Tower of London, and the Keeper of the Jewel House and take part in three daily ceremonies unique to the Tower of London: the Ceremonial Opening, the Ceremony of the Word and the Ceremony of the Keys.

At 9:00 am, the Ceremonial Opening begins and involves a military escort and the Duty Yeoman Warder opening the Middle and Byward Towers, after which the public can enter. The Ceremonial Opening takes place every day except Sunday, with a section of the Tower Guard, including an NCO and a Yeoman Warder. At 3:00 pm, the Ceremony of the Word, known as the Word, takes place. This sees the Officer of The Guard and

Preparing for Parade

escort march to the Byward Tower, the main entrance used by visitors to the Tower of London, to collect the Word. The Word is the password for after-hours entry to the Tower of London, used by Tower staff, residents and the soldiers on duty. The Byward Tower acts as the great gatehouse of the Outer Ward of the Tower of London. It was built by Henry III between 1238 and 1272. It was designed to provide an additional defensive layer to the central Keep. The Word is changed every twenty-four hours, issued by the Ministry of Defence, and collected daily from the Byward Tower by the Officer of the Guard and escort. Once they arrive at Byward Tower, the Officer collects the Word, carried in a leather pouch, from the Duty Yeoman Warder and delivers this to the Resident Governor.

The Ceremony of the Keys, perhaps the most famed of all three ceremonies, is performed at precisely 9:52 pm every night by the Chief Yeoman Warder. The exact date of when the Ceremony of the Keys began remains unknown. However, some forms of ceremony have taken place since the fourteenth century. Today's ceremony is likely to date to the nineteenth century when the institution of the Yeomen Warders was reformed by the then Constable of the Tower, Field Marshal Arthur Wellesley, 1st Duke of Wellington. This ceremony is used to ensure the fortress remains secure, to prevent the escape of any of its prisoners, and to lock the outer gates for the night. The Chief Yeoman Warder is accompanied by four Tower Guards, with one carrying a lantern rather than a weapon. The lantern plays a pivotal role in the ceremony, lighting the way and used to reveal any lurking enemy of the state who may be hell-bent on causing acts of anarchy and chaos. The Chief Yeoman Warder will lock the three gates that control access to the causeway over the moat. Before The Chief Yeoman Warder can enter the fortress proper, they must respond to the following challenge issued by the sentry at the Bloody Tower arch:

Who goes there?
The Keys
Whose Keys?
King Charles's Keys
Pass, King Charles's Keys

The party marches into the courtyard, where the Main Guard salutes the Keys on the Jewel House steps. Then, the bugler presents arms as the party enters and plays *the Last Post*. With the clock striking at 10:00 pm, Chief Yeoman Warder cries, 'God preserve King Charles,' to which the assembled Guards respond, 'Amen.' To end the ceremony, the Keys are delivered to the monarch's representative in the Tower, the Resident Governor, whose previous post holders include former Scots Guard Major General Sir Digby Raeburn (1915–2001), whose commands included the 1st Guards Brigade Group between 1959 and 1960.

When they escort the sovereign, the Yeomen Guards will exchange their blue undress uniform for their Tudor scarlet and gold several times a year. This includes an annual Roll Call and the Sovereign's Inspection every four years. They will also attend the sovereign on other occasions, including the annual Royal Maundy service and the Epiphany Service in the Chapel Royal at St. James's Palace. They are also present for installations of Knights of the Garter as well as investitures, lying-in-state, the funeral of the sovereign, and summer garden parties held at Buckingham Palace. But it is for one service they are most famed for: the ceremonial search of the cellars of the Palace of Westminster before the State Opening of Parliament, lest a recurrence of the Gunpowder Plot occur.

The guard duties at Windsor Castle, the largest inhabited castle in the world and the oldest in continuous occupation since its founding by William the Conqueror in the eleventh century, are undertaken by the Foot Guards. The Guard Mounting ceremony takes place at 11:00 am three times a week, and it is accompanied by a Regimental Band, Corps of Drums, or occasionally by a Pipe Band. The Guard will form up on the Castle Forecourt if the King is in residence. Otherwise, the changing ceremony of the Windsor Castle Guard forms outside the Guard Room. The Windsor Castle Guard usually comprises one officer, five NCOs, twenty-one Guards and one drummer when the King is in residence. Otherwise, it comprises one officer, five NCOs, fifteen Guards and one drummer. Today, sentries can be found at the Advanced Gate, St. George's Gate, George IV Gate, the Quadrangle, the Brunswick Tower and outside the Guardroom, with some posts doubled up when the King is in residence.

Today, the troopers of the Household Cavalry continue to provide the Guard at the Palace of Whitehall and Horse Guards. Every morning the mounted King's Life Guard of the Household Cavalry Mounted Regiment (HCMR) ride from their Hyde Park Barracks via Hyde Park Corner, Constitution Hill and The Mall, to start their guard duties at 11:00 am during the week and at 10:00 am on a Sunday. As in the times of Charles II, the Mounted Guards are in position on either side of the main entrance to the royal estate from the start of their duties until 4:00 pm; after that, two dismounted sentries remain on duty until 8:00 pm. The HCMR provide two distinct types of guards: the Long Guard and the Short Guard. The Long Guard is carried out when the sovereign is in London and consists of one officer and twelve other ranks, including a trumpeter and standard bearer, known as a Long Guard. The Short Guard is held at all other times, and two non-commissioned officers and ten troopers lead the guard. During the HCMR's summer camp, their duties are fulfilled by the King's Troop RHA and, on occasion, visiting troops, including the Royal Canadian Mounted Police (RCMP).

State Opening of Parliament

The Opening of Parliament is a ceremony that began out of practical necessity. By the late fourteenth century, how the King, his nobles and representatives of the Commons had begun to gather was forming an established pattern with the names of Peers attending checked against the list of those who had been summoned, while representatives of the Commons were checked against the sheriffs' election returns. The robed Peers (Lords) then gathered in the Painted Chamber at the Palace of Westminster, the King's private room. The Painted Chamber had been constructed by Henry III. It was demolished in 1851 after a series of unfortunate events, including fire and general neglect. For their part, the Commons were summoned and gathered at the Bar or threshold of the

Chamber, followed by a speech overseen by the monarch, who remained for discussions. The Lord Chancellor usually delivered the speech and explained why an assembly had been called, after which the Peers and Commons departed to discuss any matter arising.

By the Tudor period (1485–1603), the modern structure of Parliament was slowly emerging, with the monarch no longer needing to attend Parliament during routine proceedings. This led to the State Opening taking on greater symbolic significance as an occasion for the full constitution of the State (Monarch, Lords and Commons) to be seen. At this time, these parliamentary gatherings began to be preceded by the State Procession, a formal display of the Sovereign, which was dignified by a sizeable entourage of Great Officers of State and members of the Royal Household. The State Procession would proceed from whichever royal residence was being used, first to Westminster Abbey for a Votive Mass of the Holy Ghost. Afterwards, and in the company of the Lord's Spiritual and Temporal, the State Procession would walk to the Palace of Westminster for the Opening ceremony, attracting large crowds as they went.

The Tudor period saw the publication of the *Wriothesley Garter Book* in 1523 by Thomas Wriothesley (d.1534). Wriothesley was a long-serving officer of arms at the College of Arms who helped organize and participate in domestic ceremonies, including the coronation of Henry VIII. His *Garter Book* depicted Henry VIII seated in Parliament in that year and shows a visual similarity between State Openings of the sixteenth and twenty-first centuries. The Palace of Westminster ceased to be a royal residence following a fire in 1512. This then led to the use of Henry's other residences until 1530, when the ceremony returned to Westminster after Henry had moved into the Palace at Whitehall. In 1536, the State Opening was held for the first time in the White Chamber in the Palace of Westminster, which acted as a dining hall where the House of Lords sat. This saw the beginning of the custom of the State Opening taking place in the Upper House of Parliament. Since then, the ceremonial has gently evolved, with a fundamental change being the cessation of the Abby service from 1679 because of fears over a Popish Plot, a fictitious

His Royal Highness Prince William fulfils his duties as First Royal Colonel of the Irish Guards Regiment at the 2017 Colonels' Review. (Corporal Pete Brown)

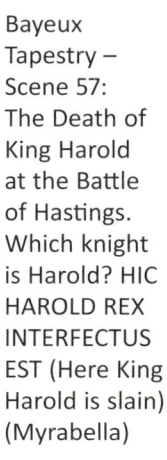

Bayeux Tapestry – Scene 57: The Death of King Harold at the Battle of Hastings. Which knight is Harold? HIC HAROLD REX INTERFECTUS EST (Here King Harold is slain). (Myrabella)

Left: Ludovick Stuart (1574–1624) by Daniel Mitjens (Dutch Golden Age). Stuart, 2nd Duke of Lennox, Duke of Richmond, and cousin of James I, is depicted in the garb of Lord Steward (1615), complete with the white staff of office. Note the Stuart ducal coronet on the pedestal. (Rasjedan)

Below: The Right Honourable Alexander Chalk in his attire as the Lord High Chancellor of Great Britain and Secretary of State for Justice, seen here at the State Opening of Parliament. (UK Parliament. Jessica Taylor, Maria Unger, Andy Bailey)

Above left: Laurence Hyde, Earl of Rochester, by Willem Wissing. Hyde, James II's Lord High Treasurer, is shown wearing the insignia of the Order of the Garter and holding the staff of office. (Holburne Museum)

Above right: Thomas Osborne, First Duke of Leeds, Lord Danby, by Thomas Gibson. Osborne, one of the 'Immortal Seven' who invited William of Orange to depose James II, is portrayed as a Knight of the Garter, holding the long white wand that signifies his role as Lord President of the Council, a title he held from 1689 until 1699. (No credit provided)

Charles III delivers the King's Speech to both Houses of Parliament on 7 November 2023. To His Majesty's right Nicholas Edward True, Baron True, Lord Keeper of the Privy Seal and Leader of the House of Lords, holding the Cap of Maintenance. To His Majesty's left is the Sword of State, carried by General John Houghton, Baron Houghton of Richmond. (Prime Minister's Office)

Admiral Sir Antony Radakin, Chief of the Defence Staff and Lord High Constable of England for the Coronation of Charles III, with Warrant Officer to the Royal Navy, Jamie Wright (with pace stick), and Senior Enlisted Advisor to the Chiefs of Staff Committee, Richard Angove (behind). (Katie Chan)

Above left: Edward William Fitzalan-Howard, 18th Duke of Norfolk, in the garb of the Earl Marshal and his robes as Duke of Norfolk, flanked by two heralds at the Palace of Westminster. (Annabel Moeller)

Above right: Algernon Percy, 10th Earl of Northumberland, Lord High Admiral of England, depicted in a maritime setting by Anthony van Dyck. (Private Collection)

Above left: Richard Wellesley, 1st Marquess Wellesley, by Martine Shee, in his Garter Robes, carrying the white staff of office as Lord Steward, with Westminster Abbey in the background. Wellesley is presumably dressed for the coronation of William IV on 8 September 1831. (Royal Collection)

Above right: David Cholmondeley, 7th Marquess of Cholmondeley, wearing the ceremonial dress of Lord Great Chamberlain and holding a white staff of office. (Allan Warren)

Samuel Vestey, 3rd Baron Vestey, Scots Guards, Master of the Horse from 1999 to 2018, seen in all his finery riding to the Queen's Birthday Parade in 2012. (Carfax2)

Following Her Majesty Queen Elizabeth II after Trooping the Colour of 1st Battalion, Coldstream Guards. From left: Crown Equerry Colonel Toby Browne, Equerry in Waiting Lieutenant Colonel Sir Alexander Matheson of Matheson, Equerry Major Nana Kofi Twumasi-Ankrah, Blues and Royals Regimental Colonel of the Coldstream Guards, Lieutenant General Sir James Bucknall. (Katie Chan)

The Military Knights of Windsor on parade. (Phil Allfry)

Members of the Honourable Corps of Gentlemen at Arms march alongside the casket of Her Majesty Queen Elizabeth II on 19 September 2022. (James Boyes)

A unique photograph featuring all the Sovereign's Body Guard: His Majesty's Body Guard of the Honourable Corps of Gentlemen at Arms, the King's Body Guard of the Yeomen of the Guard (with baldricks) with their Standard Bearer, the Yeomen Warders of His Majesty's Royal Palace and Fortress the Tower of London, and Members of the Sovereign's Body Guard of the Yeoman Guard Extraordinary and The Royal Company of Archers, also with Standard Bearer at the coronation procession of His Majesty King Charles III. The Royal Watermen walk in the centre. Of note is the new Royal Cypher. (Katie Chan)

Above: US Secretary of Defence Leon E. Panetta enjoying a chuckle and a pint with Yeoman Warders Dave Coleman (left) and Rob Fuller in the Yeoman Warders' Mess at the Tower of London. The Yeoman Warders are in their blue working dress. (DoD photo by Erin A. Kirk-Cuomo/Released)

Left: Heralds in procession to St George's Chapel, Windsor Castle, for the annual service of the Order of the Garter in 2006. From left: Wales Herald of Arms Extraordinary Michael Siddons; Somerset Herald of Arms in Ordinary David White; Maltravers Herald of Arms Extraordinary John Robinson; York Herald of Arms in Ordinary Henry Paston-Bedingfield; and Windsor Herald of Arms in Ordinary William Hunt. (Philip Allfrey)

Above: Henry Dymoke as the Honourable the King's Champion, as he appeared at the coronation banquet of George IV on 19 July 1821, on his borrowed circus horse. (Print by Edward Hull)

Right: The Lord Lieutenant of Greater London, Sir Kenneth Olisa OBE, in a jovial mood. (Ben Skipper)

A Grenadier Guard Sergeant assists a Coldstream Guard WO2 in preparation for the coronation procession of His Majesty King Charles III. Of note is the Sergeant Major's slashed cap peak, a modification favoured by the Household Division that encourages the wearer to stand straight. (Katie Chan)

Senior figures of the British Army and London District stroll past the Band of the Welsh Guards. From left: Chief of the General Staff General Sir Patrick Sanders (Rifles) with Ben Wallace (Scots Guards), Garrison Sergeant Major Andrew 'Vern' Stokes (Coldstream Guards), and Major General Christopher Ghika (Irish Guards), Major General commanding the Household Division and General Officer Commanding London District in 2022. (Sergeant Donald Todd)

A mounted division of the Life Guards leaves Horse Guards Parade. (Oast House Archive)

Above: The Massed Bands of the Household Division perform in the fireworks finale at Beating Retreat 2013. (Unknown)

Right: Anne, Princess Royal, riding on horseback along The Mall towards Horse Guards Parade in her role as Colonel of The Blues and Royals and Gold Stick-in-Waiting during the 2023 Trooping the Colour. (Katie Chan)

A Battery of The Honourable Artillery Company fires its guns at the Tower of London to honour HRH The Prince of Wales' 71st birthday with a sixty-two gun salute. (Sergeant Paul Randall)

The King's Troop, Royal Horse Artillery, riding towards Buckingham Palace after Prince William's Colonel's Review as Colonel of the Irish Guards Regiment, 2017. (Sergeant Rupert Freer)

The Mounted Band of the Household Cavalry at the 2007 Trooping the Colour in their State Dress. Note how the Kettle Drummer salutes the Dais, and the reins attached to his stirrups. (Jon)

The Pipes and Drums of the Band of the Scots Guards perform at the Pentagon, 2009. (Master Sergeant Stan Parker)

The Band of the Welsh Guards at Windsor Castle. (Ibagli)

Welsh Guards Changing the Guard at Buckingham Palace with the King's Colours. (km30192002)

Life Guards changing the dismounted guard at the Palace of Whitehall. (David Crochet)

The Queen's Bargemaster and a Royal Waterman (with a royal footman standing behind them) on the carriage conveying the Imperial State Crown to the Palace of Westminster for the State Opening, 2015. (John Pannell)

The search begins. The Yeomen of the Guard prepares to seek out miscreants and ne'er-do-wells in the cellars at the Palace of Westminster. (Houses of the Oireachtas)

Wreaths are laid by members of the Royal Family during the Remembrance Sunday service at the Cenotaph in Whitehall, London. (Sgt Dan Harmer)

Guards from 1st Battalion, the Irish Guards, conducting a live firing exercise deep in the Belize Jungle. (Sergeant Rupert Frere)

The casket of Her Majesty Queen Elizabeth II is seen here on a gun carriage, towed by 142 members of the Royal Navy, a tradition dating back to the funeral of Queen Victoria. (DCMS)

Left: Drum horse Mercury in a lighter mood, showing off his 'Movember' moustache with this fine handlebar effort. 'Movember' is an annual event that raises money for men's health and is heartily supported by the Household Division. (Sergeant Adrian Harlen)

Below: Farewell. The King's Troop fires its 13-pounder guns at Hyde Park during the Funeral Procession of Her Majesty Queen Elizabeth II. (Corporal Rob Kane)

conspiracy to assassinate Charles II invented by Titus Oates (1649–1705) an Anglican priest.

The monarch's role in the proceedings has changed over time. Initially the sitting monarch would introduce the ceremony before calling upon either the Lord Chancellor or Lord Keeper to address the assembly of Peers and representatives of the Commons. James I was accustomed to public speaking and capable of doing so at great length, with the result of dispensing with the Chancellor's services. During the Interregnum Cromwell would deliver the opening speech. With the Restoration of the monarchy, it soon became the custom for the monarch to speak, with Charles II doing so from 1679. Since then, the monarch (if present) has given the speech, except George I, whose poor command of spoken English precluded him from addressing the gathered Peers and Commons. During the Regency of 1811–1820, George, the Prince of Wales, later George IV, attended in full state dress, making a Prince Regent's Speech.

After the destruction of the old Palace of Westminster by fire in 1834, the gutted Painted Chamber was roofed over and turned into a temporary House of Lords, pending the rebuilding of the palace. It hosted the State Opening until 1847 when the new Lords' Chamber was opened. 1852 saw the start of what has become the present ceremony, with the Victoria Tower Sovereign's Entrance being used for the first time. During the State Opening of Parliament, the Union Flag is replaced by the Royal Standard of the United Kingdom. The use of the Sovereign's Entrance would form part of a new processional route, including the Royal Staircase, Norman Porch, new Robing Room and Royal Gallery. During her reign, Victoria missed the State Opening ceremony on four occasions, each due to pregnancy, between 1837 and 1861. After the death of Prince Albert (1819–1861), overcome with an almost unquenchable grief, Victoria withdrew from the public gaze, avoiding public engagements.

However, Victoria would attend the State Opening in 1866 wearing a black dress and veil rather than her robe of state, now draped over the throne, and delegating the reading of the opening speech to the Lord Chancellor. Victoria attended the State Opening on six more occasions, wearing a small diamond crown instead of the Imperial State Crown. When not in attendance, Victoria delegated the opening ceremony and statement to the Lords Commissioners, who included her son Albert the Prince of Wales and later Edward VII. With Albert's ascension to the throne as Edward VII in 1901, the full State Ceremonial of the event was restored, and it would be George V who would resume wearing the Imperial State Crown in 1913.

The two world wars saw the ceremonial aspect of the State Opening understandably reduced, with the full ceremonial State Opening restored by 1950. During her reign, Elizabeth II opened every session of Parliament, with the exceptions of 1956 and 1963 due to pregnancy and in 2022 on medical advice.

On that occasion, Charles, Prince of Wales, and her grandson Prince William, Duke of Cambridge, in their capacities as Counsellors of State, empowered to do so by letters patent issued by the Queen, deputized for Elizabeth. The Prince of Wales would deliver the Queen's Speech from the consort's throne.

The ceremony begins

Before the State Opening of Parliament, the Palace of Westminster cellars are searched by a detachment of ten Yeomen of the Guard led by a Junior Exon and assisted by a Sergeant Major. This is a tradition that can be traced back to the failed Gunpowder Plot of 1605 led by Robert Catesby (1572–1605), a Catholic radical who sought to kill James I and replace him with his daughter Princess Elizabeth (1596–1662), later Queen of Bohemia. Since the discovery of the hapless Guy Fawkes (1570–1606) and his hidden explosives, the cellars have been searched before the State Opening of Parliament. Known as The Search, the party of Yeomen of the Guard is supervised by the Lord Great Chamberlain, and for their services, the Yeomen receive a small glass of port. To be on the safe side the security services tend to carry out the main search utilizing more contemporary methods and equipment, as opposed to lanterns and swords.

Peers and Peeresses will assemble in the House of Lords on the day of the State Opening of Parliament with the Lords Spiritual and the Lords Temporal wearing their Parliament Robes for the occasion. Also present are the senior representatives of the judiciary, who sit on woolsacks in the centre of the Chamber, and members of the Diplomatic Corps, who are seated behind the bishops. The Commons assemble in their own Chamber, wearing ordinary day dress, and begin the day, as any other, with prayers. Beforehand, the Speaker's Procession takes place in the usual way: preceded by a doorkeeper, the Serjeant at Arms, whose past incumbents have included Lord Charles James Fox Russell (1807-1894), a lieutenant-colonel of the Royal Regiment of Horse Guards (The Blues) (RHG), leads the Speaker of the House of Commons from his official residence to the Commons Chamber, followed by his trainbearer, chaplain and secretary. In the Central Lobby, a police Inspector makes the traditional cry of 'Hats off, strangers', instructing those assembled to remove their hats in deference to the highest-ranking commoner of the realm.

Delivery of Parliamentary Hostage

On the morning of the State Opening, the Treasurer, Comptroller, and Vice-Chamberlain of the Household assemble with other senior members of the Royal Household at Buckingham Palace. Of these, the Treasurer, Comptroller, and senior members of the Royal Household accompany the monarch in the carriage procession. At the same time, the Lord Chamberlain remains at Buckingham Palace to keep a single Member of Parliament, the Vice-Chamberlain, as a ceremonial 'hostage' for the duration of the state opening. This tradition ensures the monarch's safe return. The 'hostage' is entertained until the monarch returns safely. This tradition is believed to have started in the reign of Charles I due to his often-testing character. Indeed, such was the impact of the poor relationship between the monarch and Parliament that a copy of Charles's death warrant remains on display in the Robing Room. It is a less subtle reminder of what can happen to a monarch who attempts to interfere with the business of Parliament. That said, there is a counterargument that taking 'hostage' is a more recent process, dating back to the 1960s.

ARRIVAL OF ROYAL REGALIA

Before the sovereign's arrival, the Imperial State Crown, Great Sword of State and the Cap of Maintenance are brought to the Palace of Westminster in their carriage, usually Queen Alexandra's State Coach. The King's Bargemaster, whose task is also to assist in organizing and facilitating river pageants, is accompanied by four Royal Watermen. As a group, they travel as boxmen on coaches, guarding the regalia as it is conveyed and returned between Buckingham Palace and Westminster. This role is reminiscent of when the regalia were brought by river from the Tower of London. Other onshore duties of the King's Bargemaster and Bargemen include acting as footmen on royal carriages during State visits, royal weddings and jubilees. The Royal Watermen walk behind the King's Bargemaster at the coronation procession. On arrival at the Sovereign's Entrance, the Crown is passed by the Bargemaster to the Comptroller of the Lord Chamberlain's Office under the watchful eye of the Crown Jeweller. The regalia are then taken up a flight of stairs lined by a dismounted HCMR Guard of Honour and heralds to be displayed in the Royal Gallery. Also in the procession, usually carried in Edward VII's Town Coach, are the two maces carried by the Serjeants-at-Arms of the Royal Household, who escort the regalia in procession.

ARRIVAL OF THE SOVEREIGN AND ASSEMBLY OF PARLIAMENT

The monarch travels 'in State' in a state coach from Buckingham Palace to the Palace of Westminster, arriving at the Sovereign's Entrance accompanied by their consort and other Royal Family members. Senior members of the Royal Household follow in different carriages. The HCMR provides a Sovereign's Escort, with members from all three armed forces lining the processional route from Buckingham Palace to the Palace of Westminster. At the same time, the bands of the Household Division precede the royal cavalcade.

The national anthem is played at the moment of the monarch's arrival; a gun salute is fired in Green Park by the King's Troop. With the monarch's arrival, the Royal Standard of the United Kingdom replaces the Union Flag at the top of the Victoria Tower for the duration of the monarch's presence. On arrival, the monarch is greeted by the Lord Great Chamberlain, responsible for maintaining the royal areas of the Palace of Westminster and the Earl Marshal. The monarch and consort then proceed to the Robing Room, where they dress in the Parliament Robe of State and the Imperial State Crown. A procession is formed of heralds, Great Officers of State and members of the Royal Household. When all is ready, a fanfare is sounded by the trumpeters of the bands of the Household Division and the monarch proceeds in State through the Royal Gallery to the House of Lords. Directly ahead of the monarch walk two peers: the Leader of the House of Lords, who carries the Cap of Maintenance, and the other, often a retired senior military officer, holding the Great Sword of State. Once seated on the throne, the monarch instructs the House by saying, 'My Lords, pray be seated', with the consort sitting to the sovereign's left, with the Queen or Consort seated next to them on the dais. Interestingly, the Imperial State Crown can only be worn after the monarch has been coroneted. Otherwise, only the robe of State is worn with the crown carried on a cushion by one of the Great Officers of State.

ROYAL SUMMONS OF THE COMMONS TO THE LORDS' CHAMBER

Motioned by the monarch, the Lord Great Chamberlain raises his white staff of office to signal the official known as Gentleman or Lady Usher of the Black Rod or simply Black Rod to summon the House of Commons. Under the escort of the Doorkeeper of the House of Lords, Black Rod then proceeds to the Members' Lobby of the House of Commons and reaches the doors of the Commons. The role of Black Rod was created in 1350 by letters patent, and the post holder is principally responsible for controlling access to and maintaining order within the House of Lords and its precincts, as well as for ceremonial events within those precincts. Today, Black Rod, a post held by Sarah Clarke since 2018, the first woman to hold the post, leads a department that plays a vital role in the day-to-day running of the House's sittings. Black Rod is also responsible for organizing and delivering ceremonial events, including the State Opening and state visits to Westminster, liaising with external partners such as London District and the Household Division where relevant. Other tasks include the daily administration of the King's residual estate in the Palace of Westminster that covers the management of the Chapel of St. Mary Undercroft, the Robing Room, and the Royal Gallery.

On Black Rod's approach, the Doorkeeper of the Commons orders that the doors are slammed shut against them; this seemingly rude act is symbolic of the rights of Parliament and its independence from the monarch. Black Rod then strikes with the end of their ceremonial staff, the Black Rod, three times on the closed doors of the Commons Chamber. Today, a mark on the door of the Commons shows the repeated indentations made by Black Rods over the years. At this point, the doors are opened, and Black Rod is admitted, being introduced by the Chief Doorkeeper of the House of Commons. At the bar, Black Rod bows to the Speaker before proceeding to the table, bowing again, and announcing the monarch's command to attend the Commons in the House of Lords.

This rather dramatic ritual is strongly associated with Charles I storming into the House of Commons in 1642 in an unsuccessful attempt to arrest five Members of Parliament, including John Pym (1584–1642), widely considered to be one of the founders of the modern English Parliamentary system. Charles I's actions were the last time a British monarch entered the House of Commons when it was sitting. Interestingly, Thomas Erskine May, 1st Baron Farnborough (1815–1886), Clerk of the House of Commons, stated that the door-closing ritual predated Charles I's outburst, symbolizing the independence of the Lower House, but its primary purpose was for the Commons to establish Black Rod's identity.

State Visits

Formal State visits by overseas Heads of State occur twice a year, usually in the spring and autumn. They are intended to strengthen the United Kingdom's external relationships, with invitations sent to the relevant Head of State on the advice of the Foreign and Commonwealth Office. As the sovereign hosts the visiting Head of State, they will stay at Buckingham Palace, Windsor Castle or the Palace of Holyrood House in Edinburgh. Formal State visits will start with a ceremonial welcome attended by the King and other senior members of the Royal Family and include the inspection of a Guard of Honour. After the inspection, the visiting Head of State will travel with the King in a Carriage Procession back to Buckingham Palace, should the inspection occur at Horse Guards Parade. On the evening of the day of arrival day, the Head of State will also attend a State Banquet in their honour.

CHAPTER FIVE
THE RELATIONSHIP BETWEEN MONARCH AND GUARDS

'I dislike my sentries at Buckingham Palace being marched to their posts by anyone wearing only one stripe. In future let them wear two.'

Queen Victoria

On the morning of 29 May 1660, the residents of Blackheath and folk from as far as thirty miles (forty-eight kilometres) away had gathered to witness something unusual and, at the same time, familiar: the return of the monarchy to Britain. This crowd, some 120,000 strong, and Blackheath were used to history's many comings and goings. Still, the arrival of Charles II, accompanied by his brothers, James, Duke of York (1633–1701) and Henry, Duke of Gloucester (1640–1660), was nothing short of spectacular. Some 20,000 men, mounted or on foot, accompanied the three, all moving onwards to London whilst brandishing swords and shouting joyously. The crowds continued to gather along the route, and soon, Charles II's triumphant return was lined with garlands, cheers and goodwill. Church bells were rung in celebration as the column drew nearer to the country's capital; this was a spectacle like no other.

The Lord Mayor and the city's Aldermen had gathered to welcome Charles before riding at the head of the column after the necessary customs were upheld and making for Whitehall. There were gathered nobles and lords, liverymen and a vast crowd; Charles and his entourage were welcomed by trumpet calls and cheers. Such was the crowd's size that the column took some seven hours to pass through the city, finally breaking free at nine that evening. At Westminster, effigies of Oliver Cromwell and his wife Elizabeth were burnt upon a sizeable bonfire.

With the return of Charles, there was bound to be a return to the days of glorious celebrations, especially after the Rule of the Major Generals. This period, between 1655 and 1657, sought to restrict the rights of individuals and groups and saw the use of the New Model Army (NMA) as an aid to enforce those restrictions. This was an unprecedented period in British history, where militarism, led by religious belief, targeted the remaining Royalists with near constant harassment and punitive taxation. Another key driver for establishing the Rule of the Major Generals had been the defeat of the expedition to Hispaniola, now known as Santo Domingo, the Dominican Republic, in April 1655. When Cromwell got news of the defeat the following July, he became convinced the defeat was a punishment from God for not enforcing England as a more religious and godlier place. This, in turn, led to a stricter, more puritanical joining of Church and State, thus, in the mind of Cromwell and his eager Major Generals, an opportunity to complete the reform of the Protestant church that had begun little over a century before. It was also an opportunity for the more ruthless of their number to consolidate their power base over the population of the British Commonwealth.

This new belief saw the subsequent clamp-down on overzealous alcohol consumption, music, dancing and joyous celebration, including Christmas, by the NMA, who had become representatives and enforcers of an invigorated Christo-fascist dictatorship. Whilst the Rule of the Major Generals was a thankfully relevantly short period of the Interregnum, scuppered by their desire to increase taxation, it is the one that remains the most remembered in the popular consciousness of the nation when identifying life under Cromwell and the Puritans.

Thankfully, with the Restoration of Charles II in 1660, there was also the restoration of civil rights and a total return of those facets of society that made life a little more bearable. Now, the subjects of the new monarchy were reinvigorated by the welcomed return of the arts and religious and civic celebration; they embraced overzealous drinking in some cases, and general gaiety was to be had for all. Charles was keen to capitalize on making his mark; the gradual standing down of the NMA, Britain's first Standing Army, was one such mark. On 14 February 1661, General George Monck (1608–1670) and his Coldstreamers gathered for one final time as members of the NMA at Tower Hill. This would be a formal farewell to arms of the regiment that had ushered in the return of the monarchy.

While proclaiming to be no politician, Monck was certainly politically wise enough to realize that such an event should not pass with a simple signature scrawled on velum to be rolled up and placed in store. This was to be the start of a renewed period of pomp. His regiment's symbolic laying down of arms as members of the NMA marked the end of an era of darkness, mistrust and pain for many. On bending down and taking up arms as King's men of the General Monck's Regiment of Foot Guard and the Lord General's Troop of Horse Guards, they had performed a very public display of loyalty to Charles and the new order. The sense of theatre and symbolism would now become a vital element of the Guards' routine and one for which they would become renowned.

With Charles experiencing daily threats to self, the importance of the Guard could not be understated. The roles of Gold Stick and Silver Stick remained as crucial as ever. Now, they were backed up by regiments of Guards, professional soldiers and experienced veterans; as with all things, the symbolism of those early years of service would find its way onto uniforms and customs. The Life Guards, for example, would adopt the acorn as a symbol of their loyalty to the Crown, a nod to the oak in which Charles hid from Cromwell's troops after the Battle of Worcester in 1651. The acorn would be incorporated into the Life Guards' uniform and be the title of the regimental magazine between 1966 and 1991. The officers' mess of the Scots Guards would eschew finger bowls due to the deposing of James II as King of England and Ireland and King of Scotland as James VII during the Glorious Revolution of 1688. This resulted from officers showing loyalty to the exiled James II and his son James (1688–1766), known as the Old Pretender, by drinking from the finger bowls at the Loyal Toast.

James ascended the throne with Charles's death in 1685 and inherited an invigorated, professional and experienced military machine. His faith and friendship with Louis XIV also rendered any further military operations in Europe obsolete. Regardless of his son-in-law, the Protestant William of Orange's machinations that would culminate in the Glorious Revolution three years later, James felt secure in his position. So secure that he introduced Irish Catholic officers and proposed a wholly Catholic troop of Horse Guards, combined with the birth of his son James in 1688 (d. 1766).

William's Glorious Revolution saw many in the army, including John Churchill, now a Major-General, abandon James and side with William. James would flee into relative comfort in France, supported by Louis XIV. With William III taking the throne in 1689, things changed, and under William, England began to strengthen its hand within the British Isles and Continental Europe. For thirteen years, William was driven by an almost pathological hatred of Catholicism, embarking on a series of battles and wars mainly against Louis XIV and aided by Protestant allies in Northern Europe, including French Huguenot soldiers.

William was impressed by the performance of his English soldiers but less so by his English officers. The purchasing of a commission by an individual was often accompanied by a bribe to either be placed within a preferential regiment or a position that attracted either social or financial gain. To curtail such behaviour, which degraded the moral and intellectual quality of the Officer Corps, William made those purchasing a commission swear that they had done so without making any 'present or gratuity'. This prudent move would later be forgotten, and the purchase of commission and each step in rank up to and including Lieutenant-Colonel would continue well into the nineteenth century, with disastrous results for the British Army, especially in the Crimean War. It wouldn't be until 1871, with the enactment of the Cardwell Reforms, led by Secretary of State for War Edward Cardwell (1813–1886), that the practice of purchase of commissions was finally abolished. Under William, the Guards would fight in Europe and the British Isles with the Coldstream and Scots Guards as the 2nd and 3rd Regiments of Foot Guards, earning Battle Honours.

British military prestige and ability were improving at the time of the ascent of Queen Anne to the throne in 1702 who was keen to capitalize on this military rebirth. After pressure from courtier and royal favourite Sarah Churchill (1660–1744), Duchess of Marlborough, she bestowed the title of Captain General (Commander-in-Chief) to Sarah's husband John Churchill (1650–1722), 1st Duke of Marlborough. Marlborough had an interesting military and political career, first defeating the Monmouth Rebellion in 1685, which helped secure James II as King, and then becoming a key player in the removal of James just three years later. This was a wise move by Anne as it secured the loyalty of Britain's ablest commander of the time and the support of the broader military community, which supported the seemingly unstoppable Duke during his campaigns of the period.

As a Stuart, and ultimately the last of that line to sit on the throne, Anne held a close affiliation with her grandfather Charles II's regiment, the Scottish Regiment of Foot Guards. Anne was keenly aware of the regiment's history and service to the House of Stuart. So, she ordered that the regiment be listed as the first of her three regiments of Foot Guards. Understandably, both the Grenadiers and Coldstreamers were less than enthusiastic about the change, both protesting vociferously. Anne backed down, making the Scots the Third Regiment of Foot Guards.

In 1711, Marlborough was caught in the fallout of the disintegration of the relationship between his wife and Anne and was dismissed as Captain General. The new incumbent would be cavalryman James FitzJames Butler, 2nd Duke of Ormonde (1665–1745), who became Colonel of the 1st Regiment of Foot Guards in January 1712 and Captain General the following February. A further change saw Anne's husband, Prince George of Denmark and Norway (1653–1708), awarded the title of Field Marshal to outrank the now-fallen Marlborough.

By the time the 54-year-old George I came to unified Britain in August 1714, he was, at that time, the oldest successor to the English throne. Whilst politically acceptable, George I was far from popular with his new subjects; his reputation of being foul-tempered and understanding rudimentary English went down like a proverbial brick. George felt constricted by his lack of English, relying on his son George to translate or communicate with ministers in French or Latin. George oversaw a more rigorous process of purchasing commissions with ranks and appointments at fixed prices. A fundamental change was the dismissal of Ormonde as Captain General, Colonel of the 1st Regiment of Foot Guards and Commander in Chief of the Forces in 1714, with the first two posts returning to Marlborough.

It would be George II who would help shape the physical appearance of Guards when he was introduced to Frederic William II's Prussian Guards. The Prussian Guards were of considerable stature, beautifully turned out, well drilled, and it was remarked, docile to the point of being moronic. Unperturbed by a lack of giant men in the British Isles, George pressed on and ensured his new guards were among his army's tallest and finest turned-out soldiers. He also standardized and added a new Hanoverian refinement to the English drill; the slow march. The goose step, which the Prussians used as an early morning sobriety test, was omitted by George. George would be the last British monarch to lead an army, doing so on 27 June 1743 at the Battle of Dettingen during the War of the Austrian Succession which took place in modern-day Bavaria. The Battle Honour Dettingen was awarded to the 1st Life Guards, 2nd Life Guards, the Royal Horse Guards, the Royal Dragoons (1st Dragoons), Grenadier, Coldstream, and Scots Guards.

The Hanoverian shaping of the army, and the Guards in particular, continued under George III, or to be correct, his son, Prince Frederick, Duke of York and Albany (1763–1827). The Duke of York was given free reign regarding military matters. He was aware of the duties the Guards of the Royal Household undertook daily, especially the Guards mounting parades on Horse Guards Parade. The Duke took the opportunity to use this parade to merge it with the Sovereign's Birthday Parade for one of the King's birthdays. This parade would use the King's second birthday as the occasion for the parade. The second birthday tradition was started by his grandfather George, who was born on 30 October, and realized good weather for a parade could not be guaranteed in late autumn. As a result, he decided to hold a second birthday in June, when the weather was more conducive to an outdoor parade.

The Duke was keen to use this date to combine a series of traditions to deliver a ceremony worthy of a king, and the first Trooping the Colour was deemed an appropriate way the king's birthday could be celebrated. The Duke's influence on the Guards did not stop there, and the rank of Private Gentleman was dissolved, which affected the Mounted Guards in particular. This now left the Horse Guards with a missing link between the new rank of Private, later to become Troopers and commissioned officers. The new non-commissioned officers would not be known as Sergeants or Sergeant Majors but as Corporals of Horse and Corporal Majors. On 23 April 1805, George would gift the Royal Regiment of Horse Guards a pair of silver kettledrums.

The Duke of York, who would later become the army's Commander-in-Chief during the Napoleonic wars, pushed on with his martial reforms. These included matters concerning the well-being of those in the rank and file throughout the British Army, who concerned him greatly and were welcomed by the men. On the other hand, his insistence that all commissioned officers adhere to a code of honour was taken with a wry smile, especially as the Duke was known to have a mistress, Mrs Mary Anne Clarke. This relationship was marked by further scandal when it was revealed the Duke had permitted her to sell commissions and promotions by Member of Parliament Lieutenant-Colonel Gwyllym Wardle (1762–1833). Mrs Clarke's performance at the subsequent House of Commons enquiry into the matter, held in 1809, wowed society. Still, the damage to the duke's reputation resulted in his resignation from various appointments, and his relationship with Mrs Clarke ended. Despite all of the controversies and not personally furnishing the British with any victories over France, the Duke's work established an army that helped Field Marshal Arthur Wellesley, 1st Duke of Wellington, beat Napoleon.

With George III's collapse into madness, George, the Prince of Wales took on the role of Prince Regent on 5 February 1811. The prince was renowned for many things, including his sartorial elegance, influenced by the likes of the famous Dandy Beau Brummell (1778–1840). Such influences rubbed off on the king and, in turn, onto those closest to him, including the Guards. The prince further demanded that relatives relay any details of military fashions worn by the Hanoverians and Prussians that could be incorporated into military dress. Numerous changes were followed to the uniforms, which, up to this point, were often little more than modifications of the contemporary civilian outfits. The prince introduced decorative headwear, jackboots and breeches; for the officers, he introduced lower-leg conforming breeches, similar to cavalry jodhpurs. Another addition was the cocked hats which were worn in any number of manners and were available in several sizes. These hats were not the most suitable for some roles, and in 1812, the Household Cavalry, who seemed to lose their headdress in even the slight breeze, were issued a Dragoon helmet.

This was followed in 1814 by a second edict from the prince that the Second Regiment of Life Guards was to wear a black lacquered cuirass. However, the moment it was revealed to the prince, he instantly disliked it, and the cuirass was abandoned. This period saw the introduction of the Napoleonic Imperial Eagle by the Blues and Royals, worn on the left sleeve of their dress tunics, and remains in use today. The use of the Napoleonic Imperial Eagle dates to the afternoon of 18 June 1815 at the Battle of Waterloo, when Serjeant Francis Styles rode against attacking French forces. Styles, alongside his squadron leader, Captain Alexander Kennedy Clarke, were soon in the midst of the fighting, during which they seized one of the two eagles captured at Waterloo, not only writing their names into regimental legends but also giving the regiment a visual reminder of their bravery.

With George's death in 1820 and the ascension to the throne of George IV, the Royal Household moved between London, Windsor and Brighton. On each move and during each residence, the Royal Household was escorted and guarded by the Life Guards or by the Blues. Whilst undertaking duties in Brighton, officers were instructed to only appear in public in what George termed 'Full Dress'. The Brighton sojourns were often graced by musical performances by the King, where invited officers would be sung to, wearing their full dress and epaulettes to signify the importance of the occasion.

The First Regiment of Foot Guards, who had become the First or Grenadier Regiment of Foot Guards, were the first of the Foot Guard regiments to be allowed to be officially furnished with bearskin caps by George. The Coldstream and Scots Guards followed suit in time, with the caps growing ever larger. The cuirass, last worn, except for the short trial in 1814, during the reign of William III, also returned to the Household Cavalry, this time with additional adornments. George was every bit the eccentric, so much so that many thought he had succumbed to the madness that had consumed his late father. George now appointed himself Colonel-in-Chief of all three regiments of the Household Cavalry, who he commanded to accompany him everywhere. At the same time, he stated that members of his Foot Guards must stand between 178 and 185 centimetres, thus ensuring a pleasing uniformity in appearance when arranged in rank and file.

With the death of George in 1830, and his younger brother William IV becoming monarch, the army, at least, had a moment to pause as the new King's interests remained purely naval. In truth, aside from assuming command of the Home Fleet at Weymouth on one occasion, William's interest in the military bordered on apathy. Unlike his elder brother, any matter regarding military uniforms and appearance was of little interest during his seven-year reign. William did take up the mantle of Colonel-in-Chief of the Household Cavalry, presenting the Life Guards with their silver kettledrums and the Blues with a guidon. The Third Foot Guards became known as the Scots Fusilier Guards and a redesign of headdresses across all the Guards regiments to one less likely to be toppled by wind or movement took place.

With William's death in 1837, the British said goodbye to a line of monarchs who had either been disinterested, of questionable sanity or simply unlikeable. As he had no living legitimate children, William's passing saw the throne pass to niece Victoria, the daughter of the fourth son of George III, Prince Edward, Duke of Kent and Strathearn (1767–1820).

The Relationship between Monarch and Guards

Despite many contemporary assumptions regarding the relationship between Victoria and the Guards, both Cavalry and Foot, Victoria seldom appeared before her Guards. Neither did she take the appointment of Colonel-in-Chief of the Household Cavalry as her predecessor had, though Victoria would appear mounted at her Birthday Parade. Many military tasks the monarch had hitherto undertaken were delegated to male family members. That is not to say Victoria was disinterested in the Guards; she expected and continued the tradition of the mounted Household Cavalry escort whenever she moved. When moving by train to Windsor, Victoria would be met by a detachment of Blues at Slough station, who escorted her carriage to Windsor Castle. The Queen and Guards relationship led to a strong kinship between Victoria and the Blues. This would benefit the Blues later when Victoria visited the Blues lines at Clewer Barracks in 1864.

What awaited Victoria was a sight worthy of the worst of urban slums. The horrified Queen ordered the barracks be rebuilt and renamed after cavalryman Field Marshal Stapleton Cotton, 1st Viscount Combermere (1773–1865). Combermere Barracks was spread over twenty acres (eight hectares) and featured more extensive barracks and married quarters for the dependants of privates and non-commissioned officers. Meanwhile, the customs of the Guards continued, and the Grenadier Guards began to march at attention as they crossed Hyde Park Corner, a custom they retain to this day. This custom has its roots from when the Duke of Wellington lived at 149 Piccadilly, Apsley House, with the troops of the Brigade called to attention whenever they passed by.

Victoria's relationship with the Foot Guards remained distant. After the death of her consort, Prince Albert, in 1861 who had undertaken most of Victoria's duties, this relationship collapsed. The annual Birthday Parade was subordinated to her uncle George, the Duke of Cambridge (1918–1904), while other responsibilities withered. Victoria remained keen-eyed regarding certain aspects of the military and the Guards' life. In 1871, her Royal Warrant abolished the purchase of commissions, and in 1877, the Scots Fusilier Guards became the Scots Guards. In 1887, after celebrating her Golden Jubilee, Victoria retired the Blues' guidon gifted to them by William IV. The main driver behind this retirement lay in the guidon's finial of solid gilt depicting St. George and the infamous dragon. This adornment made the guidon top heavy, leaving it a struggle to support, and only by the regiment's strongest.

A decade later, in 1897, the Coldstreamers were allowed to increase in size from two to three battalions by Royal Assent; this addition increased the Foot Guards' size to nine battalions, three of whom were billeted in the Mediterranean region. The following year, the Third Coldstream Battalion, alongside the Scots Guards Regiment, was presented with their colours by Victoria. Amazingly, despite Victoria's seeming aloofness and the fact she only addressed the Foot Guards twice, once in 1856 upon their return from Crimea and forty-two years later, at the presentation of the colours, she remained popular with all members of the Household Cavalry and Foot Guards. This popularity was strengthened by her addressing the Blues contingent of a composite regiment bound for South Africa, wishing them well and a safe return. Victoria did not witness their return, dying on 22 January 1901. When they did return, they returned to an enlarged brotherhood as the Irish Guards had stood to on 1 April 1900.

Her son Edward VII took to the throne as the head of the largest empire in human history. British interests and influences were manifest, but these would be tested by many social and political changes that were to mark the twentieth century as one of change. Edward was a *bon viveur* whose interests in anything military were second to many other interests, from food to horses. His main input in the life of the Guards was to declare that the rank of Private in the Household Cavalry be changed to Trooper. His wife, Queen Alexandra of Denmark (1844–1925), would start the royal tradition of handing out shamrocks to the Irish Guards on St. Patrick's Day (17 March) in 1901, a tradition that continues today. With defence cuts affecting the Scots Guards Third Battalion, Edward promised to preserve the colours at Buckingham Palace until they were needed again. With the death of Edward in 1910 and the ascent of George V, who was seen as a somewhat brusque king, the Empire was entering a period of almost unparalleled change.

The Relationship between Monarch and Guards

As monarch George, an officer in the Royal Navy earlier in life, was now the Colonel-in-chief of all the regiments of Household Cavalry and Guards. Perhaps due to his naval background, George had excellent attention to detail. In 1913, whilst observing manoeuvres of the Blues, he noted they lacked a cap badge. To correct this error, the King offered his cypher. So, the Blue's first cap badge became the royal cypher ringed by the regimental title. As the Blues left to go to war the following year, Queen Alexandra, now the Queen Mother, bade the men farewell. Very few would return. The First World War saw the Guards, both Mounted and Foot, swell in size, aided by the formation of the Welsh Guards on 26 February 1915. The sacrifice of the Guards Division, in particular, was noted, and at the war's end, George stated that the rank of Private in the Foot Guards be replaced with that of Guardsman. With the war's end, the foundations for today's Household Division and the supporting units of London District were in place. The public and escort duties remained throughout the war, but Trooping the Colour was paused for the duration of the war. Interestingly, the Household Cavalry and Foot Guards continued to wear their ceremonial Full Dress.

After the First World War, the most apparent social change that impacted the Guards was the widespread use of motor transport and, more importantly, the motor car. This impinged on the safe movement of the King's Guards and Sovereign's Escorts and necessitated a move for the Household Cavalry from their Regents Park Barracks to their Knightsbridge Barracks, which they had first occupied in 1795. Upon their return, the Life Guards were greeted by a telegram from George saying, 'I welcome my Life Guards back to their old home.' Another important royal decision was to commemorate the Armistice of the First World War. In 1919, the Royal Household established the practice of two minutes' silence at 11 o'clock as a service of Silence and Remembrance, making the announcement on 7 November. The original idea had come from Australian journalist Edward Honey (1885–1922), who suggested a five-minute silence be observed in a letter to the *London Evening News* on the first anniversary of the Armistice. After much deliberation between George and Prime Minister David Lloyd George, 1st Earl Lloyd George of Dwyfor (1863–1945), two minutes was settled upon as being the ideal length of time to hold the silence.

The 1930s saw the Guards exercise their duties to their fullest. In 1936, they led the State Funeral of George, worked with the uncertainty of the short reign of Edward VIII in 1936 and celebrated the Coronation of George VI before the men of the Household Cavalry and Foot Guards once again departed for the front lines.

Ceremonial duties were put on hold between 1940 and 1946; the Guards returned to a far different United Kingdom than that which had existed in 1939. The men of the Mounted and Foot Guards, including musicians, were all in their khaki service dress and peaked caps as they paraded past the mounted King and Heir Presumptive, Princess Elizabeth. Upon his return to Buckingham Palace, George and his entourage were greeted by members of the United States Army. It would be three more years until the return of the full-dress uniforms of bearskin caps, scarlet tunics and cuirass to Horse Guards Parade. On 17 April 1946, the Riding Troop of the Royal Horse Artillery was formed at the request of George to provide support for State Ceremonial. On 24 October 1947, during an inspection by George, he took out a pencil, struck through the word 'Riding' and over the top wrote 'King's', thus changing the name. The new name stuck, and the King's Troop has remained thus ever since.

Like his grandfather, George's reign was marked by significant changes: the slow withdrawal of the Empire and the continued growth of the Commonwealth of Nations. Post-war Britain was also gripped by austerity and the wounds of war, which had hit home almost unabated for the entire duration. Despite all of this at its head, the Empire, as it was, was led by a well-liked King and, at home at least, and a popular government keen to change the lives of ordinary Britons for the better. The marriage of Elizabeth to Prince Philip of Greece and Denmark on 20 November 1947 gave the men and women of the Royal Household, London District and the United Kingdom a moment of light relief. It was also an opportunity to show it was still capable of incredible feats of pageantry. All captured by newsreel and television, the royal wedding, which took place in grey and overcast weather, featured the mounted Guard Escorts of the Household

Cavalry in full dress riding alongside the coachman-driven state coaches. The Princess was cheered on by enthusiastic crowds outside Buckingham Palace as she departed for Westminster Abbey.

With the death of George, Elizabeth II led the nation for seventy years, ensuring the men and women of the Household Division and London District maintained their high standards. Elizabeth was renowned for her attention to detail and insistence on excellence, especially in all matters relating to equitation. Overseeing numerous State Ceremonial and public events through a period of significant social change, Elizabeth became the acme of the all-knowing Sovereign in such matters.

With the ascent of Charles III in 2022, the relationship between the Royal Household, the Household Division, and the London District remains as strong as ever. Although times have changed, and the increased influence of social media in the twenty-first century provides us with almost unfettered access to events, past and present, there is still a bit of magic in State Ceremonial and Public Duties that cannot be found anywhere else in the world.

OF POMP AND CIRCUMSTANCE

'Is the sovereign not the natural guardian of the honour of the country?'
Prince Albert of Saxe-Coburg and Gotha

Trooping the Colour, among other ceremonies associated with State, can be traced back to the Middle Ages, when the bearing of arms by heralds and nobles allowed for easy recognition during the heat of battle. As the British Army grew, so did the need for individuals to easily recognize their regimental colours, that would be the rallying point for any regiment should they become fractured in battle. In peacetime, the colours, which were unique to each regiment, would be unveiled and paraded regularly, giving the latest recruits the opportunity to study and remember the design for future reference. As an official ceremony, the Trooping the Colour did not start until 1805. It wasn't until Robert Gascoyne-Cecil, 3rd Marquess of Salisbury (1830–1903), a Conservative politician, complained about the apparent lack of regal pomp in 1861 that the Royal Household began to give serious consideration to providing more spectacle.

Given that Victoria remained deeply withdrawn from more significant social events, with relatives fulfilling her role, building a repertoire of awe-inspiring ceremonies was slow. It wasn't until 1911, at the Coronation of George V, that the monarchy and State Ceremonial came into its own, as 60,000 troops lined the route from Buckingham Palace to Westminster Abbey.

The State Ceremonial and Public Duties made by London District's regiments continue to stand out and shine. Today, it is safe to say the men and women of all units involved are at the top of their game, leading a legacy that has entertained and enthralled in good times and bad.

Victory and Remembrance

The first British Victory Parade occurred in late June 1815, days after the Allied victory at Waterloo on 18 June. The Allied victory was confirmed with the delivery of the news of victory, accompanied by two French Eagles, presented to George, the Prince Regent, by Wellington's Aide-de-Camp, Major Henry Percy (1785–1825), who had charged from the battlefield to London. The Prince Regent gave thanks for victory, wept for the fallen and promoted Percy on the spot. Contemporary records depicted a relieved populace drunk on the wine of victory. Indeed, the initial stories to come away from Waterloo were of defeat for the Allies, which had led to some despondency. However, thanks to the efforts of Percy, many, like the Prince Regent, wept for the fallen, while most celebrated with drink and song.

The parade, of which no defined date can be found, took place shortly after. It would feature some 15,000, mostly British, troops parading in celebration at Hyde Park at the defeat of Napoleon Bonaparte (1769–1821) and his subsequent exile to Elba.

Despite the Allied victory being a key milestone, the recently appointed American ambassador, John Quincy Adams (1767–1848), would later remark; 'In the evening we all rode round the streets to see the illuminations for the great victory of the 18th. They were not general, nor very magnificent. The whole range of their variety was, "Wellington and Blücher," "Victory," "G.P.R.," and "G.R." The transparencies were very few, and very bad.'

We'll never know whether Adams felt sympathy for the defeated and exiled Bonaparte or was looking in the wrong place.

The next Victory Parades, referred to as Peace Parades, would occur over a century later, in 1919. There would be two parades in London, sanctioned by George V, one on 19 July and a second by the Indian Army, delayed because of logistical issues and an outbreak of influenza, on 2 August. Once again, the first parade was led by 15,000 Allied soldiers, who marched past the wood and plaster Cenotaph, a term from the Greek words for 'empty tomb', on Whitehall, London. This was designed by architect Sir Edwin Lutyens (1869–1944) as a non-denominational focal point for the parade. The parade itself, whilst short, had been intended to be a one-off, with many veterans and families keen to remember in their own way. Regardless of some disquiet in veteran's circles, the Cenotaph, initially intended to be a temporary structure, became a focal point for families' grief. Within seven days of the parade, over a million people had visited the site, with floral tributes extending ten feet (three metres) from the base of the Cenotaph. Almost immediately, there came calls to make the Cenotaph a permanent structure. After some debate, work was started in May 1920. The Portland stone Cenotaph was unveiled on 11 November 1920, two years after the signing of the Armistice, by George V. The unveiling of the Cenotaph would become part of the State Funeral for the Unknown Warrior of both events. David Lloyd George would write: 'The Cenotaph is the token of our mourning as a nation; the Grave of the Unknown Warrior is the token of our mourning as individuals.'

The service and story of the Unknown Warrior was, for a great many, undeniably beautiful and emotional. The idea of the Unknown Warrior came from Reverend David Railton (1884–1955), a First World War chaplain who had earned the Military Cross (MC) in 1916 for saving three men under fire. His desire to mark the memories of the many soldiers whose identities were unknown, in particular, drove him to lobby Field Marshal Douglas Haig, 1st Earl Haig (1861–1928), for the suitable recognition of these men. There was no response from Haig, but this drove Railton on, and the idea remained.

Like many men who had returned from the war, Railton struggled to adjust to peacetime. Perhaps seeking satisfaction from his service experience and his post-war transition, he pursued his idea to remember 'An Unknown British Soldier' once more in the early summer of 1920. Writing to the Right Reverend Bishop Herbert Ryle (1856–1925), then Dean of Westminster, the letter proposed the burial of the body of one of the many unknown men. Railton further requested that, if permitted, one of his own Union Flags that had accompanied him during his war service be used as a 'war' flag rather than a new flag. Given that Railton did not know Ryle, his request was extremely bold. Within days, the Dean responded to Railton in the positive, and having given Railton's idea thought, he went as far as to propose the flag be hung in St. Faith Chapel after the service. Ryle acknowledged that while similar ideas were proposed, Railton's was the best. Ryle would approach his chapter and the government to discuss the concept and how best to proceed but cautioned Railton against getting his hopes up regarding a quick resolution.

Preoccupied with ecumenical matters, Railton was more than surprised when, on 19 October, he received a letter from Ryle. On 22 October, *The Times* announced the official unveiling of the Cenotaph on Armistice Day. It also mentioned a committee led by Lord George Curzon, 1st Marquess Curzon of Kedleston (1859–1925), charged with reinterring the body of an unknown warrior, with the two ceremonies being interdependent. On 25 October, Ryle once again wrote to Railton confirming that his war flag, if suitable, would be used in the ceremony. Another touch shared with Railton was that soil from France's battlefields would fill the grave once the casket had been lowered. This thoughtful touch was further added to by an invitation to preach at Westminster Abbey later that year. Several holes in the flag would be patched by Railton's wife Ruby before its final journey on 3 November and consequent solemn duty. As an Honorary Chaplain, Railton brushed down his service uniform in preparation for 11 November. On the eve of Armistice Day, *The Times* ran two articles on Railton's endeavours, one on the War Flag and one on the Unknown Warrior, which included the following sentence: 'Thus, the Unknown Soldier returns to-day to English shores bearing with him the banner of a victory greater than any victory of the sword.'

As Armistice Day approached, the preparations for the return of the Unknown Warrior were made. Lord Curzon's committee had carefully planned these preparations, which were turned into actions on 7 November. Six bodies were exhumed from six battlefields where British soldiers had fought, with each of the recovery parties led by a Subaltern. Once the physical remains had been correctly identified as British soldiers, typically from remnants of uniform, they were placed on a stretcher and taken to a temporary chapel, a hut, at Saint-Pol-sur-Ternoise near Arras, France, at the headquarters of Brigadier-General Louis Wyatt (1874–1955), General Officer Commanding, British Forces in France and Belgium. At the makeshift chapel, the bodies of the unknown soldiers were set to rest and received by the chaplain from the Imperial War Graves Commission (IWGC), Reverend George Kendall (1882–1961). Kendall performed a final inspection to ensure the remains belonged to British soldiers. Once his task was complete, each of the bodies was covered with a Union Flag. His task done, Kendall left the chapel, locked the door and the sentries stood to. At midnight on 7 November, Wyatt, accompanied by Lieutenant Colonel Edward Gell (1875–1951) of the Directorate of Graves Registration and Enquiries, entered the chapel. Wyatt selected a body randomly, placed in a plain pine coffin by Wyatt and Gell and set before the chapel's altar. Kendall removed and took away the remaining bodies for reburial.

The following morning, chaplains from the Anglican, Roman Catholic and Non-Conformist faiths held an official service. At midday, the coffin was removed and taken by military convoy to Boulogne, some fifty miles (eighty kilometres) from Saint-Pol. As the convoy entered Boulogne, it was greeted by the citizenry and French soldiers, who lined the route to the French Army HQ at Château de Boulogne-sur-Mer. The ambulance that carried the coffin halted in the courtyard and was greeted by eight soldiers from different British and Commonwealth regiments who stood sentinel for their fallen brother-in-arms. The eight men, all from the ranks, then carried the coffin of the Unknown Warrior, known as the *Tommy Anonyme* by the French, to the Château's library, their route lined with French soldiers. The library had been converted into a *chapelle ardente*, decorated with flags and palms, a custom normally afforded only to heads of state and senior dignitaries. For his final night in France, the Unknown Warrior was guarded by the cream of the French Army, the highly decorated 8th Infantry Regiment, holders of the Légion d'Honneur.

As the French stood their watch, two British undertakers, Mr Horace Kirtley-Nodes (1876–1959) and Mr John Sowerbutts (1875–1955), began their work. They had brought a casket made from oak from Hampton Court Palace and provided by the British Undertakers' Association. The casket featured iron bands and handles, and the lid was topped with a sixteenth-century sword from the Royal Collection personally selected by George V. The sword was held in place by an iron shield bearing the inscription 'A British Warrior who fell in the Great War 1914–1918 for King and Country'. The empty casket, which had already been to Westminster Abbey to ensure a perfect fit on the floor of the Abbey, weighed some 225 lb (102 kg), was opened. The two undertakers carefully lifted the pine coffin into the casket. They then sealed the casket and quietly left the men of the 8th to their solemn duty.

The following morning, 9 November, Marshal Ferdinand Foch (1851–1929) stood with the Adjutant General, Lieutenant-General George MacDonogh (1865–1942), who acted as the King's representative, in the Château's courtyard. The pair waited for the eight pallbearers from the previous day to load the casket onto a waiting French Army wagon. The casket was carefully loaded onto the wagon, drawn by six black horses, and finally draped with Railton's Union Flag. At 10:30 am, the French infantry and cavalry trumpets gave their final salute, the *Aux Champs*, followed by Chopin's *Funeral March*. The wagon was preceded by a mile-long procession of children, soldiers and marines, followed by numerous wreaths.

At last, the wagon made its final journey through Boulogne and down to the Quai Gambetta, where HMS *Verdun* waited with a white ensign at half-mast. The eight pallbearers carried the casket onboard and piped aboard with an Admiral's call. They were watched by an emotional Foch, who had just delivered a speech to the ship's company and the silent crowds gathered on the quay. As the band finished playing the *Marseillaise* and *God Save the King*, the French wreaths were laid upon and around the casket. Finally, four sailors moved into position to guard the coffin at each corner of the caskets, rifles reversed, heads bowed.

At 11:45, in an almost eerie silence, HMS *Verdun* cast off to *God Save the King* and the nineteen-gun salute that was usually reserved for the salute of Field Marshals. HMS *Verdun* made her passage across the channel accompanied by French torpedo boats, aircraft and a special escort of six destroyers. The destroyers took up their stations, three in line ahead of HMS *Verdun* and three in line astern, their ensigns lowered. The convoy made such good time on the calm waters that they were forced to lay up for two hours before finally moving off and letting HMS *Verdun* slowly enter Dover through its western harbour, watched by crowds, who were extraordinarily quiet according to a *Times* reporter. Once again, the nineteen-gun salute was fired, this time from Dover Castle, welcoming the Unknown Soldier home. HMS *Verdun* approached Admiralty Pier silently; the waiting troops stood to attention, rifles reversed.

The casket was carried off HMS *Verdun* by six veteran Warrant Officers from all branches of the military and followed by MacDonogh. A procession of military officers and civilians soon formed as the casket was carried to Dover Marine Railway Station. There, the casket was loaded onto South Eastern & Chatham Railway (SECR) General Utility Van No. 132, which had previously carried Nurse Edith Cavell (1865–1915) and Captain Charles Fryatt (1872–1916), civilians whom the Germans had executed during the war. After loading the wreaths, Van No.132, with its special white roof and attending passenger car with its guard of Connaught Rangers, departed with the 17:50 Dover to Victoria boat train. As it left, the

Guard of Honour from the Connaught Rangers presented arms. This act of respect was repeated minutes later as the train passed through Dover's Harbour Station as the Royal Irish Fusiliers paid their compliments. The Guards of Honour and crowds continued along the route despite the cold.

At 20:32, the train arrived at Platform 8, Victoria Railway Station; the attending Connaught Rangers handed over the responsibility of the casket to the King's Company, Grenadier Guards. The Grenadiers began their duties, one either side of the van's luggage door, head bowed, rifles reversed. Their guard lasted throughout the night, with guards changing every thirty minutes. Platform 8 was sited next to the Buckingham Palace Road entrance, and it was there that the gun carriage for the State Funeral would collect the Unknown Warrior. The crowds gradually left.

The combined events of the State Funeral and the unveiling of the Cenotaph had been organized by the General Officer Commanding (GOC) London District and Major General commanding the Brigade of Guards, Grenadier Guard, Major General George Jeffreys (1878–1960). Jeffreys had been the wartime GOC of the 19th (Western) Division to whom Railton had served as Senior Chaplain. Jeffrey and his staff at Horse Guards had found themselves placed not only in a unique position that enabled the Guards to draw on their ceremonial and planning expertise but also in charge of a one-off dual ceremony of enormous importance to so many. While Lord Curzon can be credited for establishing the annual Remembrance ceremony at the Cenotaph, it should be Jeffreys and his staff at Horse Guards who should be credited with the establishment of how State Ceremonial, including the Cenotaph's annual Remembrance ceremony, is conducted to this day.

The programme was well designed, and the orders arising from it were signed by Lieutenant–Colonel R. Luker. These covered every detail of movement once the Unknown Warrior arrived at Victoria Railway Station and came under the charge of the London District. The orders were meticulous, containing written and visual instructions regarding timings, the placing of military mourners at the Cenotaph, identifying who marched with the gun carriage and from the moment the casket left Victoria Railway Station.

The Relationship between Monarch and Guards

The morning of 11 November found central London shrouded in a thick mist. The change in weather failed to keep the crowds away, and by mid-morning, the Grenadier Guards, who had kept vigil throughout the night, were relieved by men from the 3rd Battalion, Coldstream Guards. These men were the bearer and firing parties, and at 9:20 am, the Sergeant in charge of the party entered Van No. 132. Once inside, he placed a Brodie Helmet, synonymous with the British soldier, and a web belt complete with a Pattern 1907 sword bayonet, on top of the Union Flag. The bearer party then advanced and removed the casket to the waiting gun carriage belonging to N Battery, Royal Horse Artillery (RHA), drawn by six black horses, a task carried out by the King's Troop, RHA today. As the casket was loaded, the Officer-in-Charge of the firing party ordered the Present Arms as the final preparations were made to move towards the Cenotaph. The bearer party then fell in behind the gun carriage, and the distinguished pallbearers paid their respects and fell in on either side of the gun carriage, with Haig taking his position to the right. Other high-ranking officers included the Admiral of the Fleet, Earl David Beatty (1871–1936), as well as Field Marshals Sir Henry Wilson (1864–1922), who would later be assassinated by members of the Irish Republican Army (IRA), and John French, later to become 1st Earl of Ypres (1852–1925).

At 9:40 am, the order was given for the firing party to right turn, reverse arms and slow march. As they marched forward, the massed bands played Chopin's *Funeral March*. As the firing party came level with the bands, the latter fell in behind the firing party. The casket then passed through the military mourners from all three services that waited close to the station entrance on Buckingham Palace Road, who then followed the gun carriage as it moved forwards. Finally, some 400 veterans, who had assembled on the platform, fell in as the rearguard. The moment the order to move was given, the remaining guns of N Battery fired a nineteen-gun salute from Hyde Park.

As the cortège emerged onto Buckingham Palace Road, it was greeted by thousands of soldiers, with arms reversed and heads bowed. Behind the silent sentinels were untold thousands of mourners, sometimes up to twenty deep, many in tears, their black dress broken by the colourful wreaths and flowers; men removed their hats as the cortège passed, taking the Unknown Warrior to his final resting place. The cortège's initial two-and-a-half mile route, planned by Luker, went to the Cenotaph via Hyde Park Corner, The Mall and Whitehall. At Hyde Park, the pipes of the Scots Guards broke the silence as the cortège passed; its length was such that it would take five minutes to pass any given point.

At the Cenotaph, where George V and others waited patiently, the cortège came to a halt on Whitehall. Watched by ticket holders, chosen at random from the bereaved wives and parents of servicemen, the King, positioned on the north side of the Cenotaph in the uniform of a Field Marshal, stood alone. The choreography that followed was textbook Guards planning. The cortège split with followers taking up preordained positions, marked by members of the military police, while the gun carriage halted opposite George V, all under the command of a single officer from London District. By 10:50 am, all movement was complete, and as the gun carriage halted, George V approached and laid a wreath of red roses and bay leaves on top of the casket. Behind the King stood the Cenotaph, its north and south faces covered with two huge Union Flags. On the east and west sides were placed the Royal Air Force Ensign, Union Flag, Red Ensign on one side, and the Blue Ensign, Union Flag, and White Ensign on the other.

As Big Ben made the first strike at 11:00 am, the King turned and pressed a button that released the two huge Union Flags. The flags were quickly gathered, and the two-minute silence began on the final bell stroke. Across the Empire, millions joined in with the silence until it was broken by the *Last Post*, called by eight buglers from the Brigade of Guards. Once the last note had been played, George V laid a wreath at the foot of the Cenotaph, followed by Lloyd George, key members of government and the Houses of Parliament. With the final wreath laid, the second part of the ceremony began, and the Coldstream Guards firing party, followed by the bearers, continued their duties as Chopin's *Funeral March* was played once more. The cortège grew as the massed bands followed the Coldstreamers, and the Archbishop of Canterbury, Randall Davidson (1848–1930), and his party fell in behind the band. Now followed by the

Archbishop, the gun carriage was once more flanked by the pallbearers. Directly behind the gun carriage marched the King and members of the Royal Family, including Prince Edward and Prince Albert. They were followed by 130 'Distinguished Personages', who were followed by mourners from each of the armed services, and finally, veterans. Once this group had passed the Cenotaph, four sentries from each of the three branches of the armed forces took position at each of the four corners of the Cenotaph, facing outward and arms reversed.

Whilst the cortège made its way to Westminster Abbey, every seat had been filled by the mothers and widows of the men lost, with 100 seats reserved for women who had lost both their husbands and all their sons. Lord Curzon was keen that the day was used to commemorate the fallen by those closest to them and not be turned into a high society event. The moment most definitely belonged to the women and not the politicians. The gathered women were entertained from 10:00 am by the band of the Grenadier Guards. The choir then sang from 10:45 am until 11:00 am. After the two-minute silence, Ryle read three collects. Afterwards, the choir once more stood and sang. At this point the Ryle and Chapter of Westminster moved to the North Porch in preparation to receive the Unknown Warrior.

The firing party had arrived and arranged themselves, standing heads down, and arms reversed whilst the bearers stood to attention awaiting the gun carriage. Once it arrived, the casket was carried feet first to the waiting Dean and Chapter. Inside the Abbey was arranged a unique Guard of Honour commanded by Lieutenant-Colonel Bernard Freyberg of the Grenadier Guards and holder of the Victoria Cross. The Guard of Honour was filled by ninety-six men who had won gallantry awards during the war, including seventy-five Victoria Crosses. The bearers, followed by the pallbearers, advanced further into the Abbey; the sobs of the 2,000 women and men gathered there almost drowned out the choir. Meanwhile, the accompanying gun carriage, the firing party, massed bands and service mourners quietly left.

The bearers reached the grave and carefully lowered the casket onto the iron bars placed over the grave, which was situated at the far western end of the Nave, only a few feet from the entrance. The pallbearers took up their positions on either side of the casket. George V, with his two sons, took their positions at one end of the grave. Ryle, Davidson and Arthur Winnington-Ingram, Bishop of London (1858–1946), stood at the other, facing the assembled congregation. The band of the Grenadier Guards then played Beethoven's *Equale for Trombones,* followed by two readings, the last of which was given by Ryle. As he did so, the bearers removed the Brodie Helmet, sword-bayonet and Railton's Union Flag. The bars were removed, and the Coldstreamers slowly lowered the casket as Ryle began the committal. The King was then handed a silver shell case containing some of the soil from France, sprinkling it onto the resting casket. The service was ended by the Guards' buglers who played *The Reveille.* At the end of the service, the band of the Grenadier Guards struck up once more, and the king, members of the Royal Family and other dignitaries left via the Great West door. The fog that had started the day had now cleared.

Outside, the now dispersed cortège and service personnel were replaced by thousands of members of the public in a line stretching back to the Cenotaph. With the Royal Family and other dignitaries gone, Freyberg led the Guard of Honour past the grave to pay their respects. Once the congregation had dispersed, the Abbey was sealed, with policemen covering the entrances to make sure no one entered.

The grave was now prepared for public viewing, being covered by an 'Actor's Pall' given by the Actors' Union to honour their fallen members. Railton's Union Flag was spread over the pall. The Brodie Helmet and sword-bayonet were placed upon it with wreaths from the Dean and Chapter of Westminster and the War Graves Inquiry Bureau. As a wooden barrier was placed around the grave, four large candles were lit, and like the Cenotaph, four sentries from each of the three branches of the armed forces took position at each corner of the grave. At 12:40 pm, the doors to the Abbey were opened, and thousands of mourners filed silently past.

The grave remained open until 18 November, after an estimated 1.2 million people had visited to pay their respects. The casket was covered with the French soil that had arrived in 100 sandbags, then covered with a York stone slab before being capped with a slab of black

Belgian marble. It now became the only tombstone in the Abbey upon which it is forbidden to walk.

The marble would be inscribed with the words of Ryle, which read:

Beneath this stone rests the body
Of a British warrior
Unknown by name or rank
Brought from France to lie among
The most illustrious of the land
And buried here on Armistice Day
11 November 1920, in the presence of
His Majesty King George V
His Ministers of State
The Chiefs of his forces
And a vast concourse of the nation
Thus are commemorated the many
Multitudes who during the Great
War of 1914–1918 gave the most that
Man can give life itself
For God
For King and country
For loved ones, home and Empire
For the sacred cause of justice and
The freedom of the world
They buried him among the kings because he
Had done good toward God and toward
His house

Surrounding this inscription were four New Testament quotations:

At the top: The Lord knoweth them that are his (2 Timothy 2:19)

To one side: Unknown and yet well known, dying and behold we live (side; 2 Corinthians 6:9)

To one side: Greater love hath no man than this (side; John 15:13)

At the base: In Christ shall all be made alive (base; 1 Corinthians 15:22)

A year later, on 17 October 1921, the Unknown Warrior was awarded the Medal of Honor, presented by General of the Armies of the United States John Pershing (1860–1948). On 11 November 1921, the American Unknown Soldier was reciprocally awarded the Victoria Cross by the British.

With the laying to rest of the Unknown Warrior, a new royal tradition was started three years later when Elizabeth Bowes-Lyon (1900–2002) laid her bouquet at the tomb on her way into the Abbey to marry Prince Albert on 26 April 1923. The future Queen Mother laid the flowers in tribute to her brother, Captain The Honourable Fergus Bowes-Lyon (1889–1915), who had died at the Battle of Loos in 1915 and whose name was listed among the missing on the Loos Memorial. Before she died in 2002, Queen Elizabeth, the Queen Mother, expressed the wish for her wreath to be placed on the Tomb of the Unknown Warrior, a wish her daughter Elizabeth II fulfilled the day after the funeral.

Today, Royal brides married at the Abbey or elsewhere have their bouquets laid on the tomb the day after the wedding. Railtons's war flag would remain at the foot of the grave until 11 November 1921, when it was removed and hung, as promised. Today Railton's flag, known as The Padre's Flag, now hangs in St George's Chapel close to the Unknown Warrior's grave.

Rites and ceremonies

State Funerals
The history of the State Funeral, with its strong heraldic themes, can be traced back to the late Middle Ages, with the Tudors and Jacobeans following suit. In these instances, the Exchequer provided lengths of

black cloth to all those taking part in the funeral cortège regardless of social rank. The quality and amount of material used to make the mourning garments were strictly regulated by the College of Arms, with lengths of fabric indicating the social position of the wearer. For example, a seventeenth-century Duke was permitted sixteen yards of cloth at ten shillings a yard. In contrast, a knight would be given a mere five yards at the cost of six shillings and eight pence. The only colour seen was provided by heralds, who placed their tabards over their mourning cloaks and carried the late sovereign's achievements in the procession. The achievement fully displays all the heraldic components to which the later sovereign was entitled. The cortège also featured Heraldic banners carried at various points in the procession. The pall-covered coffin, which in turn may be covered by a canopy, was borne on a horse-drawn bier, with all horses, including any accompanying mounts, dressed in black; black drapes would also be hung along the procession route.

By the thirteenth century, a lifelike wood and wax effigy of the deceased individual would be carried on or near the coffin, replacing the embalmed body that would have been on view during the proceedings. The effigy would often wear the deceased sovereign or queen consort's coronation robes and regalia. For effigies of notable individuals, their robes of state or armour may have been placed on the effigy.

Edward II was the first sovereign to be honoured with an effigy, and the last sovereign to be given an effigy was James I at his funeral on 7 May 1625. The use of an effigy was replaced with a crown on a cushion, which in turn was placed upon the coffin, a tradition begun at the funeral of Charles II. Today, the few surviving effigies can be seen at the Queen's Diamond Jubilee Galleries in Westminster Abbey; these include the armour from the lost funeral effigy of General George Monck, father of the Coldstream Guards (1608–1670).

State Funerals were also occasions for royal almsgiving, with early funerals featuring a contingent of almsmen walking in the procession and offering prayers for the deceased's soul.

For the funeral of Elizabeth I, a contingent of 266 poor women led the funeral procession between Whitehall Palace and Westminster

Abbey, with Elizabeth's Lord High Almoner, Anthony Watson, Bishop of Chichester (c. 1549–1605), delivering the final service. Elizabeth's funeral also included over a thousand participants, including peers and their families as well as servants, including 'children of the scullery', the 'yeomen of the boiling house' (bakery) to seamstresses, and the Maids of Honour of her Privy Chamber. Also in attendance were the Great Officers of State, the chief justices, the Lord Mayor and Aldermen of London and numerous clerks and officials. The Master of the Horse, Edward Somerset, 4th Earl of Worcester (1550-1628), later Earl Marshal of James I and later Lord-Lieutenant of Glamorgan and Monmouth, followed this procession, leading a Palfrey of Honour. The Palfrey was a highly valued, often lightweight horse known for its smooth gait that followed directly behind the coffin. This act continued a medieval tradition whereby the late sovereign's horse would follow them into the church, where it would be given as a gratuity, or compensation, to the Abbey. The Master of the Horse followed the chief mourner, Elin Ulfsdotter Snakenborg, the Marchioness of Northampton (1548/4–1635), as senior peeress after Lady Arbella Stuart (1575–1615) refused to undertake the role for political reasons, as James I had not yet arrived in London in preparation to take the crown. Women rarely attended a funeral, though the women and ladies of Queen Anne's household would walk in her funeral procession. Bringing up the rear of the funeral cortège, carrying their white staves of office in the procession, marched the men of the Yeomen of the Guard. At the end of the funeral service, in a scene much recorded, the Yeomen would break their white staves of office across their knees, casting them into the grave as a sign that their duties had ended.

Many of these funeral practices were maintained into the nineteenth century, with occasional tweaking. At the funeral of George IV, the Sword of State and Cap of Maintenance were carried before the coffin. Of interest, until the twentieth century, a sovereign would not attend their predecessor's funeral. However, William IV would break that tradition and attend the funeral of George IV. By the time of the funeral of William, the chief mourner and his attendants still wore black mourning cloaks, the coffin covered by a purple velvet pall, featuring the Royal Arms covered by a black canopy. The crowns of the United Kingdom and Hanover were carried on cushions in the procession that followed a route marked by black drapes. The crowns would be placed on the coffin for the service, while the heraldic banners followed the coffin. As it was customary for State Funerals to take place after sunset, the funeral cortège of William started at 8:00 pm. The Brigade of Guards lined the processional route, a tradition that continues, with one in four of the Guards holding a torch. The regimental bands played George Handel's *Dead March* from the oratorio *Saul* (HWV 53) as the procession passed their positions. Today, officers and troops bearing arms, either as route liners or as part of the cortège, held them in reverse as a sign of mourning. Another martial tradition, echoing the gun salute, known as the Death Gun Salute, is fired to honour the death of a sovereign. Today, the Death Gun Salute is fired by the King's Troop (RHA) and A Battery, the Honourable Artillery Company. The Death Gun Salute is followed by firing the 'minute guns'. This 300-year-old tradition still takes place during the funeral procession, with a single gun being fired every minute until the end of the funeral ceremony.

By the time of the State Funeral of Queen Victoria in February 1901, a remarkable sixty-four years had passed since the previous royal funeral. Fully aware of this and nodding to the social changes during her reign, Victoria left strict instructions and alterations regarding the service and its ceremonies that set a new model for how state (and indeed ceremonial) funerals have occurred since. As Victoria disliked black, the cloak, drapes, and canopy were removed from the service, and her coffin was draped in a simple white pall. This indicated the late Queen's request to be buried as 'a soldier's daughter', a nod to the service of her father, Prince Edward, Duke of Kent and Strathearn (1767-1820). As a young officer, Prince Edward had taken leave without absence, a move indicative of later, somewhat questionable behaviour as an officer that often led to confrontation. Most notably, and in contrast to his earlier behaviour as a Subaltern, the prince's excessive discipline led to the Gibraltar Mutiny of 1802 that effectively ended his military career. With Victoria's changes, the procession took on a more martial mood, with the Peers, Privy Counsellors and Judiciary no longer taking part en masse. The pallbearers were Equerries, and the gun carriage was now employed to convey the monarch's coffin.

Having died at Osborne House, Isle of Wight, Victoria's body was conveyed by HMY *Alberta*, followed by other yachts that conveyed Edward VII and other mourners. As the funeral flotilla made its passage from Cowes to Gosport minute guns were fired by the assembled fleet as the yacht passed. On arrival at Gosport, Victoria's body remained on board HMY *Alberta* with Royal Marine guards before being transferred by gun carriage to the railway station for her journey to Waterloo Station. It was moved by gun carriage to Paddington Station, where it was taken to Windsor for the funeral itself. On arrival in Windsor, a new tradition that continues to this day, was born after the horses that had been formed up to carry Victoria refused to move, much to the anger and embarrassment of the Royal Artillery. This led to the Royal Guard from HMS *Excellent*, a Royal Navy shore establishment, being gathered and pulling the coffin with ropes. After the funeral service in St. George's Chapel, Windsor, Victoria's body lay in state for two days under a military guard before joining the late Prince Albert of Saxe-Coburg and Gotha in the nearby Royal Mausoleum at Frogmore at Windsor Great Park, once again towed by the Royal Guard at the request of Edward.

Today, State Funerals continue to follow the template set by Victoria, with the lying-in-State with Westminster Hall being used for this purpose since the death of Edward in 1910. The move to Westminster Hall proved popular, with over a quarter of a million people taking the opportunity to file past Edward's coffin in 1910, securing its future use for such moments. Edwards's funeral was just as memorable as his mother's, with the gun carriage in use once more, pulled by sailors, and flanked by members of the Guards Division. The rear party of the gun carriage was followed by Edward's riderless charger, the late King's boots placed reverse in the stirrups, a gesture symbolizing the fallen leader looking back on his troops for the last time. The charger was immediately followed by Caesar, Edwards's favourite fox terrier, escorted by a suitably attired Highlander handler. There followed the

State Procession, accompanied by nine kings and forty foreign princes. After the funeral service, the processions left for Paddington Station, taking an astonishing two hours to cover the three-mile distance between the two locations. At Paddington Station, the mourners and King's Body boarded the Royal Train bound for Windsor for the funeral. The same processional route was followed in 1936 and 1952, but not for the funeral of Elizabeth II.

The traditions were added to over the twentieth century, and at the lying-in-state of George V, the Vigil of the Princes took place. Gathered around the coffin of the late King were his four surviving sons: Edward VIII, who had served with the 1st Battalion, Grenadier Guards in Flanders and Italy, and Albert the Duke of York, and later George VI. They were joined by Prince Henry, Duke of Gloucester (1900–1947), and Prince George, Duke of Kent (1902–1942). Prince George would later die on active service when the Short Sunderland he was a passenger on crashed on Eagle's Rock Dunbeath, Caithness, Scotland. Prince George was the first royal to die on active service in 450 years. The Vigil of the Princes was repeated once again at the lying-in-state of Queen Elizabeth, the Queen Mother, with her grandsons Prince Charles (b.1948), then Prince of Wales, now Charles III, Prince Andrew (b. 1960) the Duke of York, Prince Edward (b. 1964) the Earl of Wessex, and David Armstrong-Jones (b. 1961) Viscount Linley. The four children of Elizabeth II, including Anne (b.1950), Princess Royal, Colonel of the Blues and Royals and Gold Stick in Waiting, stood guard at her lying-in-state twice: once in Edinburgh and once more at Westminster Hall.

The State Funeral of Elizabeth II marked the culmination of ten days of national mourning. During that time, the Royal Navy, Army, and Royal Air Force readied themselves to perform their final duty to Her Majesty. Given the size of the task ahead and this being the first sovereign's funeral since 1952, London District had their work cut out for them. Facing numerous challenges, from the route layout to the number of individuals involved, London District's efforts focused on the problem-solving skills of Garrison Sergeant Major (GSM) Andrew 'Vern' Stokes (Coldstream).

The military elements of the State Funeral were planned with a precision that has long been a hallmark of the Household Division. At the end of the period of lying-in-state, shortly after 10.35 am, a Bearer Party formed of troops from The Queen's Company, led by The Captain, Major Johnny Hathaway-White carried Her Majesty's coffin from the catafalque in Westminster Hall to the State Gun Carriage maintained and provided by King's Troop. Elizabeth's coffin had been constructed more than thirty years before the funeral. Made of English oak, it was lined with lead to protect the coffin and the remains from moisture damage. Due to the weight of the coffin, eight pallbearers were required to lift and carry it rather than the usual six.

As is the tradition, the State Gun Carriage was drawn by 142 Royal Navy ratings. The cortège was led by the massed Pipes and Drums of Scottish and Irish Regiments, the Brigade of Gurkhas and the Royal Air Force. The massed bands were followed by The Kings, Heralds and Pursuivants of Arms, officers, and senior members of The Queen's household. The State Gun Carriage, now flanked by the Bearer Party, the Service Equerries to The Queen acted as pallbearers, as well as detachments of The King's Body Guards of the Honourable Corps of Gentlemen at Arms, the Yeomen of the Guard and the Royal Company of Archers. Charles, along with members of the Royal Family, the King's Household, and the Prince of Wales, walked behind the coffin. The Royal Standard of the United Kingdom served as a pall, upon which was placed the Imperial State Crown, the Sovereign's orb and sceptre and a wreath with greenery and flowers from the gardens of Buckingham Palace, Highgrove House, and Clarence House was placed on the coffin, together with a note from Charles which read 'In loving and devoted memory. Charles R'.

Following a route lined by the Royal Navy and Royal Marines, the cortège passed through Parliament Square on its way to Westminster Abbey. At Parliament Square, a tri-Service Guard of Honour had formed consisting of members of Nijmegen Company, Grenadier Guards, the Royal Navy and The King's Colour Squadron of the Royal Air Force, each with their colours draped and accompanied by a Band of the Royal Marines. Before the funeral service, the tenor bell of Westminster Abbey was rung once a minute for ninety-six minutes, each toll symbolizing each year of Elizabeth's life.

The coffin arrived at Westminster Abbey at 10:52 am, marking the beginning of the State Funeral Service conducted by the Dean of Westminster, David Hoyle, that began at 11:00 am. Following the Commendation and Blessing, the *Last Post* was sounded by State Trumpeters of the Band of the Household Cavalry wearing the State Dress Gold Coat from the steps of The Lady Chapel inside Westminster Abbey. A two-minute silence followed before being broken by *Reveille*. The national anthem was then sung, followed by the bagpipe lament *Sleep, Dearie, Sleep*. This marked the end of the ceremony and was performed by the Piper to the Sovereign, Pipe Major (Warrant Officer Class I) Paul Burns, Royal Regiment of Scotland, the seventeenth Piper to hold the title of the Piper to the Sovereign since the role was introduced by Victoria in 1843. Then, as now, the Piper's primary duty is to play at 9:00 a.m. for fifteen minutes under the Sovereign's window and on state occasions.

The Bearer Party carried Her Majesty's coffin through the Great West Door to the State Gun Carriage outside, accompanied by Johann Sebastian Bach's (1685–1750) *Fantasia* in C minor (BWV 906). A Sovereign's Standard of the Household Cavalry followed the coffin. Charles then followed, leading members of the Royal Family, followed by mounted elements of the Household Cavalry and representatives of the civilian services. At 12:15 pm, the cortège of some 3,000 military personnel, accompanied by seven military bands, began their slow march to Wellington Arch. As the cortège slowly marched towards Wellington Arch, Big Ben could be heard tolling each minute, and the traditional Minute Guns were fired from Hyde Park by the King's Troop. At the front of the cortège were representatives of Commonwealth forces led by mounted members of the Royal Canadian Mounted Police (RCMP) on horseback, followed by representatives of the Royal Air Force, the Army, and the Royal Navy and Royal Marines. Then the defence staff and armed forces chaplains, Officers of Arms, and the Royal Household. Elizabeth's coffin followed, again on the State Gun Carriage pulled by Royal Navy ratings and surrounded by an escort party. Again, Charles and members of the Royal Family followed. At the rear of the procession were representatives of civilian services.

The column now stretched for over a mile. The funeral cortège left Westminster Abbey, passing down Whitehall, with Standards lowered, and those in the procession gave salutes as they passed the Cenotaph. The cortège then navigated the tight turn and narrow arches of the Palace of Whitehall, a source of concern during the planning phases. The funeral cortège then made its way up The Mall, passing Buckingham Palace. There, the King's Guard gave a Royal Salute to the Victoria Memorial. Palace staff gathered outside the gates, bowing as the funeral cortège passed and moved towards Constitution Hill before stopping at Wellington Arch at Hyde Park Corner. At Wellington Arch, the coffin was transferred with a Royal Salute to the State Hearse for Elizabeth's final journey to Windsor. The hearse, accompanied by Princess Anne and her husband, Vice-Admiral Timothy Laurence (b. 1955), travelled on quieter roads instead of motorways to allow the public to line the route and pay their respects.

At 3:00 pm, the coffin arrived in Windsor, where a final cortège involving 1,000 military personnel followed the Long Walk to St. George's Chapel. The State Hearse was flanked by the Pall Bearers and an Escort Party of Guards from the 1st Battalion Grenadier Guards. On its journey along the Long Walk, the cortège passed the Queen's fell pony, Emma, who wore the Queen's scarf on her saddle. Emma was attended by the Queen's groom, Terry Pendry, who would later be installed as a Military Knight of Windsor. Also present were two royal corgis, Muick and Sandy, a breed synonymous with Elizabeth. The cortège was led by a dismounted Detachment of the Household Cavalry Mounted Regiment (HCMR), followed by a mounted Division of the Sovereign's Escort. This was followed by a massed Pipes and Drums of Scottish and Irish Regiments, the Bands of the Coldstream Guards and The Household Cavalry and officers of the Household Division.

After being complemented by the Windsor Castle Guard, Charles and the Royal Family joined the procession in the Quadrangle, during which the Sebastopol Bell, one of two large bells captured at the Siege of Sebastopol in 1855, and the Curfew Tower bell tolled. In addition, the King's Troop fired minute guns from the East Lawn of the castle. At the end of the procession, the coffin was taken to St. George's Chapel via the West Steps. The 1st Battalion Grenadier Guards formed the Guard of Honour in the Horseshoe Cloister. This was joined by a Step-lining Party, comprising members of the HCMR lined on the West Steps of St. George's Chapel and on arrival at St. George's Chapel, Windsor, the Bearer Party carried Elizabeth's coffin up the West Steps for the Committal Service, conducted by the Dean of Windsor, David Connor (b. 1947), who had served as Bishop to the Forces between 2001 and 2009.

The committal service began at 4:00 pm in the presence of 800 guests, primarily made up of the Royal Household and staff from the Queen's private estates, as well as members of the Royal Family, Governors General and Prime Ministers from the Commonwealth realms, and members of foreign Royal Houses. As the service neared completion, the Imperial State Crown, orb, and sceptre were removed from the coffin and placed on the altar. The Queen's Company Camp Colour was then placed upon the coffin before the Lord Chamberlain, Andrew Parker, Baron Parker of Minsmere (b. 1962) symbolically broke his wand of office and placed its halves atop the coffin.

After this, the Garter Principal King of Arms, David White (b. 1961), recited the styles of Elizabeth and Charles, between which a lament, *A Salute to the Royal Fendersmith*, was played by the Sovereign's Piper, as the Queen's coffin was lowered into the Royal Vault. The singing of the National Anthem marked the end of the ceremony.

OTHER FUNERALS

In the United Kingdom, it is customary for State Funerals to remain the sole reserve of the sovereign. However, a State Funeral may be held to honour a highly distinguished individual, but only after approval of both the Sovereign and Parliament, the latter being responsible for approving the expenditure of public funds for the exercise. The last non-royal State Funeral in the United Kingdom was Sir Winston Churchill (1874–1965) on 30 January 1965.

Other funerals, including those of senior members of the Royal Family and high-ranking individuals, may be given a Ceremonial or Public Funeral, an occasion that shares characteristics of a State Funeral. By the nineteenth century, Ceremonial Funerals had become like State Funerals, even down to a herald reading the style and titles of the deceased and leading members of their household carrying white staves and breaking them at the graveside. One exception to this practice was the public funeral of William Gladstone (1809–1898), which took place without military involvement. Instead, members of the Lords and the Commons walked in the funeral procession, each House led by their respective presiding officer.

Ceremonial Funerals have been held for Louis Mountbatten, 1st Earl Mountbatten of Burma; Diana, Princess of Wales; Queen Elizabeth the Queen Mother; Margaret Thatcher, Baroness Thatcher; and Prince Philip, Duke of Edinburgh. While Ceremonial Funerals tend to follow the ritual patterns of a State Funeral on a somewhat smaller scale, the Ceremonial Funeral of Prince Philip was muted due to COVID restrictions at the time of the funeral. This meant that the number of mourners was restricted to thirty. A service of thanksgiving took place at Westminster Abbey on 29 March 2022, with Elizabeth II in attendance along with foreign royalty and politicians. The royal couple's bodies were interred together in the King George VI Memorial Chapel at St. George's on the evening of 19 September 2022, after Elizabeth's State Funeral.

CORONATION

Since the Coronation of Edward the Elder (c. 874–924) in 899, the essential elements of the ceremony have remained unchanged since the time of William the Conqueror. The recognition and oath, anointing, investing, crowning, and finally, enthronement and homage are all vital elements of the Coronation story. Still, without the support of the men and women of the London District, the Household Division and the wider military family, the splendour of the journey from Buckingham Palace to Westminster would not be possible. Since the Restoration of 1660 and the gradual expansion of the Empire, Coronation processions

The Relationship between Monarch and Guards

became more than celebrations; they have become visual reminders of Britain's martial and wider political power. Indeed, such was their draw that the Coronation of Victoria on 28 June 1838 was delayed by forty-five minutes after the Queen's Procession fell foul of London's traffic. This delay, among other events, earned Victoria's Coronation the unenviable nickname the Botched Coronation. This led to a complete overhaul of the ceremony, including the rediscovered rites that had taken place during medieval Coronation and the introductions of rehearsals. The prospect of a monarch having to endure a five-hour service was too much for Edward VII, and by the time of his Coronation, a plan was much in place. Involving 30,000 soldiers from Britain and the Empire, the Coronation also set a precedent for following monarchs when Edward and Queen Alexandria (1844–1925) appeared on the balcony of Buckingham Palace to greet the crowds.

In 2023, almost seventy years after the Coronation of Elizabeth II, the first to be televised, some 6,000 men and women from British and Commonwealth armed forces gathered in support of the Coronation of Charles III and Queen Camilla. These 6,000 men and women would either line the procession's passage or participate in the two processions unique to Coronation: the King's Procession and the Coronation Procession. Both processions are led by the mounted Brigade Major, who precedes the brakeless four-tonne Gold State Coach on its journey to and from Westminster Abbey by approximately 1,500 metres (one mile). On the day of the Coronation, there will be two processions. The first, known as the King's Procession, is the smaller of the two, featuring 200 troops, centred on the Sovereign's Escort of the Household Cavalry Mounted Regiment. This travels from Buckingham Palace down The Mall towards Trafalgar Square. At the end of the Mall, the procession turns onto Whitehall before marching to Westminster Abbey. Despite being the smaller of the two processions of the day, it is still 1.42 miles (2.3 km). Over 1,000 street liners from all three armed forces services, supported by civilian police, are positioned to flank this route.

After the Coronation service the larger Coronation Procession returns to Buckingham Palace along the same route. The 2023 Coronation

Procession of Charles now featured over 4,000 armed forces personnel. It also included 400 personnel from the armed forces of forty Commonwealth countries and overseas territories, making it the largest military procession in London for seventy years. Within this mass of colourful and historic uniforms were riders of the Royal Canadian Mounted Police (RCMP), including the Riding Master, who led the way for the Sovereign's Escort. The procession was formed into eight processional groups and included twenty different military bands, their arrangement reflecting their seniority. The Household Division was closest to the Gold State Coach, reflecting their military seniority. The Household Division was followed by the Royal Navy (RN), the Army, and the Royal Air Force (RAF). The Army contingent of the Coronation Procession was broken down further, with regiments and corps parading by the British Army's Order of Precedence, which ranks regiments by seniority. A further traditional implication of the positioning of regiments involved is the Royal Artillery (RA) presence. Despite the Household Cavalry being listed first and usually parading at the extreme right of the line, the presence of the King's Troop, Royal Horse Artillery (RHA), parading with its guns, took precedence over the Household Cavalry. As a result, the Coronation Procession, led by the Brigade Major, Household Division, and his retinue, were followed by the King's Troop.

Following the King's Troop were the Commonwealth and overseas territories contingent, accompanied by the Massed Pipes and Drums, flanked by 110 flag bearers carrying the Commonwealth flags. This cohort was followed by members of the RAF, accompanied by a Massed Band made up of personnel from the Central Band of the RAF, the Band of the RAF Regiment, the Band of the RAF College and the Band of the Royal Auxiliary Air Force. The RAF also provided fourteen musicians to perform specially composed fanfares during the Coronation Service, and the Band of the Royal Air Force Regiment provided musical support to the RAF street-lining contingent.

The RAF was followed by the Army, led by Brigadier Alex Potts, Head of Arms and Services, behind who paraded the men and women, including

The Relationship between Monarch and Guards

the Corps Sergeant Major, of the Royal Armoured Corps (RAC). The British Army Band Tidworth and British Army Band Catterick provided musical accompaniment to this part of the procession. They were followed by the Army's Corps and Infantry, led by Colonel Infantry, Colonel Peter MacMullen, Irish Guards and accompanied by the Band of the Royal Regiment of Scotland, the Highland Band and the Lowland Band. The Army's Corps and Infantry included representatives from the Royal Corps of Signals (RSIGS), the Mercian Regiment (MERCAN) and the Royal Gurkha Rifles (RGR), as well as various Corps Sergeant Majors. The final procession group of the Army was led by Colonel Army Air Corps (AAC), Colonel Julian Facer, who led soldiers from several corps, including the Royal Army Chaplains' Department (RAChD), Royal Army Veterinary Corps (RAVC) and the Royal Military Academy Sandhurst (RMAS). This group was supported by the Band of The Rifles and the Band of The Brigade Gurkhas. The Army groups were followed by sailors and marines of the Royal Navy and Royal Marines, including the Royal Marines Band Service.

After the parade of the armed forces came the Household Procession led by Commander Foot Guards, Colonel Guy Stone, Welsh Guards, and the Massed Bands of the Household Division and followed by the five Foot Guards Regiments and the two regiments of the Household Cavalry. The remainder of the Household Procession comprised dismounted elements from the Household Cavalry, the Major General's Retinue, 1st Division of the Sovereign's Escort and the 2nd Division of the Sovereign's Escort, HMRC. The Gold State Coach followed and was flanked by the Royal Watermen and King's Body Guard of the Yeomen of the Guard, representatives of the Armed Forces of the Realms, Gold Stick, Standard Party, the Royal Canadian Mounted Police, and the 3rd Division of the Sovereign's Escort. This was followed by the Carriage of the Prince and Princess of Wales and the Carriage of the Duke of Edinburgh. Due to the weight of the Gold State Coach, the standard quick march of 116 paces a minute was slowed to 108 paces and set by the bass drums of the bands throughout the Coronation Procession. Using a unique radio earplug metronome system, the architect of the parade, Garrison Sergeant Major

(GSM) Andrew Stokes, Coldstream Guards, ensured the beat remained constant. It also allowed the Coronation Procession to compress the group, allowing for a heightened visual impact.

One final aspect of the parade was the design and introduction of a unique drill manoeuvre by GSM Stokes that reduced the width of the marching groups from a twelve abreast frontage to six abreast. This enabled the procession that had filled the width of The Mall to move smoothly through the gates of Buckingham Palace. Once assembled in the gardens of Buckingham Palace, the troops gave three cheers to the newly anointed Charles and Queen Camilla. This was followed by the now traditional balcony appearance, with the Royal Air Force's Red Arrows adding a final splash of colour and pageantry to the occasion.

Chapter Six
Trusted Guardians

'To be a guardian is to be trusted. To be trusted, all must be tested.'
Erin Morgenstern

From the triumphant return from exile to the deserts of South West Asia, every Trooper and Guardsman is, first and foremost, a soldier. For almost 500 years, the soldiers of the Household Division have flitted between parade ground shine and field grime, carving an envious legacy of excellence as they did so.

The end and the beginning

'A few honest men are better than numbers.'
Oliver Cromwell

Charles I's last day on earth was a cold one. He asked for an extra shirt to cover his slight frame, lest his trembles in the winter's air be mistaken for fear by the soldiers and crowd which had gathered around the hastily assembled black-draped scaffold which had been erected in front of the Banqueting Hall at the Palace of Westminster. His final address to the silent crowd could barely be heard as the ranks of soldiers surrounding the scaffold made it impossible to listen to the King's voice. His final sentence, without the normal stammer, was one that he would be best remembered by, 'I shall go from a corruptible to an incorruptible Crown, where no disturbance can be.'

A man who had misused his power and acted in such duplicitous ways that he brought chaos and bloodshed to the three kingdoms now showed he could also behave with a brave dignity. His address finished, Charles turned to the executioner, saying a few words, prayed and lay his head upon the block. The tension must have been almost unbearable as the crowd watched Charles stretch out his hands, his signal to the executioner that he was ready to die.

The executioner's blade fell, and some bystanders rushed forward to dip their handkerchiefs in the fallen king's blood. Charles' head was shown to the shocked crowd in silence. On 9 February, Charles, his head reattached to his body, was buried at St. George's Chapel, Windsor Castle. Before his committal, Oliver Cromwell is said to have visited the King, who lay in his coffin and uttered, 'Cruel necessity!'

Thus, the start of Cromwell's rule was ushered in by cheering soldiers and groaning civilians. England had become a Commonwealth at a single stroke, no longer hindered by royalty, the House of Lords or the trappings thereof. Britain now became the British Protectorate, a republic formed by the countries of England, Scotland and Ireland, and what followed over the next decade was little short of a disaster.

Cromwell exhibited the traits of a tyrant aided by the New Model Army (NMA), now a byword for brutal subjugation, especially in the Celtic countries, as he wielded power like an iron fist in a chained glove. Cromwell's rule as Lord Protector was marked by regicide and religious and social persecution. It also witnessed the slow change of the much-vaunted NMA from a disciplined fighting force into a sharpened instrument of state terror. By 1652, both Ireland and Scotland had been subjugated by the NMA. Those Catholic landowners, in Ireland in particular, that survived the NMA onslaught were treated harshly. Their land and titles were taken from them, and deportations were occasionally meted out. The NMA also gained territories in France for the first time since the loss of Calais in 1558, making Britain a leading military power in Europe.

Despite the military power Britain could wield, including a resurgent navy, and the gradual return to normality at county levels with the law being upheld once more, it was all for nothing without equal political power. Parliament, despite its best efforts, was unable to meet the needs of the NMA. Funding was easily met but demands to simplify the country's laws to make them more accessible, on top of demands for religious and financial reforms, was adding stress. To further compound Parliamentary woes, the NMA was demanding that Parliament be dissolved, and new elections held.

The Levellers, despite being considerably diminished as a significant political force, remained strong enough to exert some influence on NMA lobbying, especially around suffrage. The military's desire to instal Godly Members of Parliament was at odds with members who felt the wider populace could not select suitable candidates. By April 1653, Cromwell had had enough and dissolved the Rump Parliament, established in 1649 due to members' hostile attitude to the Grandees' intention to try Charles for high treason. There followed a six-month experiment of holding a Parliament known by various terms including the Nominated Assembly and the Parliament of Saints.

The 140-strong Parliament, whose members had been selected by Cromwell and the Council of Officers, would be wound up by Cromwell, reforming as a new Council of State. In December 1653, the Instrument of Government, which officially afforded Cromwell the title of Lord Protector, was accepted by the NMA. A brief but significant Royalist uprising in 1655, known as the Penruddock Uprising, led by Colonel John Penruddock (1619–1655), a member of the Sealed Knot, a secret Royalist association, saw Royalists taxed heavily. This was followed by a period known as the Rule of the Major Generals, which saw England and Wales divided into ten regions, with each of the new regions governed by a Major General, who answered to the Lord Protector, Cromwell.

This period was one of sustained abuse of military power and one the Parliamentarians would be best remembered for. Targeting what they felt were typical ungodly Royalist pastimes, such as race meetings, the Major Generals exerted their puritanical and authoritarian religious beliefs on an otherwise placid populous. Any act was carefully carried out within the boundaries of the law and led by Cromwell's now-established single-person executive. This period became the pinnacle of military power that was to be termed the Interregnum State, and any show of political normality was just that: a show.

Cromwell was keen to prevent his role as Lord Protector turning England into an authoritarian state but would act dictatorially when it suited him. He was faced with two choices: pleasing a military eager for more Godly reforms or a return to the old method of governance, that appealed to the broader population. In 1657, after turning down the offer to be crowned to avoid offending the NMA, Cromwell established the Protectorate as a hereditary position. At the same time, the Other House, a second chamber, was established despite the NMA's apparent political power.

With his death on 3 September 1658, Cromwell's rule passed, somewhat ironically, to his son Richard (1626–1712). Unlike his father, Richard was no heavy hand and lacked any real authority on account of the NMA's lack of trust and respect for him. Richard was quick to restore old constituencies along with a type of governance many would have been familiar with in the pre-Interregnum period. Despite his best intentions, by the end of May the following year, Richard was out of office.

The NMA now had complete control of the country. However, it still needed a Parliament, if only to give the façade of legal governance and to raise taxes. The NMA also remained wary of the electorate and reinstated the Rump Parliament. This arrangement failed the test of time, and the Rump was expelled from Parliament. As with all things, the world comes at you fast if you've not been paying attention, and now the NMA was perceived as weak and spent.

The population and mechanisms of law and order were breaking down. Taxes were not paid, magistrates went on strike, the navy blockaded the Thames, and the common soldiery had become targets of ridicule. Naked military rules were not going to be tolerated, and the Rule of the Major Generals had shown it was incapable of good governance. The ending of 1659 was the breaking of an already demoralized military and the Council of State as the country began to collapse around them.

Meanwhile, in Scotland, General George Monck gathered his men. On 1 January 1660, he crossed the River Tweed into England and entered the village of Coldstream. With this single act, Britain found itself on the road to restoration.

REGAINING A FOOTHOLD

The Stuart Restoration ushered in the Age of Enlightenment, and for many Britons, it was also a return to sense. The pains of the Reformation era, which Martin Luther (1483–1545) had unleashed on Northern Europe after he nailed his *Ninety-five Theses* to the door of All Saints' Church in Wittenberg, Germany, on 31 October 1517, were far from over. In Britain, the Stuarts remained treading a fine line between dogmatic Protestantism and Catholicism, culminating in the crowning of Charles II.

With Charles II's return, establishing a professional army was considered urgent. Despite being respected by Charles II for professionalism, the NMA of the old regime had all but disappeared by early 1661. On 14 February, Monck's Coldstreamers, a NMA regiment, performed their symbolic act of laying down arms as men of the old regime as part of the Declaration of Breda, only to pick them up once more as soldiers of a new English Army. At this moment, they joined the ranks of the Guards who had returned from exile with Charles.

Charles's first foray into political games supported by the Guards took place shortly after his marriage to Catherine of Braganza (1638–1705), daughter of John IV of Portugal (1604–1656) in 1661. As part of the dowry, Charles was gifted Tangier, located on the north coast of Morocco. Almost instantly, Parliament refused to take steps to protect the new territories. Charles successfully argued that Tangier's importance was in accessing the trade with the Levant to the east, home of numerous goods. As a result, a force consisting of 240 First Foot Guards, 120 Coldstreamers and 240 other troops was detached to protect Tangier. The dispatched troops would return four years later when the riches of Araby failed to materialize.

Charles remained keen on deploying his Guards, and in May 1664, fifty Coldstreamers were sent to Guinea. The following year, 300 Foot Guards and the bulk of the Household Cavalry were sent to join a Royal Navy fleet assembled to counter the Dutch threat during the Second Anglo-Dutch War. The Guards fought as Marines as the British attempted to blockade Dutch waters. Despite early Royal Navy victories, the war reached a stalemate in 1666. On 31 July 1667, the Treaty of Breda was signed by all parties, ending a period of political and commercial antagonism that had started with the first Anglo-Dutch War of 1652 to 1654. Regardless of the Treaty of Breda, there was a further clash of arms between 1672 and 1674, known, somewhat imaginatively, as the Third Anglo-Dutch War. The main driver of the war had been the Dutch capture of New Amsterdam in 1673. There was also the matter of the Dutch increasing their naval raids, which resulted in the loss of more British ships than Dutch. This time, Charles quickly let experience override integrity and invited his long-time adversary Louis XIV (1638–1715) to join him as an ally. This newly found and unlikely military alliance saw a company of Coldstreamers sent to France 'for the service of the King of France'. The First Regiment of Foot Guards would join them.

The Treaty of Westminster concluded the Third Anglo-Dutch War, which went badly for the Dutch, on 9 February 1674. This saw the return of the colony of New Netherland to English hands. It also included a provision for a mixed commission to regulate commerce, particularly in the East Indies. On the face of it, the treaty was little more than a formality; the English were growing increasingly war weary and Parliament, no longer happy to supply further financial backing for the war, was also alarmed by backroom deals that had been carried out between Charles and Louis. Parliament had also become aware of the hitherto secret Treaty of Dover signed on 1 June 1970, a treaty which required that Charles convert to Roman Catholicism at a future date and that he would also support Louis with his conquest against the Dutch Republic by supplying sixty naval ships and 4,000 soldiers. In exchange for his support, Louis would furtively grace Charles a yearly pension of £230,000. This was in addition to a further sum payable upon Charles's declaration of his religious conversion. In the event of any resulting rebellion, France would send 6,000 troops to support Charles.

This revelation led to Members of Parliament petitioning for the reduction in the size of the Household troops, who it was now felt were tainted by Charles's duplicitous dealings with Louis. Parliament's request was formalized by the Quest of Grievances. The list stated that the Household troops were now a refuge for Papists, were unlawful, expensive, and now surplus to requirements for Charles's continued reign. In short, given the discovered Treaty of Dover, their presence scared Parliament, whose memory of the Rule of the Major Generals remained fresher than ever. Charles quickly realized the danger he had placed himself in by his dealings with Louis, no matter how they'd been arranged. He quickly ramped up his dedication to maintaining the Protestant cause and the anti-French rhetoric.

At this point, Colonel John Churchill, a rising star in the Foot Guards and a seasoned campaigner, was dispatched to Flanders, where he was to command two battalions of Foot Guards. The intent had been, along with Dutch, German and Spanish allies, to attack France. Sensing the tide had turned against him and aware of Charles's almost empty purse, Louis bribed Charles to stay his hand, which, of course, happened, much to the chagrin of England's allies, especially the Dutch. Charles's withdrawal of troops was made independently of parliamentary oversight, and whilst the Guards returned to the Old Somerset House on the Strand in London, the Dutch and French began fighting once more.

With James II becoming king on 6 May 1685, there was already disquiet. James had become a convert to Catholicism at some point between 1668 and 1669. Despite this, James continued to attend Anglican services, finally abandoning these in 1676, perhaps due to the Test Act of 1673, which sought to curtail the liberties of Catholics and non-conformist Protestants. Underlying this Act was the principle that only people taking communion in the Church of England were eligible for public employment, and the severe penalties pronounced against those who refused to attend Anglican services. Not only did this exclude many in the Scottish and Irish communities but also members of non-conformist congregations such as the Religious Society of Friends (Quakers), who had faced almost uninterrupted State harassment since the mid-1650s.

James's Catholic beliefs saw him gain unlikely allies from many quarters in Scotland and Ireland, including the Scots Guards; it would also hamper his ability to command and rely upon the broader military and, more importantly, political circles. The fear of James instituting an absolute monarchy led to what became known as the Exclusion Crisis, which occurred between 1679 and 1681 with the key political parties of the Whigs and Tories having differing concerns over James's reign and subsequent succession. The culmination of several years of political manoeuvres would deliver what was to become known as the Glorious Revolution, hastened by the unexpected birth of an heir to James II, James Stuart, on 10 June 1688 (d. 1766). James Stuart's birth was political and religious dynamite, for it assured the continuation of the Catholic Stuart line, something the Anglican members of Parliament would not entertain.

As a result of James Stuart's birth, the husband of James II's daughter Mary, Prince William of Orange, was invited to 'rescue the nation and the religion' by a mixed group of Whigs and Tories known as the Immortal Seven. William agreed, and on 5 November 1688, he landed at Torbay, Devon, with around 15,000 men, consisting of around 11,000 infantry, including 5,000 members of the Anglo-Scots Brigade and Dutch Blue Guards, 3,660 cavalry and a sizeable artillery train of twenty-one cannon. The force was further augmented by 5,000 volunteers, consisting of British exiles and Huguenots, French Protestants.

With the advent of William's arrival, James, his reputation marred by his religious leanings, could not command the very Guards he should have been able to call upon to protect him. As William advanced upon London, the Royal Army established by Charles II melted away. This seems even more remarkable given that as Duke of York, James had led the Guards during the Great Fire of London in 1666. During that event, he would direct his fire brigades to create a fire break by destroying properties while evacuating Londoners from the seemingly unstoppable fire. In doing so, he showed himself as a more than capable leader and incredibly brave.

Although he had marched his army to Salisbury to meet William in battle, James was keenly aware that a bloody battle would be in no one's interest, least his own. Now seemingly resigned to his fate, his men fleeing left, right and centre and mentally unprepared, James was happy to let the events unfold around him. James returned to London and, by December, had fled into exile to the safety of France and Louis' court. With James in exile, William of Orange became William III, and his invitation to become monarch now severed the hereditary Stuart monarchy.

In January 1689, the Convention Parliament attempted to use the political uncertainty of having the rightful king in exile and their chosen replacement in Britain to its advantage. The Convention Parliament now considered James's act of taking exile in France his abdication. The Tories, many of whom remained supportive of the hereditary monarchy, were reluctant to hand the Crown to William and Anne. As a compromise, it was suggested that William and Mary should become regents until the death of James, given the latter's lack of formal abdication. William, whose troops now patrolled London, was beginning to enjoy growing support nationwide. Therefore he flatly refused the role of regent. He had been invited as monarch, and monarch he would be. Parliament relented but took the opportunity to reframe the powers of the monarchy, using William's ascent to the throne as the start of this process.

In 1688, Parliament drafted a Declaration of Rights in light of the Glorious Revolution, which became the Bill of Rights in 1689. The Bill removed William and Mary's hereditary and conquest rights to the throne, reasserting that Parliament had ordained their regal position. Parliament now checked royal authority, the dream of many English politicians; included in these checks were two elements that would give Parliament future control over any errant monarch: control of the Crown's finances and removing the monarch's right to maintain a standing army. Other checks included free elections every three years and freedom of speech within Parliament. The Scottish and Irish were excluded from the Anglican-dominated Bill of Rights. There was also the assumption that William and Mary would have children, securing their royal line. As it was, Queen Mary would die childless, and William would remain unmarried until his death. Mary's sister Anne would go on to succeed William in 1702.

Now it had a constitutional Protestant monarch, England began to flex its political and military muscles once more. William was far from a shy and retiring monarch. He was keen to assert his rule against a backdrop of unrest in Scotland. He was also faced with the ever-present threat of the Catholic James Stuart's return, supported by France. The situation would see the Guards using their battle skills again. The first challenge to William's authority came in 1689 when pro-Stuart John Graham, 1st Viscount Dundee (1648–1689), took up arms and led a force of Catholic Highlanders against a Williamite force at the Battle of Killiecrankie. Regardless of his death in the battle, for Graham, Killiecrankie was a success for the Jacobite cause, and he became one of its first heroes.

However, with Graham dead, the Jacobite cause soon collapsed. William quickly asserted his authority over Clan leaders, demanding their loyalty to him and him alone. On 13 February 1692, thirty members and associates of Clan MacDonald of Glencoe were brutally put to the sword by government forces, allegedly for failing to pledge allegiance to William and Queen Mary. This was the beginning of a bloody reign for William and the beginning of the loss of his popularity.

Ireland was to fare no better with the dogmatically driven William arriving in the summer of 1690 intent on relieving the Catholic siege of Protestant Derry, led by James. Leading a mixed army of Protestant soldiers, William defeated James at the Battle of the Boyne on 1 July. At this stage, William's use of Northern European troops stemmed from his belief that English and Scottish soldiers remained politically unreliable; with the real possibility that many remained loyal to James.

His domestic battles were, for William, little more than a distraction from his main desire to restrain the expansionist aims of Louis. On 20 December 1689, along with Holy Roman Emperor Leopold I (1640–1705), William formed the Grand Alliance, an alliance that would see England become involved in its first continental war since Elizabeth I. Once William felt that he had secured his Irish flank, he rapidly turned his attention to continental Northern Europe, ready to provide complete support and fulfil his obligations under the terms of the Grand Alliance. Departing with his army for Flanders, William waged a seven-year campaign against Louis. This war, waged almost exclusively during the summer months, would end inconclusively. After Williams's death from pneumonia, a complication from a broken collarbone following a fall from his horse, Anne, his sister-in-law and cousin, ascended the throne on 8 March 1702 as Queen of England, Scotland, and Ireland. Anne continued the family's crusade against France, throwing her weight behind the War of the Spanish Succession that had started in 1701 and sparked by the childless death of Charles II (1661–1700) of Spain and the subsequent nomination of Philip of Anjou, a grandson of Louis as heir. Charles VI (1685–1740), the Holy Roman Emperor and ruler of the Austrian Habsburg monarchy felt he had a rightful claim to the throne and support from the Grand Alliance. He went to war against Spain and her French allies.

The ensuing war changed the fortune of the fledgling Great Britain and her military over the next twenty years. In 1704, John Churchill, Lord General Marlborough, was dispatched to Portugal with the First (Grenadiers) and Coldstream Guards. Simultaneously, twenty-five Foot Guard companies were assembled in the Dutch Republic, with a third of the companies later dispatched to Spain, where the French besieged the latter in Barcelona. With the return of peace in 1713, there was a real hope to reduce the size of the army, but this was short lived; with the 1715 Jacobite Rising by James Stuart (1688–1766), also known as the Old Pretender, the son of James II, ensuring a well-maintained army. This brought about an expansion of a battalion each to the regimental rosters for the three Foot Guards regiments. This was also the start of the rule of the House of Hanover with George I. From 1720 to 1740, the British experienced a period of relative peace until the War of the Austrian Succession, which lasted from 1740 to 1748.

The War of the Austrian Succession saw a new, modernized army take to the field. George II joined his troops at the Battle of Dettingen on 27 June 1743. This was the last time a British monarch would take to the battlefield and lead their forces, though princes would continue to go to war. Simultaneously, the British fought the French in North America in what was to be called King George's War (1744–1748) and against the Spanish in the War of Jenkins' Ear (1739–1748). It would be the harsh conditions and appalling treatment of the American settlers who were drafted to fight the latter of the two wars in particular that would stir the ire of the survivors, a rage that would follow them home. To add to his headaches, George II's army, which he had assumed control of in 1743, despite its modernization, still lacked leadership among the field officers and medical care, and in comparison to his French counterparts, the British soldiers were often subjected to brutal punishment.

At the Battle of Dettingen, George's force engaged French troops, with George maintaining visibility among his forces from the onset despite being under fire by French forces. George ignored all pleas to seek shelter and safety as the French fire increased in intensity, resulting in many of the British horses panicking, throwing their riders in a vain effort to escape French shot. George was able to control his horse despite early difficulties, and tired of trying to control the fractious mount, he dismounted and continued the battle on foot. His presence on the lines invigorated his infantry lines, and soon the British were charging at French positions, causing a hasty withdrawal and forcing the hand of the much-feared French Household Cavalry into the battle. As the French cavalry charged the British lines, they were met by British light cavalry, who fearlessly charged into the midst of the French cavalry, breaking them as they did so. Time and again, the French aimed to shatter the British lines, each failed attempt weakening the French. At this decisive moment, the Allies, who had assembled their cavalry, including the Horse Guards, struck. The French were routed, and their retreat towards the River Main provided the Allies with an opportunity to destroy France's army. George called off his army from destroying the rapidly retreating French forces and retired to eat cold mutton under an oak tree. At that moment, Dettingen was added to the Household Cavalry and Foot Guards battle honours.

After Dettingen came the Battle of Fontenoy in 1745, the result of which was a resounding French victory regardless of the bravery and sacrifice of the British infantry. Not only would this leave some in the British camp regretting their reticence in not destroying the French two years before, but it also spurred a final Jacobite rebellion known as the Forty-five Rebellion. The British Army, led by Prince William Augustus, Duke of Cumberland (1721–1765), the youngest son of George, former Colonel of the First Regiment of Foot Guards and now Captain General of the British land forces, returned to England. The Brigade of Guards, bolstered by a recent recruiting spree that a generous bounty had enhanced, was preparing to defend London. Regardless of early successes, Charles Stuart (1720–1788) and his rebellion were far from welcome, with even the pacifist Quakers throwing their support behind armed resistance to the Catholic Pretender's incursions. At Derby, with support now lacking, Charles was forced to turn back and make for the coastal town of Montrose, north of Edinburgh, where he hoped to link up with a French invasion force.

The ensuing chase by British forces, led by a recently returned Cumberland across northern England and Scotland, culminated on 16 April 1746 at Culloden Moor. Here, the Jacobean troops were soundly defeated, their leaders captured and executed, and many of the survivors either sent overseas to the colonies or banished. Cumberland's actions in the immediate aftermath of the battle were equally bloody, with the abandoned wounded survivors of the Jacobite army put to the sword and livestock taken and sold. Enraged by France's support of the Stuarts' final rebellion, George sought satisfaction and sent his soldiers back to Europe. Rather than find the glory of battle, the soldiers in Europe engaged in little more than armed walks.

1756 saw the start of the Seven Years' War. This conflict saw the European powers engage in a global war across Europe and the Americas. The Seven Years' War was also the first where Britain entered a conflict because of a political prerogative led by William Pitt, 1st Earl of Chatham (1708–1778), rather than royal, though George III would reclaim this prerogative during his reign. Despite serving as a Coronet in the King's Own Regiment of Horse, Pitt lacked the necessary military acumen but could rely on his cunning political machinations to help bring victory to Britain. The Seven Years' War events peaked in 1760 at the Battle of Warburg. Colonel John Manners (1721-1770), Marquess of Granby and Colonel Royal Horse Guards (Blues) led twenty-two squadrons of horse ahead of the advancing infantry. Whether or not Granby became infected with the cavalier's tendency to become excited and charge at everything, he lost his hat and wig in the charge. This later led to Granby having to salute his commander without his headdress and start a tradition among the Blues and Royals (Royal Horse Guards and 1st Dragoons) (RHG/D), making them the only soldiers of the British Army who may salute without headdress. Granby's use of horse, man and artillery would be the undoing of the French, winning the battle for Britain and her allies. The war itself would drag on until 1763. At its conclusion, it would leave Britain with experienced soldiers who were now bravely led but lacked a sense of morality that would hinder its progress in the Americas.

When George III ascended the throne in 1760, Britain had started an intellectual, industrial, political and social revolution. Its empire was growing by the moment, and its military rapidly gained an enviable experience. George was keen to reclaim some of the throne's power from the politicians, and inevitably, clashes occurred, with disastrous results. An ocean separated the valuable American colonies and a political class keen to establish its rights of determination. Allied to this were the lingering headaches that could be traced to Charles I's sale of Canada to France and Charles II's relinquishing of territories along the Hudson River. Although the French occupants of Canada and beyond had been gradually evicted by the commercial pressure of British traders by the seventeenth century, the region remained politically explosive. With William III's war against France spilling into the North Americas, fighting between British and French colonists broke out, though not to any measurable intensity. For seventy years, the two sides had squabbled, the larger British contingent well supported by its motherland, and the smaller French colonies left to fend for themselves. While support was welcome, how that support was given was not. In New England, resentment among the colonists grew over the caveats and behaviour that came with the soldiers sent to protect them. The French, unlike the British settlers, had made allies with the First Nation people of Canada, and under French prompting the First Nations began attacking British colonies in 1689. The following year, the British settlers retaliated and began a series of raids.

For almost twenty years, the two sides sniped and fought until 1709, when a petition was sent to Queen Anne asking for help to overpower Canada and Nova Scotia. In the next two years, both territories were conquered. The French had now moved to Quebec and had begun to build a series of riverside forts. In 1753, a Virginia militia Major, George Washington (1732–1799), was sent as an envoy by Robert Dinwiddie (1692–1770), the Lieutenant Governor of Virginia, to order the French to remove themselves from what was perceived as British territory. By all accounts, the bemused French soldiers refused to vacate their forts, sending Washington away. The following year, skirmishing began once more, and keen to be rid of the French, the Governor of Virginia, Lieutenant-General Willem Anne van Keppel, 2nd Earl of Albemarle (1702–1754), who had been commissioned into the Coldstream Guards in 1717 and later led the Royal Horse Guards, sought help from Britain. Albemarle was no figurehead or weak leader and had fought at Dettingen, Fontenoy and Lauffeld, where he had commanded the British infantry with considerable skill. In response to this call to arms, Britain sent Major General Edward Braddock (1695–1755), commissioned as an Ensign in the Coldstream Guards in 1710.

In a tale as old as time, the seasoned veteran Braddock struggled against fighting a well-organized militia in woodland and mountains. In his advance to contact the unseen militia, Braddock would lose five horses, his force of two regiments steadily taking casualties from French/First Nation musket fire. On 9 July 1755, Braddock and a small force made contact with a French force dispatched from Fort Duquesne near the Monongahela River. Initially, Braddock's men performed well but were soon overcome by the enemy force, and despite repeated attempts to rally his disorganized troops, Braddock was felled by a shot to the chest. Washington, who was part of Braddock's expedition as a volunteer officer, bore the mortally wounded Braddock to safety. As a token of thanks,

Braddock gifted Washington his two pistols and ceremonial sash, which Washington wore as commander of the Continental Armies.

With Major General James Wolfe's (1727–1759) final victory against the French in Quebec in 1759, British military prestige in North America was again asserted. Sadly the reputation and actions of the British soldiers among the settlers would undo Britain's opportunities in North America, as well as taxation and lack of representation. The first experience of clumsy politics occurred in 1677 when a force of First Foot Guards and Coldstreamers were sent to quell a settler's revolt. A century later, little had changed, and George III faced the possibility of having to send over troops to bring the colony to heel once again. In 1770, nine British soldiers shot into a crowd of some 400 in what was to be later called the Boston Massacre, killing five. In April 1775, some 300 British soldiers died in what were to become known as the Battles of Concord and Lexington after a failed attempt to disarm the settlers. Two months later, the Continental Army was raised and commanded by Washington. The British Prime Minister, Frederick North, 2nd Earl of Guilford (1732–1792), a former Lord Lieutenant of Somerset, tried to reason with the new Congress, but to no avail. In response, a 1,000-strong body of Foot Guards, including reinforcements of Hessian troops, was raised and dispatched by April 1776. These would support the Commander-in-Chief of British land forces, General William Howe, 5th Viscount Howe (1729–1814).

Washington's forces adopted guerrilla tactics by echoing the tactics of the French and First Nation militia. Once again, the British had forgotten the lessons of the previous two decades. Initially, the combined army and navy force did well, which was surprising given that no formal command structure was in place. After the usual winter lull, fighting started once again in June, but little progress was made, and Howe found himself replaced by General Sir Henry Clinton (1730–1795) of the Coldstream Guards. The Guards continued to arrive in North America, but the country they found themselves in was hard to occupy. A gradual withdrawal to New York ensued in 1778 and a recovery of fortunes under Lieutenant General Charles Cornwallis, 1st Marquess Cornwallis (1738–1805) of the First Foot Guards at the Battle of Camden on 16 August 1780 was achieved. This recovery was short lived and merely delayed the inevitable as Washington and his French allies slowly turned the screw on the British forces culminating in the siege of Yorktown and the subsequent surrender of Cornwallis little over a year later, on 19 October 1781.

THE AGE OF REVOLUTION

'If you build an army of 100 lions and their leader is a dog, in any fight, the lions will die like a dog. But if you build an army of 100 dogs and their leader is a lion, all dogs will fight as a lion'
Napoleon Bonaparte

On 21 January 1793, Louis XVI (b. 1754) left his prison cell for the last time, bound for the scaffold erected at the Place de la Révolution in Paris. Madame Guillotine and her operator Charles-Henri Sanson (1739–1806), who had been the royal executioner, now continued his work for the First French Republic. Louis XVI left his carriage and mounted the steps of the scaffold, where he was prepared for his execution. Louis turned to address the watching crowds but his voice was drowned out by the assembled drummers. Only at the moment of Louis' death, combined with restricting access to ports, did the British truly take events in France seriously.

While Britain's empire was gradually expanding and strengthening, its military was still very much licking its wounds from the loss of the American Revolutionary War. The Royal Navy and the Army remained underfunded and morale low. Still, the effect of France's declaration of war upon the British and Dutch on 1 February 1793 was little short of electric, with the British dispatching Frederick, Duke of York, second son of George III, to Flanders to take on the French. In what was to become known as the War of the First Coalition (1792–1797), the Duke of York led a command that included the Brigade of Guards and a cavalry force that included the Blues. The Foot Guards were soon taking the battle to the French; memories of fighting in North America were still fresh, and they adopted a new doctrine of fighting in light companies, carrying less personal equipment and shorter, therefore, lighter muskets. This innovation also allowed for rapid deployment and increased mobility. The French also remembered the lessons of fighting the British in North America and continued the fight throughout the winter months. This drew on the British resources, and by the spring of 1794, they had withdrawn to England.

1794 also witnessed the start of a new type of warfare, one hinted at in the past but now very much in the mainstream: propaganda. Pitt was declared 'an enemy of the human race' by the French, with the violent anti-monarchist Maximilien Robespierre (1754–1794) of the First Republic making inflammatory remarks that demanded the rules of chivalry were not applicable when fighting the British, the English in particular. The Duke of York responded quickly, promising an unholy wrath upon those Frenchmen and their families who took Robespierre's remarks as instruction. Meanwhile, a young Corsican artillery officer, Napoleon Bonaparte (1769–1821), who was descended from Italian nobility, had been noticed by Robespierre's younger brother Augustin (1763–1794) after Bonaparte's plans had given the French success at the Second Battle of Saorgio (24–28 April 1794). Bonaparte's links with the Robespierre brothers were deemed not strong enough to warrant his arrest and possible death in the chaotic events of early summer in Paris of 1794 as Robespierre's Reign of Terror was violently ended. The young Bonaparte was placed under house arrest, but after a plea of innocence to fellow Corsican Commissaire Antoine Saliceti (1757–1809), Bonaparte was acquitted of any wrongdoing. Despite his early successes, Bonaparte's involvement to recapture Corsica from the British failed but did flag him up to British diplomatic and military intelligence circles.

The war that until now was seemingly trundling along, soon exploded. A failed attempt by the British that included sending eight light companies of Foot Guards to destroy gates and sluices of the Bruges Canal allied to the outbreak of disturbances in Ireland soon saw the Brigade of Guards spread thinly. Regardless, the British dispatched a force of Guards to the

Netherlands after the declaration of war by the Dutch, culminating in the Battle of Callantsoog on 27 August 1799. It wouldn't be until 1801, when the British landed in Egypt, that they would lock horns with Bonaparte. On 8 March, a British force, including the 1st Battalion of the Coldstream Regiment of Foot Guards and the 1st Battalion, Third Regiment of Foot Guards, led by Major General George Ludlow (1758–1842), 1st Foot Guards, landed near the Nile Delta. There, they fought and won the Battle of Abukir, which opened the way for the battles of Mandora on 13 March and Alexandria on 21 March and culminated in the siege of Alexandria (17 August–2 September 1801). The end of the campaign would see Bonaparte vanquished and the rise of perhaps one of the Guard's most famed sons, Major General Richard Lambart, 7th Earl of Cavan (1763–1837), who had been commissioned into the Coldstream Regiment of Foot Guards in 1779. Meanwhile, Bonaparte returned to France and plotted an invasion of England.

By 1804, Bonaparte's grand plans of invading England were becoming a memory; his focus was subjugating mainland Europe, and to cement his authority, he crowned himself Napoleon I, Emperor of the French, at Notre-Dame de Paris Cathedral on 2 December 1804. French intimidation soon rippled through the continent, causing the collapse of governments. The Iberian Peninsula was one of the first to fracture after Bonaparte invaded Portugal on 19 November 1807 to prevent the British use of the port of Lisbon. Not only did this lead to the flight of the Portuguese Royal Family to Brazil, but it would bring chaos to Spain the following year as unexpected French border crossings with Spain led to the withdrawal of Spanish support in Portugal. Spain was rapidly embroiled in political and constitutional turmoil as Charles IV (1748–1819) abdicated in favour of his son, who would become Ferdinand VII (1784–1833), and who forced his hand in an aborted coup in 1807 after a series of scandals. To regain his throne, Charles IV appealed for Bonaparte's intervention, only to be dismissed by Bonaparte, the latter installing his brother Joseph (1768–1844) as the King of Spain. On 2 May 1808, the French showed the Spanish how they would govern as a protest by the citizens of Madrid was ruthlessly put down.

The situation in Portugal and the increasing tensions in Spain sparked a British intervention. What became known as the Peninsula Wars (1807–1814) saw the Guards perform admirably, with all six regiments of the Household Cavalry and Brigade of Foot Guards earning honours in August 1808. Despite numerous logistical and political issues for the British, such as Lieutenant General Arthur Wellesley's drive and the quality of the men under him, Portugal was considered liberated by 3 April 1811 with battle honours gained at Corunna (16 January 1809) for the Grenadier Guards. With the arrival of the Household Cavalry towards the end of the Portuguese campaign, they could join Wellesley's campaign in Spain, but first, they had to organize themselves into an efficient fighting force. Such was the turnaround from the rabble Wellesley had witnessed upon their arrival in Portugal, that he raised his hat to them as they crossed into Spain. On 22 February 1812, Wellesley was made the Earl of Wellington in the county of Somerset; he then became Marquess of Wellington on 18 August the same year.

The fighting would become immeasurably harder as the French remained as stubborn now as they did in 1808. However, the campaign progressed well, with the help of Bonaparte, who made the mistake of invading Russia with his Grande Armée on 24 June 1812. Not only did this split the forces of the French and its allies, but it also removed Bonaparte's attention from the rapidly deteriorating situation in Spain. The Allies were quick to capitalize on Bonaparte's arrogance, winning the Battle of Salamanca on 22 July 1812 and earning the Coldstream and Scots Guards their next battle honours. Regardless of how hard the French fought in Spain, the pressure exerted upon their dwindling numbers by the Allies slowly began to show. By 1813, the French victories had slowed, and by the end of the year, the Grenadier and Coldstream Guards could add the Battle of the Nive (9–13 December 1813) to their battle honours. On 11 December, Joseph Bonaparte abdicated as King of Spain with his brother following on 6 April 1814; this was followed on 4 June by the surrender of the last French garrison at Sant Ferran Castle. Bonaparte found himself confined in exile to Elba, an island off the northeast coast of Italy; now seen as the all-conquering hero Wellington was made Duke of Wellington, together with the subsidiary title of Marquess Douro of Somerset on 3 May 1814. Wellington's subsidiary title drew its name from the River Douro, the largest river of the Iberian Peninsula.

The events that followed were as dramatic as it was shaping for the men of the Household Cavalry and Foot Guards as any so far. Bonaparte returned to the French mainland spurred by rumours of relocation to a remote island in the Atlantic and by the devastating news of the death of his ex-wife Joséphine on 29 May 1814 (b. 1763). Bonaparte's triumphant return to Paris on 20 March 1815 galvanized the Allies, with the British, Russians, Austrians and Prussians all swearing to defeat the errant Emperor once and for all, with Wellesley leading the defence. Bonaparte's force was formidable while Wellington lamented his; even junior officers in the Foot Guards privately lamented their lack of training but quickly recognized the quality of their non-commissioned officers. Worse still were the standards of personal fitness among the officer corps, whose consumption of rich foods had led to such obesity that they often struggled to escape contact with the enemy, leading to capture or worse. Alcohol abuse was also an issue, with port, sherry and fine wines being consumed in such quantities as to make Bacchus blush.

THE BATTLE OF WATERLOO

> 'Our officers of cavalry have acquired a trick of galloping at everything. They never consider the situation, never think of manoeuvring before an enemy, and never keep back or provide a reserve.'
>
> Arthur Wellesley, Duke of Wellington

The events that took place on 18 June 1815 at Waterloo, then in the United Kingdom of the Netherlands, were to change the fortunes of the Household Cavalry and Brigade of Foot Guards. The struggle with regaining prestige after their American misfortunes crowned by the surrender of Yorktown still affected the psyche of the Foot Guards almost thirty-five years later. In one day, that was to change. Wellington had reconnoitred the likely site of the battlefield, about two kilometres (1.2 miles) from the town of Waterloo and about fifteen kilometres (9.3 miles) south of Brussels. During his analysis, Wellington quickly recognized that the upcoming battle would be an infantry battle. Wellington had the advantage of holding the higher ground, forcing Bonaparte to attack an easily defended forward slope that would hide his reserves. To Wellington's east lay the Château d'Hougoumont complex, with its orchards and outbuildings; to the west, the Bois de Ohain and Bois de Paris, and the direction from which the Prussians would arrive.

The Hougoumont complex was fortified and manned by the Foot Guards, Hessian and Nassau troops. A terrible storm raged the night before the battle, swamping the battlefield and leaving all desperately trying to sleep but cold and uncomfortable. The following morning, the cold and tired defenders of Hougoumont stood to, roused by the start of the French advance, accompanied by music. The initial French attack on Hougoumont quickly evicted the Hessian and Nassau troops from their defensive positions in the orchard. Still, the moment of triumph was abruptly interrupted by a counterattack by the First, Coldstreamers, and Scots Guards who slammed into the French, rapidly pushing them out of the orchard with an outstandingly aggressive fighting spirit.

To the rear centre of Wellington's line, waiting unseen behind the ridgeline, were the two brigades of British heavy cavalry. The 1st Brigade, known as the Household Brigade, commanded by Major General Lord Edward Somerset (1776–1842), consisted of Guards regiments: the 1st and 2nd Life Guards, the Royal Horse Guards (the Blues), and the 1st (King's) Dragoon Guards. The 2nd Brigade, known as the Union Brigade, was commanded by Major General Sir William Ponsonby. Its unique name came from the regimental make-up of the Brigade that consisted of an English (the 1st or The Royals), a Scottish (2nd Scots Greys), and an Irish (6th or Inniskilling) regiment of heavy dragoons. Both brigades fell under the command of Lieutenant General Henry William Paget, Earl of Uxbridge (1768–1854), who would lose his leg to grapeshot towards the end of the battle, resulting in the famous exchange; 'By God, sir, I've lost my leg!' to which Wellington replied, 'By God, sir, so you have!'

Uxbridge, who had eloped with the wife of Wellington's younger brother Henry (1773–1847), Lady Charlotte Cadogan (1781–1853), was an exceptional cavalry and infantry commander. But even the hardest-won acumen would not prevent the chaos that ensued once he'd let slip the dogs of war under his command. On Uxbridge's command, some 2,000 men and heavy cavalry horses were let loose upon the French lines, falling upon them like banshees, breaking the French cavalry, who were desperately trying to destroy the infantry squares. The 1st Life Guards and Scots Greys then slammed into the French infantry, somehow escaping the mass of infantry that rapidly swarmed around them, more by luck than judgment. Meanwhile, the 2nd Life Guards fell upon the French artillery, wreaking havoc before being subjected to a French cavalry counterattack. The 2nd Life Guards now faced an unholy onslaught by the French cavalry.

Meanwhile, command and control had utterly broken down in the divisions of the Blues, voice and trumpet calls being virtually impossible to hear in the clamour of battle. This left the Blues fragmented, with troopers reduced to fighting private battles. Despite this, there remained a sense of cohesion as the Blues desperately tried to organize themselves into an effective force once more and relieve the 2nd Life Guards. Such was the French onslaught only 250 Life Guards were able to return to their lines. The French cavalry was now desperately trying to break the resolve of the infantry sqaures that continued to mow down their mounts. Those cavaliers who were dismounted quickly found themselves in trouble as the soft ground and unsuitable attire led to fallen troopers being mercilessly picked off by musket fire. By late afternoon, the British heavy cavalry had reorganized and was once more in the fray, their efforts securing a gap in the French line at the farm complex of La Haye Sainte.

At Hougoumont, the orchards had fallen, and the smoke from the burning haystacks began to obscure the field of view for all parties. The French were trying to force entry through the main gate. The interior of the Château was now home to a combined force of Coldstream and Scots Guards, with officers and men holding firm under increasing French pressure. The Coldstream and Scots Guards had formed an impressive mutual defence strategy to hold the line at Hougoumont. The French continued their attacks, and soon, the wives and women who had accompanied their men into battle and were treating the wounded, came under fire themselves. Meanwhile, the First Guards Light Companies had left Hougoumont to join the rest of the First Guards at the centre of the line.

By mid-afternoon, Wellington was planning to draw in the cream of Bonaparte's troops, the Imperial Guard, knowing that defeating these elite soldiers would devastate the French morale. Sure enough, the Grenadiers of the Imperial Guard were now advancing on the British, who had withdrawn behind the ridge line. The bearskins, worn to intimidate man and beast, slowly came into view. The steady sound of the footfall of the Imperial Guard accompanied by drum heralded their approach. On the other side of the ridge lay the recumbent First Guards, commanded by General Peregrine Maitland (1777–1854), who at the Battle of Quatre Bras two days earlier had given Wellington a tactical victory despite Marshal Michel Ney, 1st Prince de la Moskowa, 1st Duke of Elchingen (1769–1815) preventing the relief of Gebhard Leberecht von Blücher, Fürst von Wahlstatt's (1742–1819) Prussians. Maitland, who had joined the 1st Foot Guards as an Ensign, ordered his men to stand and fire when the Imperial Guard exposed their torsos. The subsequent musket fire from the two battalions of guards slammed into the unsuspecting Imperial Guard. Within moments, the First Guards were on their feet and charging bayonets first into the stunned Imperial Guards. The two guards' regiments clashed in a mêlée of unmatched butchery, with the Imperial Guard soon finding the sabres of the cavalry at their backs. Within ten minutes, the Imperial Guard were fleeing for their lives, watched in horror by their fellow countrymen. The remaining defenders stood at Hougoumont, the site broken by cannon fire and heavy fighting; 2,000 guards had seen off 18,000 French veterans. The battle was won, and the shame of Yorktown was expunged from memory.

For their efforts, the First Guards became the First or Grenadier Regiment on 29 July 1815 by decree of George III in commemoration of their defeat of the Grenadiers of the Imperial Guard. They were allowed to adopt the bearskin cap. George, the Prince Regent and future George IV declared himself the Colonel-in-chief of the Household Cavalry in appreciation of their gallantry in the field. Bonaparte was excused the ignominy of execution, instead banished to Saint Helena, 1,870 kilometres (1,162 miles) from the west coast of Africa, dying there on 5 May 1821. Ney was tried and sentenced to death for his role in the events that culminated in Waterloo, later known as the Hundred Days. On the day of his execution by firing squad, 7 December 1815, Ney refused a blindfold and was given the right to provide the order to fire. Wellington's legacy was the striking of a medal to be awarded to all British soldiers who participated in the Waterloo campaign, which became the Waterloo Medal. This was authorized and distributed to all ranks in 1816. In accordance with the Treaty of Paris, Wellington was appointed commander of the multinational army of occupation based in Paris that included the Household Cavalry and the Guards Brigade. This was Wellington's final active command, which he led until its dissolution in 1818.

DREADNOUGHT: THE VANGUARD OF EMPIRE

> 'to strive, to seek, to find, and not to yield.'
> *Ulysses*, Alfred Lord Tennyson, 1842

The post-Bonaparte world saw a shift in global politics. Britain and her burgeoning empire grew in confidence and influence, and stability returned. By the 1830s, the edge of the Guards and most of the British Army had slowly dulled, with everyday life evolving into an endless round of routine and mundane tasks. To the east, the Russian Empire also grew in confidence. It was keen to continue to subject the neighbouring Ottoman Empire, which had been slowly shrinking since the mid-1800s, to its demands of territory and domestic political influence. Disagreements between the Russians and Ottomans had been the source of numerous wars from 1568, finally ending in 1918, with the source of Russian hostility in the 1850s being a disagreement over the rights of Christian minorities in Palestine. Regardless of a local compromise between the French-backed Roman Catholics and the Russian-backed Eastern Orthodox Church with the Ottoman authorities, neither Napoleon III (1808–1873) nor Tsar Nicholas I (1796–1855) initially accepted any formal agreement regarding rights. Nicholas I was keen to protect the Orthodox Christians as if they were Russian subjects. The British stepped in, eager to maintain regional peace. The initial political plans were deemed successful until the Ottomans' requested changes, which, in turn, infuriated Nicholas, who walked away from negotiations.

In July 1853, the Russians entered Ottoman territory known as the Danubian Principalities in modern Romania and began an advance on Constantinople, the capital of the Ottoman Empire. Despite fighting a defensive battle, the Ottomans were pushed back. Still, it wasn't until 16 October that, with Anglo-French support, the Ottomans formally declared war on the Russians. The Ottomans were fortunate to be led by Omar Pasha (1806–1871), who halted the Russian advance at Silistra in northern Bulgaria. Pasha's actions failed to stop the Russians completely. At the Battle of Sinop on 30 November 1853, a Russian navy squadron caught an Ottoman squadron at anchor at the southern edge of the Black Sea.

The following January, alarmed by growing Russian military power, the British and French fleets entered the Black Sea in a show of force. By June, the Anglo-French pressure was wearing, with a Baltic blockade bottling up the Russian Fleet and keeping large numbers of troops in place to protect St. Petersburg, the capital of Russia, from a seaborne attack. In the Black Sea theatre of operations, Austria threatened to support the Ottomans against Russian aggression unless Nicholas I left Ottoman territory before either side could engage one another. Remarkably, the threat worked, and the Russians began to pull back. Still, public opinion now directed politics and demanded satisfaction against Russian aggression.

Meanwhile, the Ottoman, French, British and Sardinian forces made plans to attack the Russian Black Sea Fleet at its Sevastopol base in Crimea. The British were led by Field Marshal FitzRoy Somerset, 1st Baron Raglan (1788–1855), a contemporary of the Duke of Wellington. Raglan's mission was to defend Constantinople and take the war to the Russians. On 14 September, the Allies achieved a surprise landing at Kalamita Bay in Crimea, and less than a week later, on 20 September, Raglan had his chance to prove his quality by doing so at the Battle of the Alma River, where the Russians were waiting, using the river as a natural defensive line, led by Prince Alexander Sergeyevich Menshikov (1787–1869). The battle was hard fought with the French and British forces taking high casualties and lacking cavalry support. It was to be British musketry that would eventually drive the Russian defenders into a retreat. Still, the lack of cavalry meant the victory could not be fully secured. On 17 October, the Allies began their Siege of Sevastopol, followed, on 25 October, by the Battle of Balaclava; it was here that the failure of the Allies in preventing the escape of the Russian defenders at Alma would come back to haunt them.

The Battle of Balaclava was a Russian counterattack led by General Pavel Petrovich Liprandi (1796–1864) against the Allied redoubts surrounding Sevastopol, aiming to sever the allied lines of communication. Liprandi focused on the thinly spread British positions, parts of which were later termed the 'Thin Red Line', and slammed into the Allied positions with 25,000 soldiers. The Russian cavalry could not break the British lines and soon found themselves under pressure from the British Heavy Cavalry led by General Sir James Scarlett (1799–1871). Such was the effect of the Heavy Cavalry that the Russians were soon in retreat. However, the fog of war was not far away. A misinterpreted order led to the near annihilation of the 11th Hussars (Prince Albert's Own) in what later became known as the Charge of the Light Brigade. The battle ended with the Russian attack repulsed, but the British lines were heavily depleted.

Almost two weeks later, the Russians tried again to break the siege at the Battle of Inkerman on 5 November. The Battle of Balaclava led to Menshikov realizing that the British lines, in particular, had been weakened.

The battle was fought in terrible weather, with visibility restricting movements and many units cut off. This made the battle very much an infantry battle, leading to its unofficial name, 'The Soldier's Battle', giving its name to the third company of the Grenadier Guards, Inkerman Company. Both sides fought tooth and nail with the Guards determined to retain their strategic positions on the heights that overlooked the Inkerman valley. Menshikov dispatched a larger force of 42,000 to overwhelm the 6,200 British defenders, who knew that owning the heights was the key to the relief of Sevastopol. The Grenadier Guards stood firm as wave after wave of Russian infantry charged. They soon ran out of ammunition, resorting to bayonets and stones and using their rifle stocks as bludgeons. The Russians were equally tenacious in their assault. Still, the quality of the Grenadier won out, but at a terrible cost, with all but four of the original seventeen officers alive and unwounded. Menshikov's gamble was lost, and Inkerman was the last of the large-scale Russian attacks against the Allies.

The siege settled down, and military discipline and routine were re-established in the first instance. The Guards continued their stoic attitude towards military standards, desperately trying to stay healthy. Their key enemy soon became a lack of fresh water, and cholera was soon rife among the Allies, with many, including Raglan, struck down by debilitating sickness and diarrhoea. The misery of that winter, especially the appalling living conditions, merely added to the daily losses. Indeed, conditions were so bad that the Scots Guards, who had received 101 replacements after Inkerman, lost most of this number within eight weeks of arrival as they waited on the delivery of sheepskin coats and long boots. The wounded fared no better, with a lack of medical services contributing to an increase in death and disease. Without the interventions of Florence Nightingale (1820–1910) and Mary Seacole (1808–1881), the death rates would have been even higher.

In early 1855, the Sardinians entered the war on the side of the Allies, sending an expeditionary force to Crimea, and as winter ended, the Allies were quick to re-establish their lines of communications that had been slowed by the previous winter. With the death of Raglan on 28 June, a new commander was appointed to the British forces, General

Sir James Simpson (1792–1868), who had been commissioned into the 1st Regiment of Foot Guards in 1811 and, like Raglan, had taken part in the Peninsula Wars and Waterloo. On 8 September 1855, the French captured the Russian positions at the Malakoff Redoubt. The same day, the British engaged Russian forces in what was later known as the Battle of the Great Redan with two brigades led by Brigadier-General Charles Ash Windham (1810–1870), Coldstream Guards. The Allied victories at both battles would lead to the fall of Sevastopol three days later.

The Guards would come away from the Crimean War with Battle Honours and twelve Victoria Crosses, introduced on 29 January 1856 by Victoria to honour acts of valour made during the Crimean War.

UNDER AFRICAN SKIES

The nineteenth century was one of rapid technological change. Communications were shrinking the world, from transportation to telecommunications; technology was shaping the empire and the various government apparatus, including the military. Command and control were revolutionized, and the inevitable gaze of public and political opinion could judge military actions, as in Crimea. The British Army continued to police and support British interests, with the Foot Guards serving at home and in the Empire, where they strengthened the Canadian border in 1862 in response to the American Civil War (1861–1865). The Crimean War spurred several critical changes in the army's organization, not least of all the establishment of the role of Major-General commanding the Brigade of Guards in 1856. This new appointment replaced the role of the Field Officer in Brigade Waiting regarding the passage of orders to the Foot Guards in particular. The first appointee was Major-General Henry Robinson-Montague, 6th Baron Rokeby (1798–1883), 3rd Foot Guards, who had commanded the First Division during the Crimean War. Robinson-Montague was also responsible for the overall improvement of the army post-Crimea.

Initial plans to perform annual exercises, especially after the 1870 Franco-Prussian War, were short lived and ran for three years before being cancelled due to costs. At the same time, the Cardwell Reforms aimed to modernize the British Army began. Initiated by Secretary of State for War Edward Cardwell (1813-1886), 1st Viscount Cardwell, the reforms sought to centralize the power of the War Office. In one of his first actions as Secretary of State, Cardwell abolished flogging in 1868, followed by the withdrawal of British troops from self-governing colonies, overturning a Wellingtonian policy in 1869. Cardwell's most significant reforms were yet to come. These focused on the abolition of the purchase of officers' commissions and the creation of reserve forces stationed in Britain; this was to be achieved by establishing short terms of service for enlisted men and removing the joining bounty for soldiers. Not all changes were welcomed by many in the regular army and their supporters. In fairness, Cardwell's reforms worked. While the overall Army budget was reduced, he could increase the army's strength by twenty-five battalions and 156 field guns and establish an enviable logistics base. The reserves available for overseas service had been raised tenfold from 3,500 to 36,000 men, giving the army greater flexibility should the need to deploy troops arise unexpectedly. As sure as night follows day, the unexpected did happen in 1882 when an Anglo-Indian force was dispatched to Egypt to overturn a local mutiny that had taken place the previous year, led by Ahmed' Urabi (1841–1911), a disgruntled Egyptian officer.

Led by Lieutenant-General Sir Garnet Wolsey (1833–1913), the Adjutant-General to the Forces was dispatched with a sizeable force of 40,560 sailors, marines and soldiers. This included battalions of all three Foot Guards brought together in the 1st Brigade led by Major-General Prince Arthur, Duke of Connaught and Strathearn (1850–1942) and the Household Cavalry Composite Regiment (HCCR), which featured three squadrons from the Life Guards and Royal Horse Guards as part of 1st (Heavy) Cavalry Brigade led by Brigadier-General Sir Baker Creed Russell (1837–1911). After the naval bombardment of Alexandria from 11 to 13 July, the first clash of arms occurred at the Battle of Kafr el Dawwar on 5 August, followed by the Battle of Kassassin on 28 August, where the HCCR made their famous moonlight charge, and ended with the Battle at Tell El Kebir on 13 September. With resounding victories in all battles, Wolsey secured a British military presence in Egypt until 1956. The expedition had left Wolsey impressed by the professionalism of the HCCR. All taking part could avail themselves of the latest military innovations, including railways, the telegraph and the deployment of the volunteer Army Post Office Corps. One comment made by the Duke of Connaught and Strathearn, the third son of Victoria, was that the British soldier should be allowed to adopt a khaki uniform rather than fight in scarlet.

While Egypt was pacified, South Sudan remained restive. Major-General Charles Gordon (1833–1885) did his best to assert British influence; he needed support. The Sudanese forces facing the British were led by Muhammad Ahmad bin Abdullah bin Fahal (1843–1885), a Sudanese religious and political leader. Bin Fahal led a force that had first defeated Ottoman Egyptian rule in Sudan and was now pressing to do the same to British interests in the country. As Bin Fahal's forces applied pressure on Khartoum, a relief force led by Wolsey was dispatched. Wolsey split his force into two parts: one would use the Nile as a transit route to besieged Khartoum, and the other would travel by camel, with the HCCR supplying 120 troopers for the endeavour. Both forces would be intercepted and, despite giving a good account of themselves, would have to return to Egypt. At the same time, Gordon would be killed defending himself at Khartoum on 26 January. The British retort to the death and mutilation of the corpse of one of its own gave strength to a terrible resolve that culminated in a new force being formed: the Heavy Camel Regiment (HCR). As comical as it sounded, the HCR was to prove the HCCR's adaptability. The Household Cavalry and Foot Guards enjoyed a period of peace and returned to their ceremonial duties.

By the end of the nineteenth century, British involvement in Africa was once again headline news. In South Africa, the prospect of locking arms with Stephanus 'Paul' Kruger, a South African politician and leader of the Boer resistance against the British in the South African Republic, was increasing. With the establishment of the South African Republic (Transvaal) after the short first Anglo-Boer War of 1880–1881, there was hope that the British were content to let the Boers be. However, the British refusal to recognize the Boers as an independent nation and demands for non-Boer political representation, aided by the débâcle of the Jameson Raid from Rhodesia on 29 December 1895 and the desire to control precious metal resources, led to the mobilization of 10,000 men from India and Nepal as well as some of Britain's reserves to the region. These reserves included Household Cavalry, the Guards Brigade and, for the first time, Honourable Artillery Company (HAC) members. Incensed, the Boers demanded that the British remove their troops from the South African Republic's borders on 9 October 1899. The British ignored the Boer ultimatum, and on 11 October, the South African Republic and the Orange Free State declared war on Britain.

Militarily, the Second Anglo-Boer War was unique in many ways: khaki was now the adopted uniform in the field, with officers and men looking alike. Swords, Sam Browne belts, and anything else that would distinguish officers and NCOs from the rank and file were discarded. Brightwork on belts, uniforms and webbing was painted over to aid concealment. The British expeditionary force, led by General Sir Redvers Buller (1839–1908), a veteran of the 1879 Anglo-Zulu War, where he was awarded the Victoria Cross, was now faced with fighting irregular Boer forces. The initial contacts with the lightly armed Boers, who fought as dragoons, were constantly in their favour; they quickly learned and adopted their tactics accordingly. For their part, the British seemed unable to gain the upper hand. Lieutenant-General Paul Methuen, 3rd Baron Methuen (1845–1932), Scots Guards, commanded the 1st Division, suffering under the sting of Boer tactics that utilized the region's geography. As the losses mounted, combined with the loss at the Battle of Ladysmith on 30 October 1899, Buller was replaced by Field Marshal Frederick Roberts, 1st Earl Roberts (1832–1914). Roberts had also been awarded the Victoria Cross gained in the 1857 Indian Rebellion; he arrived in Cape Town on 10 January 1900 to a theatre the troops were unable to control. The summer brought more reinforcements, dysentery and the loss of hundreds of horses as the environment took its toll.

Initially, Roberts used contemporary military thinking to address the situation. Still, he soon adopted knowledge and skills from the 1776 American war and his personal experiences of India. Roberts had gathered a sizeable force of 30,000 infantry, 7,501 cavalry and 3,600 dragoons, together with 120 guns with which to beat the Boers. The largest British mounted division ever assembled and featuring 5,000 men and mounts was led by Brigadier-General John French (1852–1925) and charged with the relief of Kimberley. After four days that included covering 120 miles (190 km) and a fantastical three-mile charge by 3,650 men and mounts led by the newly promoted Major-General French, a route to Kimberly was opened on 15 February 1900. The integration of the cavalry as a tactic further shaped the combined arms operations that would define future warfare, and the successful use of cavalry continued into high summer. To commemorate the sacrifices made by the many Irishmen deployed in South Africa, Victoria ordered the creation of the Irish Guards (Irish or IG) on 1 April, making them the fourth Foot Guards Regiment.

In November 1900, after the defeat of conventional Boer forces, Roberts was relieved by Kitchener, who was promoted to Lieutenant-General. The war now entered its final phase; guerrilla warfare, and brutal measures to control the Boers were implemented. The rail network was soon utilized, and some 8,000 blockhouses manned by 50,000 soldiers were established along the route, with columns patrolling the lines in armoured trains, engaging Boer fighters and protecting the lines. Boer farms were levelled, and concentration camps were established with women and children interned. Kitchener had adopted what would later be termed a 'scorched earth' policy in his drive to be the man to defeat the Boers. Kitchener's approach soon drew condemnation as conditions deteriorated and famine and disease began to take hold in the camps (almost 30,000-odd Boer women and children died). The war would continue until the signing of the Treaty of Vereeniging on 31 May 1902. The Guards, whose contemporaries in Britain had said farewell to Victoria on 2 February 1901, were able to return for the delayed coronation of her son Edward VII on 9 August 1902. The Household Cavalry, Foot Guards and HAC who returned were now schooled in new ways of warfare, and all the lessons of the past century were about to be tested in ways that could not possibly be imagined.

Chapter Seven
A World at War

'It doesn't matter what you do, so long as you don't frighten the horses.'

Edward VII

For the British Empire, the Edwardian era was the pinnacle of its influence. It was led by a well-travelled King Emperor whose political awareness allowed him to exert influence on government decisions at home and abroad. His familial ties with every Royal Household in Europe meant that Edward VII was capable of calming otherwise stormy weather, except for Wilhelm II (1859–1941) of Germany, who seemed impervious to his cousin's charms. The British military of the time was a different beast from that which had ushered in the reign of his mother. Commissions were no longer bought or sold; this meant that getting sons into family regiments, or the Guards, had become more challenging, though not impossible. Aside from the ripples of charge from the Cardwell and subsequent Childers Reforms of 1881, led by Secretary of State Hugh Childers (1827–1896), the twentieth-century British military was getting to grips with new technologies and tactics. For the men of the Household Cavalry and Brigade of Guards, the reign of Edward was a truly golden era; the days of parading for a representative of the sovereign were now replaced by nearly a decade of State Ceremonial and Public Duties for a king keen to impress cousins and foreign dignitaries. For the men of the Household Cavalry, the increased use of the motor car by the Royal Household would see them quickly pass the baton of escorting to the police to prevent injury to horse and rider.

Edward's death in 1910 and subsequent lying-in-state and funeral, attended by no less than nine kings and a mass of princes and dukes, provided the Household Cavalry and Brigade of Guards with an opportunity to deliver a masterpiece of State Ceremonial, and deliver they did. The death of Edward also signified such profound social and cultural changes in the world that within a decade, many of the kings and princes who walked behind the coffin, accompanied by bearskins and colours, would either be dead or deposed. The ascension of George V to the throne would herald a steady decline in royal influence across Europe and bear witness to the death of many of the men who made up the Household Cavalry, Brigade of Guards and Honourable Artillery Company.

First World War: the birth of a division

> 'Have you news of my boy Jack?'
> *Not this tide.*
> 'When d'you think that he'll come back?'
> *Not with this wind blowing, and this tide.*
> My Boy Jack, Rudyard Kipling, 1915

In both world wars the Household Cavalry and the Brigade of Guards continued their tradition of excellence in the field and were deemed to be elite enough to be drafted in to their own divisions. To help build the necessary division both Household Cavalry and Brigade of Guards were able to field an enviable force, with the Household Cavalry having three regiments and the Brigade of Guards able to draw on no less than nine battalions. On 4 August 1914, when war was declared against the Central Powers, the Household Cavalry and Brigade of Guards were in Great Britain, spread between London and Windsor, where they were performing State Ceremonial and Public Duties. Two Foot Guards battalions were also based in Aldershot, Hampshire as part of the 1st Division, which would lose 16,000 soldiers during the First World War.

Aside from the formation of the Welsh Guards, unlike the Regiments of the Line, there would be no mass expansion at battalion level. The Foot Guards would only raise one additional battalion apiece and a special 'Reserve' battalion which was used to hold reinforcements and carry out Public Duties. The Guards Depot at Caterham, Surrey, once the largest Depot of the British Army, continued to process recruits through its twelve-week basic training course. After passing-out the new soldiers were sent to one of the new reserve battalions to continue their training. The Guards saw their high standards as key to their ethos of excellence, and a world war was not going to stop that.

The Household Cavalry would have an interesting war, not only supporting the cavalry divisions in the mounted roles, but also as dismounted infantry in the Household Battalion. With the formation of the Guards Division the Household Cavalry would go on to provide a cavalry squadron and a cyclist company. The Foot Guards were likewise spread around the British Expeditionary Force (BEF) either as individual battalions or formed into Guards Brigades fighting with the 1st, 2nd and 7th Divisions.

The war also saw the founding of the first new Guards regiment since the formation of the Irish Guards with the Welsh Guards (Welsh or WG) coming into existence with a Royal Warrant signed on 26 February 1915. The Welsh Guards was the brainchild of Field Marshal Horatio Kitchener, 1st Earl Kitchener. Kitchener was quick to realize the potential of forming an additional Guards regiment. On 6 February 1915 he instructed former Grenadier and then General Officer Commanding (GOC) London District Major-General Sir Francis Lloyd (1853–1926) to raise a regiment of Welsh Guards.

The nucleus of the Welsh Guards came from the Grenadiers who transferred five officers and 634 soldiers to the new regiment, as well as officers from line regiments, many of whom were Welsh. This influx of personnel allowed the Welsh Guards to mount a guard at Buckingham Palace on 1 March 1915, St. David's Day, led by Welshman and former Grenadier, Lieutenant-Colonel William Murray-Threipland (1866–1942), who would later become the regiment's colonel. By mid-August the 1st Battalion had crossed the channel to join their brother Guards in France.

Kitchener's experience with the Guards left more than a good impression on him and his next project was to form a Guards Division around this formidable and highly disciplined force. Kitchener was a stickler for discipline and felt the influence of the Guards with their high standards would rub off on the rest of the BEF, especially those now forming the New Army, another of his ideas. Kitchener, now familiar with the process behind forming new units, once again approached George V, who granted the idea his permission. This allowed Kitchener to make his plans, unbelievably without initially consulting the War Cabinet, and most importantly Field Marshal Sir John French (1852–1925) Commander-in-Chief BEF. French would eventually receive notification of the new division by letter in mid-July, barely a month before Grenadier Major-General Frederick Lambart, 10th Earl of Cavan (1865–1946), took command on 18 August in time for the Loos offensive.

The new division's ORBAT would see the Foot Guards battalions gathered into three brigades of five battalions each, which would be reduced to four battalions in February 1918. Also joining the new division were the Guards Brigade Machine-Gun companies, and the Household Cavalry's cavalry squadron and a cyclist company, which would be detached from mid-1916. Other service support units included Royal Engineers (RE), Royal Field Artillery (RFA), medical and veterinary services as well as the all-important divisional train. Over time the division would continue to evolve, gaining trench mortar batteries in 1916. It would be around this time that the division would be recognized by its 'Eye' insignia designed by Major Sir William Avery, 2nd Baronet (1890–1918), Army Service Corps (ASC). The insignia would return once more in 1941, representing the Guards Armoured Division until 1945.

The new division was rapidly thrust into the crucible of the Western Front, seeing its first action at the Battle of Loos on 26 September 1915. Loos would be a horrific baptism of fire for the division which was called forward to support the heavily mauled 21st and 24th Divisions. The Guards Division was able to relieve both divisions the following day and simultaneously establish a new Line of Departure (LoD) from which they were able to assault German positions, whilst under fire, including gas attacks. For the next three days men from the Grenadier, Coldstream and Welsh Guards pushed against German defenders at two points, known as Hill 70 and Puits No. 14 bis. Despite the Coldstreamers being pushed back from their positions at Puits No. 14 bis the Germans merely shelled the newly established British lines rather than physically counterattack them. It was decided to pull the Guards back from the front lines on 29 September, with relief starting that night and being fully completed by 1 October. The break, if only from the horrendous environmental conditions, including near constant rain, was short lived and within forty-eight hours the Guards were back on the line.

On 8 October Lance-Sergeant Oliver Brooks (1889–1940) Coldstream Guards, would lead a raiding party which would see him awarded the division's first Victoria Cross. His medal was later presented to him by George V on a hospital train which was taking the king back to England, who was suffering from a broken pelvis, caused by a fall from his horse. The division was relieved once more on 13 October, to return to the line forty-eight hours later opposite the Hohenzollern Redoubt, a formidable strongpoint of the German 6th Army. Elements of division would join an assault on the position alongside the 9th (Scottish) Division between 13 and 19 October 1915. Understandably the redoubt was extremely well defended, and the British assaults led to nothing, troops kept at bay by defensive fire and the worsening environmental conditions. On 26 October the division left the line for the final time to rest in the town of Bethune some seven miles (twelve kilometres) northwest of the Hohenzollern Redoubt.

That autumn the division settled into the trench life routine; their behaviour remained exemplary and silenced pre-formation critics that the Guards Division would be unable to maintain their high peacetime standards. Trenches were often handed over in a far better state than they were taken over in, with efforts made to maintain structural integrity and minimize environmental impacts leading to immersion foot syndrome, known then as 'Trench Foot', which in turn could severely incapacitate an individual, leading to gangrene and amputation of the toes or even the whole foot.

In November the division was moved to a new Tactical Area of Responsibility (TAOR) in the Neuve Chappelle region, remaining in the Ypres Salient. By February 1916, after a relatively quiet autumn and winter the division lost its commander, Lord Cavan, to promotion as a corps commander. His replacement was Coldstreamer Major-General Geoffrey Fielding (1866–1932), who would remain in command of the division until September 1918. Fielding's arrival coincided with a divisional move across the Flanders border region of France and Belgium, joining the Second Army. This move also took the Guards out of the line and for the next month they were able to decompress from the pressures of the front line. The break did not last long and a month later the division returned to Ypres Salient.

The conditions faced by the returning division on 20 March were operationally hazardous; the salient was surrounded on three sides by the Germans, who seemed to delight in bombarding Allied positions within the salient almost remorselessly. On arrival the Guards also found their trenches were in dire need for some Guards level care and attention. Barely a month later, on 19 April, the Germans attacked, briefly breaking through the lines of the 2nd Scots Guards before being repulsed. Given the restrictions placed on the division's artillery in preparation for the planned offence on the Somme, this was a feat of arms.

In May the division was relieved and moved once again into the reserve before moving to Hooge, Belgium, in June to provide reinforcements after a German assault broke through the British lines. A final stint at Ypres Salient followed and in late July the division moved south to the Somme, site of one the bloodiest battles in history, which had started at the beginning of the month. The role of the division had been to act as reserve, but they were pretty much in the thick of the battle from the moment of arrival.

The division moved to lines between Serre-lès-Puisieux and Beaumont Hamel and from 9 September, which marked the start of the Battle of Ginchy, the division began to relieve front line units. On 15 September, following a creeping barrage and accompanied by five tanks, entering the battle space for the first time, 1st and 2nd Guards Brigades took the fight to the Germans in what was to become the Battle of Flers-Courcelette. Despite strong German opposition and challenging terrain, the 2nd Guards Brigade had achieved their objective by 11:00 am. To their left flank the Coldstream Guards battalions of the 1st Guards Brigade were suffering under withering machine-gun fire, with many of their officers slaughtered within moments of leaving the safety if their LoDs. Such losses of leadership were bound to have an effect on the advancing Guards, and for a moment it seemed the Coldstreamers were about to run out of steam. Suddenly above the din of shell and machine-gun fire came the high-pitched call of a hunting horn. During the chaos, wearing a distinctive French Adrian helmet stood Lieutenant-Colonel John Campbell (1876–1944) Coldstream Guards. Campbell rallied the men, leading them in a headlong bayonet charge on the German positions, successfully overwhelming the defenders and taking charge of the captured positions. Campbell would repeat these actions once again, leading his troops on to another objective.

Meanwhile the 1st Scots Guards were busy consolidating their gains. Lance-Sergeant Fred McNess, who had led a section through heavy German fire to capture a trench, had rapidly organized a defensive position, when he became aware his left flank was threatened by a German counterattack. After forming a successful 'block' in the trench and holding his position, McNess collapsed with blood loss, his jaw and neck heavily wounded. For their actions Campbell and McNess were awarded the Victoria Cross. Such was the Guards advance they were ordered to stop and hold their ground to enable fresh troops, including the 3rd Guards Brigade, to continue the advance the following day. September 1916 was a bloody month for the division with the loss of almost 5,000 personnel and after being relieved on 17 September, it withdrew for refit.

October saw the division leave the front lines once more to give the mauled Foot Guards a chance to rest, refit and retrain. The key element of training was to develop an army that was no longer fighting a war of attrition but was an army that fought a combined arms battle. The modern age of warfare had arrived, and the Guards would be keen to be the vanguard of this modern thinking. The key element of this retraining was to develop a force that would strike and breakthrough enemy lines, taking the battle beyond the trenches. Regardless of the implementation of this new and aggressive doctrine, trench warfare remained a key part of the BEF's mission, and by the close of 1916 the Guards were rotating though the mass of trenches that crossed the Somme area of operations. Meanwhile the division artillery continued their work of providing fire support to the front line and harassing the German lines whenever the opportunity arose.

1917 saw a step change in German tactics with their withdrawal to what became known as the Hindenburg Line, a series of defence in depth positions, at places eight miles (thirteen kilometres) deep. In their wake the retreating Germans left devastation and chaos. As the Allies advanced, filling the void left by the Germans they were faced with a mammoth task of clearing the numerous obstacles left by the Germans. The German ambitions to beat the Allies were further aided by the start of the Russia Revolution on 8 March. This would lead to the eventual collapse of the Eastern Front and ceasefire on 15 December. This would effectively allow the Central Powers to concentrate their military on the Western Front, whilst Russia collapsed into years of anarchy and civil war. The culmination of having additional resources available on the Western Front would see the Oberste Heeresleitung (OHL) of Imperial Germany organize a new offensive culminating in the Kaiserschlacht or 'Kaiser's Battle' on 21 March 1918. The Russian Revolution was cause for concern for the Central Powers and the British Empire. Both were now fearful of the spread of militant Bolshevism to the rank and file at home and on the front.

April would further cement 1917's reputation for being a pivotal year in the war. On the 5th the Germans completed their withdrawal to their Hindenburg Line, bedding down in a mass of island-like hardened emplacements set in a sea of barbed wire. However, any renewed sense of relief the OHL may have had was dashed most cruelly the following day, when the United States entered the fray. America's entry into the war, which many saw as long overdue, would have long-reaching repercussions for the war on the Western Front. It also allowed the

Allies to breathe a sigh of relief as men and materiel slowly crossed the Atlantic and landed in mainland Europe. For the Guards 1917 was to be a significant year with a move away from the Somme and back to Flanders.

The British-led Second Battle of Messines at the beginning of June would see the start of the Allied push back against the Germans. It was unmatched in its ferocity for a host of reasons, not least the detonation of nineteen mines which had been dug underneath German lines and whose detonation was heard in London. This cataclysmic opening, which would claim 10,000 German lives, was followed by a combined arms assault which followed a creeping barrage laid down by artillery whose techniques now included advances in command and control and counterbattery fire. As part of XIV Corps, led by Cavan, the home corps of the Guards Division was placed in reserve.

For all its ferocity the Second Battle of Messines was a precursor to the far more important Third Battle of Ypres. It was also used to test new tactics including the all-important bunker-clearing drills, which had been finessed by the Canadians. The Canadians were increasingly innovative in their prosecution of fighting the war from the aspect of combining the technical with the technological. This new approach culminated in the Battle of Vimy Ridge (9–12 April 1917) which proved the worth of their approach and was consequently copied at Messines to great effect and with great success.

On 31 July the division, which had crossed the Ypres-IJzer Canal four days previously, left their LoD at the start of the Battle of Pilckem Ridge. The Canal is a canalized river that linked the Ypres Salient, held by the French and BEF, to the Yser Front, that was manned by the Belgians. As such it is bordered by the usual heavy tacky clay soil that can be found alongside most rivers and canals. For a military geologist such an environment was only good for fighting on when hard. On the night of the 31st the heavens opened, and the marshland surrounding the battlefield was soon turned into a muddy morass.

This sudden change saw the Guards, who had driven the Germans back a staggering two and a half miles in the first day, bogged down, quite literally. The rain continued for the next few days and attacks postponed for up to a fortnight in one case simply because the ground had become impassable. The Guards left their waterlogged lines for rest only to return at the end of August before handing over their lines once again at the end of September.

By now the Guards were truly entrenched in the Third Battle of Ypres and would join the Battle of Poelcappelle on 9 October. Once again, the terrain was against any attacking force, yet the Guards were able to extend their lines, if only by a few hundred metres. They would be relieved on 17 October and with the end of their involvement in the Third Battle of Ypres, left the field with no fewer than five Victoria Crosses. The division now headed south, and on to Cambrai.

The Battle of Cambrai took place between 20 November and 6 December 1917. Cambrai would develop the techniques that the BEF had used in Third Battle of Ypres, but on a far larger scale. Armour was now deployed on a staggering scale, with no fewer than 378 of the 476 tanks engaged in a combat role. The geography was also different. Cambrai was a relatively quiet sector of the front, and its terrain was a world away from the morass of Ypres. It was perfect tank country.

The British plan was to smash through the German lines, held by a single corps, with two of their own, featuring British, Canadian, Indian, French and American troops. Using a mass of firepower and armour the Allies would then open a doorway in the Hindenburg Line, punching through into the rear areas, where the cavalry would be free to wreak havoc and chase down the remaining defenders. Given the numbers, the weight of fire and perhaps the hubris of senior commanders, some felt this was perhaps the 'war will be over by Christmas' moment they'd been wishing for since 1914.

The battle started well, the infantry utilizing the creeping barrage advance to contact once more with very few casualties. The sucesses rolled in fast, the flabbergasted Germans completely taken unawares by what was happening; thousands of prisoners and tonnes of stores were taken by the advancing Allies. Despite the early successes the Germans soon overcame their shock and by the end of the first day were holding fast. Their tenacious defence left the cavalry, including elements of the Household Cavalry, waiting impatiently in their Forming up Areas (FUPs) to be released and run riot beyond the Hindenburg Line. The order never came.

The following day the Guards Division were released from their reserve positions and began taking over the line held by the 51st (Highland) Division, a process that took three days. There followed a series of aggressive defensive actions by the Guards and they soon found themselves under immense pressure suffering ever-growing casualties. On 28 November the division, which had lost too many men to hold their gains, withdraw from the line.

On 30 November the German defence soon turned into the expected counterattack. This time the tables were truly turned, and the Allies were left as bewildered by the ferocity of the assault as the Germans had been nine days before. Such was the aggression of the German assault that Allied positions seemed to collapse, with hard-won gains lost. The Guards stood to and held fast despite being victims of the fog of war and managed to halt the German advance and bring order to a rapidly deteriorating situation. The division was relieved several days later and moved back to the Arras area twenty-three miles (thirty-eight kilometres) to the northwest.

The winter of 1917 signalled the end of the 'Year of Crisis'. The Russian Revolution would gift the Germans fresh manpower and supplies, for its land forces at least. Elsewhere the instigation of the convoy system helped curtail sea losses from U-boat attacks, and Allied pressure in Europe and the Middle East continued to apply pressure on the Central Powers. Just when Britain should have been preparing to launch new offensives in the spring of 1918 it began to curb its military activities in France. Vital reserves were withheld, and the Guards Division lost three of its battalions, some 1,500 men, who were sent elsewhere.

The retaining of reserves, especially in mainland Britain, can in part be excused by political concerns that the violence of the Russian Revolution would spread. Therefore, retaining troops to counter any revolution was perhaps prudent by nervous politicians. The Germans were quick to capitalize on the fact that weakened BEF units had begun taking over French lines, especially in the Somme region. It was in this region that the OHL launched *Unternehmen Michael* or Operation *Michael* on 21 March 1918.

Like the Battle of Cambrai Operation *Michael* was intended to punch through the British lines and push on to the Channel ports whilst simultaneously dividing British and French forces. To achieve his goal chief of the German General Staff, General Erich Ludendorff (1865–1937), who would later perpetuate the myth of the *Dolchstosslegende*, or 'stab-in-the-back', had assembled seventy-two divisions. Facing this were initially twenty-six allied divisions, which would be bolstered by a further twenty-three French divisions.

When launched, Ludendorff's operation utilized newly designed artillery and infantry tactics, the ferocity of which drove the British defenders back over the 1916 battlefields of the Somme. The Guards were now engaged in a fighting withdrawal and were not giving ground easily. Despite their numerical superiority the seemingly unstoppable German advance was forced to fight for every step. The Guards also formed flanking formations, channelling the German advance into increasingly stronger Allied defensive positions. By 5 April Ludendorff's offensive had run out of steam, and despite the men and equipment the Germans had captured they were failing to reach key objectives, forcing Ludendorff to terminate his offensive.

The toll of Ludendorff's gamble was horrific: 239,800 men lost, including his elite *Stoßtruppen* or stormtroopers, now virtually irreplaceable. The butcher's bill for the Allies was no better, with 254,816 casualties of which 177,739 were British. Unlike the Germans, the Allies would be able to replace loses as well as out-produce a quickly ailing German war machine. The war had, inevitably, swing to the side of greater industrial output.

From high summer the Allies were relentless in their pressure on the Central Powers, and as the Allies clocked up victory after victory, with the Central Powers pushed back the inevitable was simply being delayed. At the eleventh hour of the eleventh day of the eleventh month the Armistice came into effect. The guns fell silent and for two minutes there was nothing. Somewhere, on the front line, a bird began to sing.

For the division the task of occupation awaited and on 18 November the Army of the Rhine, which included the Guards Division, was formed with the division marching into a defeated Germany on 11 December and on into Cologne. As the Guards Division, which had been led by Major-General Torquhil Matheson, Coldstream Guards, since 11 September, was slowly demobilized from February 1919 every man could rightly hold his head high, and the division returned with sixteen Victoria Crosses. These sat alongside numerous other awards and a legacy of professionalism second to none.

At the end of the war the British Army had changed, almost beyond recognition; gone were many of the pre-war habits, especially the ornate dress uniforms, though in many cases these were reserved for the regimental bands and mascot handlers. For the men of the Guards Division, it was very much business as usual, and they retained their pre-war dress for State Ceremonial and Public Duties. A further indication of their elite status saw the Privates of the Foot Guards renamed Guardsmen, at the request of George V, in 1921. With the end of the war Lambart was bestowed numerous honours from numerous Allies including Victor Emmanuel III (1869-1947), the King of Italy, in recognition of his efforts with the Tenth Army. On 22 March 1920 Lambart became Lieutenant of the Tower of London, followed by his appointment as the Aide-de-Camp General to George V on 1 October 1920. Lambart became Captain of the Honourable Corps of Gentlemen-at-Arms on 23 July 1929; he would take part in the procession for the funeral of George V on 28 January 1936. This was followed by participation in the Coronation of George VI on 12 May 1937. Lambart became the Commanding Officer of the Hertfordshire Local Defence Volunteers during the Second World War, and would pass away peacefully on 28 August 1946

After the war Major-General Sir Geoffrey Feilding would become Major General Commanding the Brigade of Guards and General Officer Commanding London District. In 1923 Feilding was made General Officer Commanding 56th (1st London) Division. He retired in 1927, passing away on 21 October 1932.

The peace, so hard fought, would be shattered as groups of aggrieved German veterans and political malcontents made their plans to avenge *Dolchstosslegende*, their actions plunging the world into the chaos of war once again.

BACK TO WORK

The British Royal Household was spared the demise experienced by the autocratic monarchies of Russia, Germany and Austria. George V was quick to focus on the use of State Ceremonial and Public Duties to strengthen the royal brand, utilizing wireless in particular, to reach out, especially at Christmas, with the first broadcast made in 1932 and written by Rudyard Kipling. Kipling had lost his only son John (1897–1915) at the Battle of Loos on 27 September. Such was the familial grief and especially the guilt felt by Kipling, he joined the Imperial War Graves Commission and wrote a two-part history of the Irish Guards, his son's regiment, published in 1923. Kipling's influence on Remembrance would extend to the use of the phrase 'Known unto God' for the gravestones of unidentified servicemen and the inscription 'The Glorious Dead' on the Cenotaph, Whitehall, London.

George V, who had eschewed all Germanic names and titles during the previous war, aimed to live simply and, except for his radio broadcasts, sought to engage in a frugal kinghood. He chose to let the men of the Household Division and Brigade of Guards provide colour and theatre to his reign, keen to show the Royal Household as servants to the Empire, not the other way around. With the passing of George V on 20 January 1936, his son, Edward, Duke of Windsor, became Edward VIII. Edward had served with the Grenadier Guards during the First World War, and despite Kitchener's best intentions, visited the front line as often as he could and was awarded the Military Cross in 1916. Perhaps George V saw the future when he said of his son, 'After I am dead, the boy will ruin himself in twelve months.' Prime Minister Stanley Baldwin (1867–1947) also shared George's concerns, and felt Edward's womanizing, often with married women and his reckless behaviour during the 1920s and 1930s, were distinctly unkingly. Edwards's dalliance with American socialite and divorcee Wallis Simpson (1896–1986) and their desire to marry caused a constitutional crisis. On 10 December 1936, in front of his younger brother, Prince Albert, Duke of York, Edward signed his abdication. Albert now found himself in the position of King Emperor and on 11 December 1936 became King George VI of the United Kingdom and the Dominions of the British Commonwealth and leading a country that was once again facing war.

THE SECOND WORLD WAR: A DOUBLE-EDGED SWORD

> 'The Guards Armoured Division went into the forefront of the battle in North-West Europe, achieved an advance unexcelled in the campaign and finally bade "Farewell to Armour" with its task triumphantly accomplished ... I am proud to have had the honour to command such a magnificent formation.'
>
> Major General Sir Allan Adair

The interwar years saw many European nations struggle with political and economic turmoil. Many governments sought to trim defence budgets to manage their respective nations' economies, convinced that there was no way the horror of the First World War could, or would, be repeated. The defeated nations, especially Germany, now compelled to repay reparations, soon experienced an increase in poverty and inequality, resulting in civil and political unrest that merely strengthened extreme politics. Now, disaffected populations sought their own resolutions to establish social and political equilibrium, and the rise of the populists in Europe, while welcomed at home, was a cause for concern among neighbouring countries.

By the mid-1930s, the power bases of Hitler and Mussolini had been strengthened by increased military power, with Germany eschewing all of its Treaty of Versailles restrictions. In the Far East, the situation was no different, with Imperial Japan heading for rule via a de facto military junta and keen to establish a new empire whose brutality would leave many observers aghast. Meanwhile, Stalin's totalitarianism was focused on bringing internal adversaries, imagined and real, to heel, culminating in the Great Terror of 1937.

America, Britian and France were not keen to be involved in another costly global war and either withdrew into semi-isolationism or tried political bargaining. In Europe, Hitler played a game of political chess, remaining one step ahead and seemingly untouchable. With the outbreak of the Spanish Civil War on 17 July 1936, between the communist-backed Republicans and the fascist-backed Nationalists, it was clear to any prudent observer that Hitler, Mussolini and Stalin were allowing their respective militaries to gain combat experience. Those analysts intelligent enough to understand the dangers this presented made the appropriate plans.

The French were acutely aware of what lay on the horizon and began constructing the Maginot Line in 1929, named after the Minister of War André Maginot (b. 1877), who died of typhoid fever in January 1932. The line was geographically limited, a fact the Germans would exploit in 1940 when Rommel pushed his 7th Panzer Division through the Ardennes, a region which General Maurice Gamelin (1872-1958) felt was impassable due to its terrain. In Britain, the political rule of thumb remained appeasement at all costs. Despite this, the calls from social and political commentators for rearmament gradually paid off. By 1938, the British were slowly improving their military capabilities with improved equipment and increased personnel numbers and a wearisome realization that war in Europe was inevitable.

America remained concerned but was safe in the knowledge that its geographic location prevented it from all but a naval attack from Europe, which could be easily intercepted. There was however a growing concern about increased Imperial Japanese aggression, especially in China, where a war of almost unparalleled brutality was taking place. To that end, the Americans slowly increased their military resources and sought to strengthen their interests in South East Asia.

Despite the best intentions of all parties of having any hope of dealing with Hitler, in particular, these would be dashed on 1 September 1939, when, along with Stalin, he invaded Poland. On 3 September, Britain and France declared war on Germany. This war was not one of attrition but one of movement on all fronts, and the Guards would find their role developing in line with changes to this new battle space. Initially, the Guards fought as infantry, fighting in Northern Europe and post-Dunkerque, North Africa. However, some Guards would remain in the United Kingdom, ready to repel any Axis invasion force.

As infantry, the Guards would earn a reputation for courage under fire, particularly in North Africa, where they initially fought Italian forces who were attempting to press British interests in Africa from 10 June 1940. The following day, the 7th Armoured Division began harassing operations against the Italians along the Egyptian border. By August, the Italians had declared a total blockade of British possessions in the Mediterranean and Africa. This followed the British withdrawal from Somaliland (Somalia) and the Italian capture of Moyale on the Kenyan-Ethiopian border. An Italian incursion of Egypt followed, and the coastal town of Sallūm was captured on 13 September, with the town of Sidi Barrani falling on 18 September.

The Guards' involvement in the Africa campaign could trace its roots back to the 22nd Infantry Brigade. This had been formed in the late summer of 1939 by the simple expedient of redesignating the month-old 29th Infantry Brigade, which, in turn, had been formed by simply renaming the Cairo Brigade. The Cairo Brigade was a Regular Army garrison stationed in Egypt and, at the beginning of the war, home to the 2nd Battalion, Scots Guards. As Italian operations in the Mediterranean and African theatres expanded, the 22nd became responsible for the Mersa Matruh Garrison, not far from the Italian front lines at Sidi Barrani. Almost a year later, in the spring of 1941, the 22nd Infantry Brigade was renamed once more, becoming the 22nd Guards Brigade. The 2nd Battalion, Scots Guards, were now joined by the 3rd Battalion, Coldstream Guards, and the 1st Battalion, Buffs (Royal East Kent Regiment). The brigade would change names twice more, first with the adoption of the 200th Guards Brigade on 14 January 1942, and finally, the 201st Guards Motor Brigade Group on 25 May 1942.

The 201st Guards Motor Brigade Group would see extensive service in the North African Campaign, first in Operation *Crusader* (18 November–30 December 1941), led by General Sir Claude Auchinleck (1884–1981), that sought to remove the Axis threat to Egypt and the Suez Canal. This was followed by the Battle of Gazala, which took place between 26 May and 21 June 1942 and not only tested Auchinleck but also the most famed of German commanders, Generaloberst Erwin Rommel (1891–1944). The outcome, against an opposing force now comfortable in its battle space and tactics, was a resounding defeat for Auchinleck. The loss of 50,000 men and a further 35,000 with the capture of the Tobruk garrison, including the 3rd Battalion Coldstream Guards on 21 June allied to the earlier failure of Operation *Battleaxe* (15–17 June 1941) delivered losses the Allies could ill afford. Despite the capture of Tobruk, some British soldiers escaped captivity, including Coldstreamers.

In the aftermath of what was to be the Panzerarmee Afrika's/Armata Corazzata Africa's final victories, the Allies quickly reorganized themselves. On 14 August 1942, the 201st became the 201st Guards Brigade, commanded by Grenadier Brigadier Julian Gascoigne (1903–1990), former Commanding Officer of the 1st Battalion, Grenadier Guards. Like the rest of the Eighth Army, the 201st began to prepare initially for defensive operations as the new General Officer Commanding Eight Army, Lieutenant General Bernard Montgomery (1887–1976) made plans that would result in the three Battles of El Alamein and witness the rapid defeat of the Axis forces in North Africa. In September 1942, the 201st was sent to Syria to train in its new role as a motorized infantry brigade, fighting with battalions made up of three rifle companies. The Coldstream and Scots Guards were joined by the 6th Battalion, Grenadier Guards on 7 October 1942. In early February 1943, the brigade became part of XXX Corps, led by Lieutenant General Sir Oliver William Hargreaves Leese, 3rd Baronet (1894–1978) of the Coldstream Guards as part of the Eighth Army.

The brigade's first action in the Tunisian Campaign, which was now ending, was at the Battle of the Mareth Line against the 1st Italian Army, led by General Giovanni Messe (1883–1968). The battle pitted the Eighth Army against a defensive force led by a skilful commander, now leading a depleted force that was suffering from a lack of resources. Messe's lines of communication were under constant harassment from the Long Range Desert Group (LRDG) established by geologist Major Ralph Bagnold (1896–1990), Royal Signals. Now commanded by Lieutenant-Colonel Guy Prendergast (1905–1986), the LRDG excelled at desert navigation, often assisting the Special Air Service (SAS), founded by the recently captured Lieutenant-Colonel Archibald David Stirling (1915–1990), Scots Guards and a veteran of the No. 8 (Guards) Commando, formed by Lieutenant-Colonel Robert Edward Laycock (1907–1968), Royal Horse Guards. Despite the actions of the British Special Forces, Messe made Montgomery fight for every inch of the ground. Between 16 and 31 March, the two armies fought, with Montgomery finally pushing the 1st Italian Army deeper into Tunisia.

For the inexperienced 6th Grenadiers, the battle was a disaster. During an attack on an objective named Horseshoe Ridge, the Grenadiers, supported by artillery, advanced with all three rifle companies. The attack resulted in a casualty rate of a staggering 70 per cent as the Grenadiers triggered anti-personnel mines and were subjected to well-laid defensive fire from enemy mortars. Regardless, the Grenadiers managed to take the ridge. To reinforce the forward companies, the commanding officer, Lieutenant-Colonel Archer Clive (1903–1995), ordered the battalion's Universal Carriers to clear a way through the minefield, intending to make it easier for Clive to reinforce the forward companies. This manoeuvre failed, with all carriers destroyed. The Germans then began to launch counterattacks, forcing the surviving Grenadiers to withdraw through the minefields they originally came, sustaining further casualties. In a similar attack, the Coldstream Guards obtained one of their objective high points, though suffering heavy casualties and losing all their Carriers. Realizing the damage his troops were experiencing, Gascoigne withdrew battalions under the cover of darkness with no further loss. The losses incurred by both battalions harked back to the battles of the First World War, with the 6th Grenadiers sustaining 279 casualties while the Coldstream suffered 136 casualties.

By May 1943, the Allies had defeated the Axis forces in North Africa and from July 1943, the 201st was attached to the 56th (London) Infantry Division, led by Major General Douglas Graham (1893–1971). The 201st was now ready to take part in the forthcoming Italian Campaign. The brigade was soon entangled in increasingly heavy fighting, suffering from equally heavy losses, and on 25 September 1943, 27-year-old Company Sergeant Major CSM Peter Harold Wright (1916–1990) 3rd Battalion, Coldstream Guards, was awarded the Victoria Cross, after assaulting three machine-gun emplacements single-handedly. The brigade continued to fight in Italy, crossing the Volturno Line, the first of a series of defensive lines established by the Germans in October, and reached the Bernhardt Line by the end of 1943. By January 1944, the 201st found themselves on the Winter Line at Monte Casino, where for the next five months, the Allies and Axis slugged it out, leaving the Guards with a high casualty rate. The lack of replacements took its toll on the brigade, and it was soon returned to the United Kingdom to become a training brigade for the Brigade of Guards. Some of the returned Guards would join their armoured brethren in the liberation of Northern Europe, while others prepared for service in the Far East. However, that adventure was cut short by the Japanese surrender on 2 September 1945.

Those Guards who had been based in the United Kingdom at the onset of war in 1939 quickly found themselves deployed with the British Expeditionary Force (BEF), led by General John Vereker, 6th Viscount Gort (1886–1946), Grenadier Guards. Upon returning to England after their successful extraction from Northern Europe in the early summer of 1940, the Guards found themselves preparing to defend the realm, waiting for an invasion that didn't come. On 17 June 1941, after the threat of invasion of Great Britain had passed, the Guards, rested from their campaigns in Northern Europe, found themselves the focus of an infantry-to-armour conversion. The 20th and 30th Independent Infantry Brigades (Guards) became, with George VI's permission, armour brigades, forming the embryonic Guards Armoured Division (GAD), which in turn fell under the direct command of the War Office. The new brigades would be the 5th and 6th Guards Armoured Brigades. Initially working with obsolete equipment, the Guards Armoured Division, led by Major General Sir Oliver Leese (1894-1978), Coldstream Guards, who would later command XXX Corps in Scilly and Italy, began learning their new craft.

Such was their eventual mastery that Field Marshal Bernard Montgomery would later comment that the GAD exercised a 'prowess in armoured war ... in a manner that had won them fresh honours and the admiration of friend and foe alike'. Before that accolade was delivered, the Guards had to get to grips with armoured fighting vehicles (AFVs) that were past their best. Initially, they trained with the lightly armed and armoured Covenanter at locations throughout the United Kingdom, including the Dukeries estates in Nottinghamshire. By the end of 1942, and now under the command of Grenadier Guard Major General Sir Allan Adair (1897-1988), the Guards Covenanters had been replaced by the slightly larger Ordnance Quick-Firing 6-pounder armed Crusader Mark III. In 1943, supplies of the American-made M4 Sherman began to arrive, with the Guards fielding both the standard M3 75-mm and the Ordnance Quick-Firing 17-pounder, installed in Firefly variants. The arrival of the Sherman was, for the Guards, a just reward after achieving combat efficiency as a division the year before. They had become masters of offensive and defensive operations and were now ready for action, and they began to prepare for the inevitable invasion of Northern Europe in earnest and confidence.

Not only had the division's equipment changed, but its order of battle had developed into a formidable battle group in three short years. The 6th Guards Armoured Brigade had become the 6th Guards Tank Brigade, an independent brigade, in 1942, while the 32nd Guards Brigade now joined the 5th in place of the 6th. GAD could now call on four artillery regiments, towed and self-propelled, an additional infantry regiment in the guise of the Northumberland Fusiliers, as well as vast service support assets. GAD now had 14,700 personnel and 3,000 vehicles in its motor transport pool, 300 of which were AFVs. It also featured the 2nd Battalion, Welsh Guards, as the division's armoured reconnaissance battalion. GAD was in reserve during the initial Operation *Overlord* D-Day landings on 6 June 1944, and it finally arrived at the Normandy bridgehead on 28 June.

From there, the 32nd advanced eastwards towards Caen via Carpiquet, engaging with elements of the 12th SS Panzer Division as part of the Second Army, led by Lieutenant General Miles Dempsey (1896-1969). During Operation *Goodwood*, between 18 and 20 July, which was to become one of the British Army's most significant tank battles, the 32nd was to experience 127 casualties, with fifteen tanks destroyed and forty-five tanks damaged. Despite the operation being contained by German forces, it was the scene of one of the more remarkable and heroic episodes of the European campaign. During an engagement at Cagny between the 2nd (Armoured) Battalion, Irish Guards and a small force of mixed German armour, Lieutenant John Gorman, whose Sherman's traversing mechanism had jammed, rammed a King Tiger by speeding down a forward slope and slamming, almost out of control, into the rear of the Tiger II. Gorman's adventures didn't stop there, and although his tank and the accompanying tank from his platoon, commanded by Sergeant Harbinson, were both out of action, he located a Firefly. He took command of it and engaged the remaining three German tanks: a Tiger I, Panther and Mark IV. Gorman's gunner successfully destroyed the Tiger II, which remained locked with Gorman's Sherman, and hit the Tiger I. The remaining two German tanks soon gathered their wits. They began firing back at the Firefly, which picked up both the crews from the destroyed Shermans and withdrew to safety. For his action, Gorman was awarded the Military Cross.

The GAD remained engaged with German forces until 22 July, after which it was placed in reserve for Operation *Bluecoat*, launched on 30 July with the intention of exploiting the American success of Operation *Cobra*. Operation *Cobra* had been launched by Lieutenant General Omar Bradley (1893-1981), commanding the First United States Army on 25 July, and sought to take advantage of the distraction caused by Operation *Goodwood*. Now it was Dempsey's turn to take advantage of a fellow ally's operation and keep the pressure on the German armoured units facing him. Initially, the GAD was placed into the operational reserves, and on 31 July, they joined the fray, marching forty-five miles as four combined armour/infantry battle groups. They were now engaged with an adversary who knew the woods and pasture lands of the bocage well enough to exploit them as additional defensive areas. For the next two weeks, the Guards fought hard against ever-stiffening resistance, and by 4 August, there was a real danger the offensive would run out of steam.

The fighting was chaotic as the Guards fought to gain the advantage. Yet the defending Germans managed to keep any meaningful advance in check. By early August, the German forces had broken contact. They were headed for Falaise, where Allied forces slowly surrounded Army Group B, the Seventh Army and the Fifth Panzer Army. Between 12 and 21 August, the Allies let loose with everything they had; artillery, armoured assault, and air attacks all hammered an area known as the Falaise Pocket. As a result of the Allied assault, the German forces lost an estimated 450,000 men, of whom 240,000 were killed or wounded, with the Allies taking 209,672 casualties.

After Operation *Bluecoat*, the GAD stood down for a rest and refit until it was ordered to advance, this time along an axis that would take them to Brussels. The end of August also saw the return of the 2nd Household Cavalry Regiment to the fold, and on 31 August, the division crossed the Somme, entering Arras the following day. At 8:00 pm on 2 September, after a seventy-five-mile dash (121 km), the GAD entered Brussels, the capital of Belgium. Adair and his Division were greeted with an almost unequalled enthusiasm by the Brusselaars, who crowded around the Guardsmen and their vehicles. The celebration continued into the following day when Adair, satisfied he had successfully liberated Brussels, pushed eastwards towards the River Dyle. The Germans, now slowly consolidating the remains of Army Group B, the Seventh Army and the Fifth Panzer Army, were waiting and starting to defend with a vigour that would mark the rest of the campaign for the division.

At this point, the Allies had advanced so quickly that their lines of communication were almost 300 miles (483 km) long. There was now a real need to access a suitable port, and for Montgomery's 21st Army Group, Antwerp was the ideal port. Yet it remained tantalizingly out of reach and pushed the normally cautious Montgomery. Perhaps, still smarting from the Battle for Caen, Montgomery devised an ambitious combined land and air assault operation named *Market Garden,* which would focus on forming a bridgehead into Northern Germany rather than push towards Antwerp.

The operation was split into two distinct elements; the first element, *Market,* saw the recently formed First Allied Airborne Army drop almost 35,000 personnel on a series of statically vital bridges and terrain between the towns Eindhoven, Grave, Nijmegen, Arnhem and the rail bridge at Oosterbeek. Meanwhile, the second, *Garden,* would see XXX Corps drive along the route of Highway 69, which ran from the Belgian-Dutch border to Arnhem. They would begin relieving and reinforcing the airborne elements in situ, and in the early stages punch out of Eindhoven and take the bridges at Son and Veghel. From there, XXX Corps would push on to Arnhem, led by the GAD; once there, the Allies would have a springboard into Northern Germany. From there, the Allies could push out, isolating German forces in the Antwerp and Scheldt estuary for later destruction. As a bonus, the operation would also destroy numerous Vergeltungswaffe 2 (V2) launch sites, from where the Germans were launching rockets against targets in Northern Europe and the United Kingdom.

The success of this ambitious operation would shorten the war and, for Montgomery, prove he was the master of combined operations. Despite some absolute awe-inspiring work from G-4 (Logistics), Montgomery's plan was hampered by a lack of firm G-2 (Intelligence) that, in turn, would affect G-3 (Operations) and G-5 (Planning) outcomes. It could be argued the G-2 gaps should have been filled by further reconnaissance, supported by the Nederlands Verzet (Dutch Resistance) and air reconnaissance. As it was, time was not on Montgomery's side, and he was keenly aware that the Germans were recovering rapidly for his advance into Germany; he needed access to a well-supported port, as well as bridges to and across the Rhine.

This lack of intelligence would hamper the *Garden* phase, almost unforgivably so, as the line of advance was dictated by the narrow road, lined on either side by floodplains. On 17 September, Montgomery's signature prelude of a heavy artillery barrage alongside air support from the 2nd Tactical Air Force (2TAF) signalled the start of the battle. Almost immediately, the leading elements of the GAD vanguard were hit by anti-tank fire. The 2TAF and supporting infantry cleared the offending anti-tank position, allowing the column to advance. This event would also be a portent of how hard the coming battle would be.

The following day, the column reached Eindhoven, held by the 101st Airborne Division; this allowed the engineers to move forward and start repairs to bridging over the Wilhelmina Canal. At this point, the GASD split, with the 5th Guards Armoured Brigade advancing to Nijmegen while the 32nd Guards Armoured Brigade stood firm and prepared to engage any counterattacks. On 20 September, the 5th arrived at Nijmegen, where they found the men of the 82nd Airborne Division, who had bravely crossed the River Waal, struggling to take the bridge. However, they succeeded in taking the northern end of the road bridge, leaving the guards, led by the 2nd Grenadiers, to rush the bridge, which was prepared for demolition. Despite this incredible bravery and the subsequent award of the Military Medal to Sergeants Robinson and Pacey, the road to Arnhem remained firmly closed.

The Guards were stopped a mere six miles (ten kilometres) from Arnhem and their brother-in-arms of the Parachute Regiment, who included the indomitable Regimental Sergeant Major John Lord, formerly of the Grenadier Guards. With the 43rd Wessex Division leading the advance, the GAD was tasked to expand the bridgehead north of Nijmegen, known as 'the Island' and remain alert to any German counterattacks. On 6 October, the GAD was pulled out of the line for much-needed rest and refit before heading seventy miles (112 km) south to Sittard, near the German border in November.

On 16 December, the Germans launched Operation *Wacht am Rhein*, otherwise known as the Battle of the Bulge, against the salient that protruded into Germany proper. Their timing could not have been better, but their decision to retrace the route they took into the Low Countries four years previously and at the start of winter was disastrous. They were using roads and bridges, unable to take the weight of their more contemporary armour designs. A lack of fuel further hampered them. The Allies, especially the Americans, had, for a moment, taken their eye off the ball, thinking the Germans could not mount such an operation. Initially, the Germans did well, but the previously mentioned environmental and logistical restrictions, stiffening Allied resistance, and a break in the weather saw the offensive rapidly lose momentum. As the battle progressed, the 21st Army Group could lend their support to operations by the First U.S. Army, whose command had been temporarily passed to Montgomery, against the Fifteenth and elements of the Sixth Panzer armies. The GAD now moved into Belgium to act as a reserve division throughout the battle.

By the beginning of 1945, the operational losses inflicted upon the Guards infantry were beginning to have an effect, and the 2nd Scots took over from the 1st Welsh. The 2nd Scots were veterans of the North African and Italian campaigns. Such were their losses they were now fielding a battalion that consisted of fifty per cent veterans and fifty per cent rebadged Royal Air Force airmen. Whilst this showed how flexible the personnel of the Citizens Army were, it was a stark reminder that the British Army's infantry continued to pay the butcher's bill in terms of losses.

8 February saw the GAD move further into Germany, occupying an area of forestry known as the Reichswald between the rivers Maas and Rhine. It was here that Operation *Veritable* saw the GAD forge a path across the Rhine as part of XXX Corps. The armoured element of the assault was hampered by the deliberate flooding of the Rhine floodplain, and despite having some of the most cutting-edge equipment, the battle, once again, became infantry led. The infantry of the 32nd Guards Brigade, consisting of the 5th Coldstream, 3rd Irish and 1st Welsh, were now attached to the 51st (Highland) Infantry Division. The subsequent assault against the Siegfried Line, which ran from the Kleve on the Dutch border down to the Swiss border, known as Operation *Veritable,* was part of Montgomery's plan to push deeper southward into Germany with the 21st Army Group.

Meanwhile, Operation *Grenade*, led by the U.S. Ninth Army, which had been part of the 21st Army Group since the Battle of the Bulge and was led by Lieutenant General William Simpson (1888-1980), was to push northeast as part of a coordinated assault. To the south, the U.S. First Army, led by Lieutenant General Courtney Hodges (1887–1966), would push his Army east. All three commanders and troops were faced with assaulting a defensive line that mirrored the Maginot Line; the 390-mile (628-km) Siegfried Line featured over 18,000 bunkers, tunnels and tank traps.

Even though the Siegfried Line sounded impenetrable, the facts were, for the German defenders at least, far from the truth. Guns had been removed to compensate for operational losses elsewhere. At the same time, the keys to many of the bunkers had gone missing, and overall maintenance was almost non-existent. That did not stop the attackers from facing some of the most ferocious fighting they had experienced. Nor were they helped by the weather, the worst winter in living memory. Within two weeks, the 32nd Guards Brigade had been reduced to two understrength battalions. Thankfully, the American breakthrough in the south gave the attacking British some breathing space, and the GAD was again formed back into its battlegroups, ready for the final push into Germany. A month after the launch of Operation *Veritable*, the GAD stood on the banks of the Rhine.

11 March saw the GAD return to Nijmegen for rest and refit, where the 1st Welsh departed, and the divisional artillery left to support the assault crossing of the Rhine, which was to take place on 23 March. The GAD, led by the 5th Guards Armoured Brigade, finally crossed the Rhine on 30 March and headed north, where it encountered the German 1st Parachute Army. As the GAD pushed on towards the town of Lingen, the defending Fallschirmjäger fought a tooth-and-nail defence. Despite their best efforts, on 3 April, elements of the 32nd Guards Armoured Brigade entered the town. The bridge that crossed the Ems River had been destroyed. At this stage, the 2nd Household Cavalry Regiment, operating as part of XXX Corps, located another river crossing four miles downstream.

The Coldstream battlegroup was now tasked with taking this valuable bridge, earning the commander of the Coldstream Infantry Company, Captain Ian Liddle (b. 1919), the Victoria Cross. Liddle's actions and engagement in capturing the bridge are worthy of mention, not only as a demonstration of how desperate the German defenders had become but also as a testament to the 25-year-olds' bravery. The bridge in question was well defended by 150 entrenched soldiers, who were supported by three 8.8-cm anti-tank guns and two 2-cm flak guns in the ground defence role; these could wreak havoc among any attacking force. The bridge had been prepared for demolition using 250-kg (551-lb) bombs.

Liddell directed his two leading platoons onto the near bank before running forward and scaling the three-metre (ten-foot) -high roadblock protecting the bridge. His plan was to deactivate the charges, allowing the bridge to be taken intact. To achieve his objective, Liddell had to cross the length of the bridge under intense fire that only increased as his intentions became apparent to the defending Germans. Whilst cutting the various wires alongside the bridge, Liddell needed to kneel, presenting the defenders with an easy target. Liddell then subdued charges that he had found underneath the bridge. Once he was satisfied all charges were neutralized, Liddell returned to the roadblock and standing on top of it, in full view of the defenders, signalled the leading platoon to make its attack. Liddell's actions ensured the bridge was captured intact, allowing for an advance across the River Ems. Liddle was killed by a sniper on 21 April.

Now, over the Ems, the GAD continued its push against stiffening German resistance to Bremen. On 14 April, the GAD halted once more, and the battle became the infantry's responsibility as men poured into Bremen. Two days later, the GAD crossed the River Weser, occupying the zone between Bremen and Hamburg. They were now fighting Kriegsmarine personnel who had been organized into Marine divisions, and who fought as bitterly as their Fallschirmjäger counterparts. April would see GAD casualties mount against defenders using every trick in the book, from booby traps to almost fanatical counterattacks. On a positive note, the advancing guards were now liberating prisoner of war camps, liberating some forty of their own, who had recently been captured as well as those captured in 1940.

From the end of April until early May, the fighting slowly subsided, and the 1st Household Cavalry Regiment now joined the GAD. With the

German surrender on 8 May, the division's gunners celebrated by firing a *feu de joie* for a full ten minutes before the ceasefire became effective.

With the war ending in Europe, the British Army began to demobilize the German forces, and the GAD worked in the Cuxhaven peninsula on the coast of Lower Saxony. On 9 May 2nd Scots assisted in taking the surrender of the island of Heligoland, home to submarine pens and artillery batteries. Meanwhile the remainder of the division was disarming German units and overseeing the terms of the Germans' surrender before moving south to Verden an der Aller, where it would police the local area.

On 9 June 1945, the division gathered, albeit without the 6th Guards Brigade's Churchills, a final time to parade past Montgomery at Rotenberg airfield, which had been cleared for bobby traps. Some 250 tanks, repainted in liberated battleship grey with coloured details and brightly coloured aerials, were arranged on either side of the airfield, stretching for half a mile in the late spring sun. In between the two rows were the vehicles of the other mobile units, including the Household Cavalry regiments. All waited as the various dignitaries landed at the airfield.

The parade was every bit the spectacle one would expect from the Guards. As the tanks passed Montgomery, they were slowly shrouded in diesel smoke, which added to the pageantry, before disappearing. As the engine noise lessened, the massed bands began to play *Auld Lang Syne*, and with that, the Guards Armoured Division, watched by military personalities, locals, prisoners of war and liberated Russians, passed into history.

The dismounted Guards followed and halted before the saluting dias in seven columns of infantry in sixes. There, Adair called the Guards Division to attention for the first time, and the end of the ceremony was indicated by the national anthem being played.

After the war, Adair served as General Officer Commanding the 13th Infantry Division before retiring on 11 March 1967. On 21 November, Adair was appointed Exon in the Yeomen of the Guard, receiving promotion to Ensign on 30 June 1950 and Lieutenant on 31 August 1951. Adair also served as County Antrim's Deputy Lieutenant and

Justice of the Peace in Suffolk. Adair retired on 14 November 1967 and passed away on 4 August 1988. With the ending of the war, the 1st and 2nd Household Cavalry Regiments were reformed as the Life Guards and Royal Horse Guards, respectively, with each regiment providing one mounted squadron each for ceremonial duties in London, with the two squadrons becoming known as the Household Cavalry Mounted Regiment (HCMR).

A Brave New World

> 'From Stettin in the Baltic to Trieste in the Adriatic, an iron curtain has descended across the continent.'
>
> Winston Churchill

The ending of the Second World War would see a new world emerge, one of mutual political distrust and arms races unimaginable at the turn of the century. The rapid pace of technology, especially that of air power and the harnessed power of the atom, saw the massed armies of the past almost relegated to insignificance. The British Empire had also begun to shrink as States started to forge their destinies after six years of war. For the men of the Guards, the war's end was the start of one of their busiest periods. They supervised the return of Soviet prisoners of war and kept the peace in Germany and Italy before moving to Palestine, where the men of the Household Cavalry and Guards Brigade were organized into the 1st (Guards) Parachute Battalion in 1946. This was formed around a cadre of staff from the Grenadier Guards and led by Lieutenant-Colonel E. J. B. Nelson. In 1948, after escorting the High Commissioner out of Jerusalem to the airport on 14 May, thus ending the British mandate in Palestine, the battalion was reduced to company strength and renamed 16 (Guards) Independent Company before finally becoming No.1 (Guards) Independent Company.

1948 was to prove a pivotal year as the new post-war order finally took shape. The Soviets, keen to assert themselves in Europe, blockaded

Berlin from 24 June 1948 to 12 May 1949 in what was to be the first international crisis of the Cold War. With the ending of the blockade, it was to be a British convoy that was the first to leave for the beleaguered city, escorted by the Blues. The same year, communist rebels sought to destabilize Malaya, resulting in the deployment of three battalions of Foot Guards, who would remain in the country for six years. In 1951, the No.1 (Guards) Independent Company deployed briefly to Cyprus. However, they would return five years later, in 1956, as part of operations against the Ethniki Organosis Kyprion Agoniston (EOKA), a Greek Cypriot guerrilla organization fighting British rule. It would also be used to occasionally flex Britain's military muscle in the Suez Canal zone, culminating in a combined airborne assault with 3 Para and the French 2e Régiment étranger de parachutists at Port Said on 5 November 1956 as part of Operation *Musketeer*. This assault was spurred on by the President of Egypt, Gamal Abdel Nasser Hussein's (1918–1970) nationalization of the Suez Canal Company on 26 July 1956. Despite the military success of the joint Anglo-French operation, the British units were ordered to return to Cyprus after mounting international pressure.

Cyprus was hardly a friendly base for the Guards, who had been deployed there before Operation *Musketeer* to find and destroy EOKA cells led by General Georgios Grivas (1897–1974), an expert in asymmetrical warfare. The political situation in Cyprus had been inflamed by the exile of Archbishop Makarios III (1913–1977), a leading advocate and lobbyist for Enosis (Cypriot unification with Greece), to the Seychelles on 9 March 1956. This was followed by a State of Emergency being declared on 26 November 1956 by its Governor, Field Marshal Allan Harding, 1st Baron Harding of Petherton (1896–1989). Harding was very much the firm hand, with the establishment of concentration camps, the indefinite detention of suspects without trial and the imposition of the death penalty for weapons offences. Harding could call upon numerous troops to support his actions, including a detachment from the Life Guards and the entire Blues. Harding's expelling of Makarios saw the insurgency balloon, with violence erupting over the next three years, with the Turks soon responding to Greek Cypriot aggression that saw the establishment of Türk Mukavemet Teşkilatı (TMT) in 1958. The Blues were quickly embroiled in the violence. They discarded their armoured cars that were easy to spot when approaching, adopting donkeys that proved helpful in stealthy approaches and traversing the Cypriot mountains when hunting EOKA operatives. Despite their best efforts, the Blues lost men, including their unarmed medical officer, during this bloody period of Cyprus's history. As the post-war period developed and the empire shrank, the Guards found themselves in action in numerous locations, including a return to Cyprus in 1963 to prevent bloodshed between Greek and Turkish Cypriots. This role would later be reprised in 1974 when a British Contingent (BRITCON) was deployed to Cyprus as part of the United Nations Peacekeeping Force in Cyprus (UNFICYP). This has since become the British military's longest-running UN mission, known as Operation TOSCA.

The 1960s would see the Household Cavalry and the Brigade of Guards further hone their skills as armoured and mechanized infantry regiments as part of the British Army on the Rhine (BAOR). The possibility of an attack by Warsaw Pact forces pouring over Germany's internal border remained high. BAOR settled into a regime that saw soldiers deployed into the field for extensive periods and training in chemical, biological, radiological and nuclear defence (CBRN). The regiments of the Household Cavalry found themselves operating main battle tanks. At the same time, the Brigade of Guards familiarized themselves with the FV432 family of armoured personnel carriers as they adapted to their role. Their roles in supporting State Ceremonial and Public Duties continued unabated, but rather than put a strain on the Household Cavalry and Brigade of Guards, both flourished.

Despite their NATO commitments, commitments in the Far East, Middle East and North Africa (MENA) continued to place the men of the Household Cavalry and Brigade of Guards in harm's way. One such flashpoint would become the Yemeni Port of Aden, which the British had administered since 19 January 1839. Since 1963 resentment toward the British administration and the proposed independence model fed local unrest. On 10 December 1963, a grenade attack by the communist

National Liberation Front (NLF) led by Qahtan Muhammad al-Shaabi (1920–1981) led to the declaration of a State of Emergency. Soon, the NLF were fighting both the British and the Front for the Liberation of Occupied South Yemen (FLOSY) led by Abdullah al Asnag for control of Aden. The region would become part of a wider conflagration known as the Dhofar War from 1963 until 1976, started by the secessionist Dhofar Liberation Front (DLF), keen to establish a state in the Dhofar province of Oman. The DLF had been founded as a communist youth collective and was led by Musallam bin Nufl (d. 2013) and Yusuf bin Alawi bin Abdullah (b. 1945). One of their key aims was to end British influence in the region. At the same time, the British and Omanis were keen to eradicate communist influence.

In November 1966, the First Battalion Irish Guards found themselves aboard HMS *Fearless*, one of the latest Royal Navy assault ships and one that would see service in the Falklands War. The mission of the Irish Guards was to land, detain and remove members of the DLF, utilizing land and sea assault. The mission got off to a shaky start as the ingestion of a jellyfish temporarily paralyzed HMS *Fearless*, but soon, the landing craft, rubber boats and Royal Air Force (RAF) helicopters were on their way. The mission was far from a success, and despite every security element being covered, the Irish Guards failed to find any members of the DLF. They could console themselves by removing some twenty surprised locals identified as possible DLF supporters. The Irish Guards then settled into a routine of counterinsurgency operations, sharing the task with the Royal Marines, fighting an enemy that only appeared at night. The patrols were split between operating in the city of Aden and the surrounding area on a six-week rotation. By the end of their tour, the Irish Guards had lost eight personnel. For the Brigade of Guards, the 1960s brought about another change, as it became known as the Guards Division on 1 July 1968. The Household Cavalry was not immune from change, and on 29 March 1969, the Royal Horse Guards and the Royal Dragoons merged to become The Blues and Royals (Royal Horse Guards and 1st Dragoons) (RHG/D). Meanwhile, the British Empire also continued to shrink.

Operation *Banner*, which began on 14 August 1969 and was formally closed on 31 July 2007, was to become the British military's most prolonged domestic operation. Throughout this period, the Household Cavalry and Guards Division men would prove themselves to be as disciplined as ever. Now operating in one of the countries of the United Kingdom, initially attempting to reassure the Catholic and Protestant communities was never going to be easy. The Welsh Guards, in particular, maintained a sense of dignity and endeavoured to maintain that sense when working among the poorer and neglected areas of their allocated areas of responsibility.

There would be losses among the Household Cavalry and Guards Division, and the Irish Guards, who were initially excused from duties in Northern Ireland, would be among the worst affected. On 10 October 1981, a remote-controlled nail bomb exploded outside Chelsea Barracks, targeting a bus carrying members of the Irish Guards band, killing two civilians and injuring 40, including 23 soldiers. The attack was carried out by a London-based Active Service Unit (ASU) of the Provisional Irish Republican Army (PIRA) in retaliation for the loss of ten prominent PIRA members, including Bobby Sands (1954–1981), during the 1981 Irish hunger strike. This attack was followed by a further nail bomb attack on 20 July 1982, in which four troopers, including the Standard Bearer and seven mounts of The Blues and Royals of the Household Cavalry Mounted Regiment, were killed by a remotely detonated bomb as they made their way to mount the Queen's Life Guard at Horse Guards Parade. For the Blues and Royals, the shock at the loss of life was almost impenetrable, with the Commanding Officer, Lieutenant-Colonel Andrew Parker-Bowles (b. 1939), and Major Noel Cardings, Royal Army Veterinary Corps (RAVC) being among the first on the scene. Their prompt actions would later save the horse Sefton (1963–1993) and other injured horses, both military and police, with Carding attending to the first battlefield injuries sustained by military horses in almost fifty years.

Despite the targeted attack on the Irish Guards, the regiment would not complete its first Operation *Banner* tour until 1992. That is not to say the Irish Guards were resting on their laurels. This period between

1969 and 1992 saw the regiment deployed to Hong Kong between 1970 and 1972, where an incursion into Chinese territory saw eight Guardsmen apprehended by the People's Liberation Army (PLA) after a navigation error. This tour was followed by a return to Caterham, Surrey, the former home of the Guards Depot between 1877 and 1960. This period was punctured by an operational tour of Belize, where they would return in 1977. In 1975, the Irish Guards were back in West Germany as part of the I British Corps, BAOR, living in Münster in North Rhine-Westphalia and ready to defend NATO's eastern flank against the Warsaw Pact forces that faced them. In 1977, recruits from the Guards Depot at Pirbright, Surrey, found themselves assisting Irish Guards in providing cover for striking firefighters during Operation *Burberry* in London.

In 1980, the Irish Guards found themselves deployed to Rhodesia as part of the Commonwealth Monitoring Force assembled to collect weapons from the local guerrilla factions and ensure free elections. The 1980s also saw the Irish Guards polish their role as mechanized infantry in West Germany, now utilizing FV432 rather than the Humber 1-ton armoured personnel carrier (APC) that they used in the motorized role of the 1960s. By the end of the 1980s, the FV432s would be replaced by the next generation of IFVs, the GKN Sankey FV510 Warrior. The Warrior was designed to replace the FV430 series but would find itself working alongside these stalwarts of the mechanized regiments. International incidents aside, the activities and duties of the Irish Guards during this period were atypical snapshots of those carried out by the other regiments of the Guards Division, who also completed Operation *Banner* tours.

THE FALKLANDS WAR

> "It is very ungentlemanly of you to refuse to shake my hand," General García said, in a widely reported exchange. "It is very uncivilized of you to invade my country," Sir Rex replied.

The Falklands War came at a time of significant cultural change in the world. In the Democratic Republic of Afghanistan, the Soviet Union was in the third year of its intervention, fighting the Afghan Mujahedeen that threatened to overthrow the Afghan government. The rise of Islamic Fundamentalism in the Middle East and South West Asia threatened not only American regional influence but also Israeli interests. United States President Ronald Reagan (1911–2004) was keen to reassert American military and political influence post-Vietnam and take the Cold War to Leonid Brezhnev's (1906–1982) Soviet Union, which he could see was starting to struggle in Afghanistan.

Meanwhile, Britain was entering its thirteenth year of performing Operation *Banner* internal security duties in Northern Ireland while simultaneously struggling to meet its commitments to NATO and its shrinking empire. For the military, despite its numerous obligations, there were rumours of yet another Defence Review, and the sheen on Margaret Thatcher's premiership was starting to dull. For all that, Britain remained a world player, but only just. Its influence industrially, politically and militarily was on the wane. While the Americans bolstered their world position, Britain seemed stuck on a gradual decline.

For the British Army, the early 1980s had entered a cycle of deployments to Northern Ireland, training, NATO and UN commitments. To many, a German posting was welcomed, if only for the improved standard of living. Despite operations in Northern Ireland providing opportunities for all teeth arms to get used to working as infantry, it wasn't considered a 'real' war. The raw appeal of the army has always been the opportunity to fight, and to the now growing numbers of unemployed young men and women, there remained the possibility of fighting a war against the Warsaw Pact, especially with an increasingly belligerent United States, not only rattling its sabres but sharpening them too.

In South America, there continued a period of intense political uncertainty that started with the Cuban Revolution in the late 1950s, soon spreading continent-wide. Socialist-inspired desires for a fair deal were becoming entrenched in the disenfranchised poor, especially in the countryside, and it was inevitable that armed clashes with government forces would ensue. Soon, Western influence and funding to those nations engaged against socialist and communist groups, funded by the Cubans or Soviets, increased, with national governments often overthrown by juntas. The late 1970s and early 1980s were the age of the proxy war by the superpowers in South America as much as they were in South West Asia. The Argentinian junta was no exception and had a long history of overthrowing the democratically elected government. Like many of its compatriots, the juntas were subject to regular changes in leadership, with each new administration promising better for the nation than the previous could deliver.

At the end of 1981, a new junta ousted the government of General Roberto Viola (1924–1994), who had been part of the junta that had overthrown the democratically elected Isabel de Perón (b. 1931) in 1976. The new junta, led by the impressionable General Leopoldo Galtieri Castelli (1926–2003), was assisted by Admiral Jorge Anaya (1926–2008), a known Anglophobe who was keen to expel the British from their South Atlantic territories, including the Falklands. Argentina had long insisted that the Falklands were theirs; now Anaya had the chance to take the British South Atlantic territories, encouraged by recent United Kingdom announcements that the British Antarctic Survey Base (BAS) at Grytviken in South Georgia and the Antarctic Protection Vessel *Endurance* were to be closed and removed, with the latter not being replaced.

Anaya took a gamble and instructed Vice-Admiral Juan Lombardo (1927–2019), Chief of Naval Operations, to plan an invasion of the Falklands. Lombardo was no stranger to the islands, having led a twelve-man team in an unlawful beach landing approximately forty kilometres (twenty-five miles) from Stanley in October 1966. Lombardo had completed his plans, aiming to land on the islands on 9 July 1982, Argentina's Independence Day; it would also see the island invaded at the start of winter, with its platoon of Royal Marines hunkered down for winter.

However, Argentine moves were not going unnoticed by Whitehall. By late March 1982, three Royal Navy nuclear submarines were en route to the region. Spooked, Anaya demanded that Lombardo modify his plan for an earlier invasion, and on 28 March, the Argentines began their preparations for Operation *Rosario*, the invasion of the Falkland Islands. On the afternoon of 1 April, the island's governor, Rex Hunt (1926–2012), received a communiqué from the Foreign Office to expect and prepare for an Argentine invasion. Hunt and the senior Royal Marines of Naval Party 8901, Major Mike Norman and Major Gary Noott, discussed the islands' defence. The Royal Marines were midway through their changeover and could count on sixty-eight marines and the eleven sailors, led by Lieutenant Chris Todhunter, Royal Navy. Twenty-two Royal Marines were dispatched to the BAS along with the remainder of the *Endurance* crew of thirteen. The Royal Marines would be captured by their Argentine counterparts on 3 April.

Meanwhile, the remaining sailors and marines prepared for the inevitable fight alongside twenty-five members of the Islands' Local Defence Force and the Islands' Governor. The inevitable happened that night, and despite a spirited defence by all, including Hunt, the overwhelming strength of numbers led Hunt to surrender. The Cabinet Office gathered in London, and the decision to launch a Task Force was made. On 5 April, the carriers HMS *Invincible* and *Hermes* left Portsmouth as part of Operation *Corporate*.

The diplomacy continued whilst both sides continued to draw their battle lines and make their preparations. A battlegroup of 7,000 was assembled, consisting of Royal Marines, the Parachute Regiment and two troops of light armour from The Blues and Royals; this was the vanguard heading south. The Blues and Royals would later support 45 Commando and 3 Para at Teal Inlet from 28 May, providing fire and logistics support as both closed to contact Argentine positions. The Blues and Royals would be joined by their fellow Guards from 2nd Scots and 1st Welsh Guards, who would arrive as part of 5 Infantry Brigade within a week.

On 3 June, the Welsh Guards landed at San Carlos, opposite Stanley, some 106 km (65 mi) away. An initial advance out of San Carlos was cancelled as the Guards began to suffer exhaustion trying to navigate the unforgiving Falklands terrain. Two days later, the Scots Guards, led by Royal Marine Major Ewan Southby-Tailyour (b. 1942), who had sailed around the islands in more peaceful times, utilized four landing craft to land at Bluff Cove, south of Stanley. During their transit, the Scots narrowly escaped being attacked by the frigate HMS *Cardiff* as it returned from delivering a fire mission against Stanley.

The Welsh Guards were on the move again by 6 June, and the inevitable fog of war set in with the battalion split between San Carlos and Fitzroy. The first move of the battalion was completed by the amphibious assault ship HMS *Fearless*. However, due to 2 Para reallocating landing craft to land supplies at Fitzroy, not all the Welsh Guards could disembark, and the captain returned the remaining Guards to San Carlos. On the afternoon of the 7 June, the remaining Guards embarked on the RFA *Sir Galahad,* a landing ship logistics vessel, arriving at Fitzroy the following morning. The officers in charge refused to disembark, insisting they join the rest of the battalion at Bluff Cover. Southby-Tailyour urged the guards to at least come ashore while stores were unloaded. Again, the officers in charge refused to disembark. Meanwhile, an Argentine observation post watched *Sir Galahad* unload its stores, and the situation was reported back to the Argentine mainland. Ten aircraft of the Fuerza Aérea Argentina (FAA) scrambled to attack the shipping at anchor in the area, with five Douglas A-4 Skyhawks making towards Fitzroy and *Sir Galahad* and other vessels unloading there, including the *Sir Galahad*'s sister ship, the *Sir Tristrum*.

The *Sir Tristrum* and the *Sir Galahad* were both hit, two bombs passing straight through the *Sir Tristrum* without detonating. Unfortunately, three bombs, launched slightly higher, slammed into the *Sir Galahad*, killing forty-six and wounding 150. This moment was the bloodiest of the war for the Task Force. Within two hours, the FAA had returned, turning their attentions to Bluff Cove, but the Scots Guards were waiting and, in 45 seconds, expended a staggering 18,500 rounds of small-arms ammunition at the attacking Skyhawks, driving them away. Deterred, the Skyhawks swung south once more for Fitzroy; this time, the air defences, which had experienced technical issues during the first attack, were ready. As the Skyhawks made their approach, seven Rapier missiles were launched. The attacking Skyhawks once again broke off their attack and headed home, much to the relief of all concerned, especially the medical services, which were the last to disembark from the *Sir Galahad* before the first attack. A single landing craft was attacked by four Skyhawks from another flight, with the loss of six crewmembers. Suddenly, two Sea Harriers screamed in and using the latest Aim-9L Sidewinders shot down three of the attacking aircraft. The Welsh Guards were still in the fight and the commander of 3 Commando Brigade, Brigadier Julian Thompson (b. 1934), could add the Welsh to 40 Commando for an attack on Argentine positions west of Stanley.

Meanwhile, the Scots Guards remained with the 5 Infantry Brigade, and by 11 June, they formed part of the wall assembled by British commanders to the west of Stanley. Their tactical area of operations was now the extreme south of the British line with 42 Commando and 1st Battalion, the 7th Duke of Edinburgh's Own Gurkha Rifles (1/7 Gurkhas) to their immediate north, and Stanley to the east. In the middle was a series of mountains, including Mount Tumbledown. On the night of 13/14 June, the Scots Guards, 1/7 Gurkhas, and 42 Commando, supported by a troop from The Blues and Royals, made their advance on Mount Tumbledown. The battle that ensued was as bitter as any, as British troops advanced, bayonets fixed, the Scots eschewing their helmets for their berets, as they advanced to contact.

Soon, the battle bogged down, and the Scots were exchanging rounds from their 66mm M72 light anti-tank weapons and Carl Gustaf 8.4 cm recoilless rifles with the dug-in Argentine forces. The battalion's commander, Lieutenant-Colonel Michael Scott (b. 1941), could call on fire support from the Royal Navy's 4.5-inch guns. The situation seemed almost hopeless, with neither side gaining any real advantage, until, at 2:30 am on 14 June, Major John Kiszely (b. 1948) stormed through the Argentine lines, bayonet fixed. His actions spurred on 14 and 15 platoons, with the assault ending on the summit of the mount, looking down upon an illuminated Stanley. Scott now urged the right flank to push on. Major Simon Price now pushed 3 Platoon, led by Lieutenant Robert Lawrence (b. 1960), and 4 Platoon into the fray, with 1 Platoon providing fire support. Lawrence was seriously wounded in the battle as he led a bayonet charge, later receiving the Military Medal for his actions.

By 9:00 am, the battle for Mount Tumbledown was over. For the Welsh Guards, their moment was just being realized as D Company 2 Para witnessed what seemed to be hundreds of Argentines converging on a point known as Sapper Hill. Remarkably, by the time the Welsh Guards arrived, Sapper Hill, complete with defence-in-depth positions, had been abandoned after the defenders had been persuaded to withdraw to Stanley by the Royal Navy and Royal Air Force. Twelve hours later, General Mario Menéndez (1930–2015), Argentine governor of the Falklands, surrendered to British forces. Former Scots Guards officer Lieutenant-Colonel Michael Rose (b. 1940), who commanded Special Air Service operations in-theatre during the war, led and arranged the Argentine surrender using skills he had learnt from the Iranian Embassy siege two years previously. Rose would be Mentioned in Despatches and promoted to full Colonel for his role in the war. The following day, 15 June 1982, Royal Marines again raised the Union Flag outside Government House. Galtieri would resign as Argentine president three days later.

As previously mentioned, two troops from B Squadron, The Blues and Royals, supported operations during Operation *Corporate* with their Scimitars, Scorpions and single Samson, making an amphibious landing at San Carlos from HMS *Fearless*. Once landed and dug in, the force provided vital perimeter security and acted as logistics carriers, moving stores over the boggy terrain, which many believed would defeat the Combat Vehicle Reconnaissance (Tracked) (CVRT). Such was their agility that the CVRTs supported 45 Commando in their yomp along the northern route and 3 Para in their tab to Teal Inlet. The CVRTs would later join in the critical battles of the 13/14th, providing fire support from their 76-mm-armed Scorpions and 30-mm RARDEN-armed Scimitars for 3 Para at Mount Longden. The two troops also provided fire support for 2 Para during the Battle of Wireless Ridge and for their fellows of the Scots Guards during the Battle of Mount Tumbledown. They would also evacuate casualties on their engine decks. On 14 June, the troops would roll through the streets of Stanley.

The Falklands War claimed the lives of eight Scots Guards and thirty-two Welsh Guards.

A World at War

THE SHADOW OF TERROR

The end of the twentieth century would see the Guards deploying globally on operations and exercises. From the famed British Army Training Unit Suffield (BATUS) in Alberta, Canada, to the sleet-swept moors of the Falklands, the men of the Guards remain the vanguards. The short-lived relief of the rapid collapse of the Soviet Union and Warsaw Pact would see the Guards operating alongside former adversaries in South West Asia and the Balkans between 1991 and 2003 as part of their Operations *Granby*, *Grapple* and *Agricola* commitments. The ferocious civil wars of the Balkans would remind all involved of how fragile peace and social cohesion was in the post-Soviet world while exposing the Guards to horrors not seen in Europe since the Second World War. It would be South West Asia, combined with massive cuts in military capacity among NATO members and their allies, that would be a test for many military organizations, including the Guards.

While NATO slowly grew as it attracted former Warsaw Pact adversaries to its ranks, so did its responsibilities. Formed in 1992 as part of the *Options for Change* defence review, the new Household Cavalry Regiment (HCR) was created by combining the Life Guards and The Blues and Royals. The HCR would lose its heavy armour and adapt to its lighter reconnaissance role by adopting the CVRT FV107 Scimitar, earning an outstanding reputation for bravery, professionalism and humanitarianism.

The many upheavals in the post-Soviet world were eclipsed by events in New York on the morning of 9 September 2001. Within weeks, the British military was supporting American efforts against the Taliban regime in Afghanistan as part of Operation *Veritas* from 11 September to 19 June 2002. On 20 June Operation *Veritas* became Operation *Herrick*. This operation ran until 2021, with the Guards forming part of a NATO-led International Security Assistance Force (ISAF) providing support to counterinsurgency operations (COIN), a task in which the British military is well versed. The HCR would be involved in *Herrick IV* (April 2006 to September 2006) fielding D Squadron as the Formation Reconnaissance Squadron (FRS). A year later, the Inkerman and Queen's companies of the Grenadier Guards would find themselves mentoring the Afghan National Army (ANA) and the Afghan National Police (AFP). These tours set the pace for the HCR and Guards Division as they became inexorably linked to operational tours in Afghanistan like most of the British military of the period. Injury and death would be commonplace for the men and women of the HCR, Guards and the Honourable Artillery Company (HAC), who had been supporting military operations since 1996 and would lose Trooper Adam Cocks (b. 1986) on 4 December 2007, in Helmand Province. The Welsh Guards would lose their Commanding Officer Lieutenant-Colonel Rupert Thorneloe (b. 1969), to an improvised explosive device (IED) during Operation *Panchai Palang* in Helmand on 1 July 2009. The Guards would also see service in Iraq as part of the Operation *Telic* (2003–2011) deployments, with the Guards Division deploying as mechanized infantry in their FV510 Warriors.

From the onset, Operation *Telic* was viewed by the army as a swift ground offensive followed by counterinsurgency operations. Initial plans and ideas envisaged a relieved local populous in the British-controlled South Zone of occupation embracing, particularly the Ahwaris of the Mesopotamian marshlands, their liberation from the Arab Socialist Ba'ath Party. Led by Saddam Hussein Abd al-Majid al-Tikriti (1937–2006), the Ba'ath Party had ruthlessly put down an uprising that had taken place in the spring of 1991, with many Ahwaris being forcibly repatriated and tens of thousands dying in the short-lived uprising. With the overthrowing of the Ba'ath Party, many Ahwaris felt that their moment of autonomy had arrived. Soon, stifled political and religious pressures filled the void left by the terrorizing control of the deposed Ba'ath Party, and the Ahwaris' frustrations boiled over. Many external players, including the Islamist Shi'a Hezbollah party, were quick to take advantage of the chaos that ensued in those early years, capitalizing on Western failures to address the basic needs of Iraqis. Street fighting and IED ambushes rapidly joined widespread civil unrest, and the British found that the COIN measures that had worked well in Northern Ireland and the Balkans failed to resolve the situation the men and women of the British military found themselves in.

Despite their best intentions, the British, like all nations in Iraq and Afghanistan, would face mounting pressure and casualties. By the time Operation *Telic* ended on 22 May 2011, the HCR and Guards Division had lost ten of their number.

The rise of the Islamic State (IS), initially led by Abu Omar al-Baghdadi (1959–2010), would see the return of British advisors, including the Guards Division, to Iraq as part of Operation *Shader*. Their return as part of a training mission has seen the Guards assist in the training of Iraqi Security Forces (ISF) and the Kurdish Peshmerga since 2014 and protect their fellow soldiers from IS.

Afterword

On 8 April 2024, history was made as members of the 1st and 2nd Infantry Regiments of the Garde Républicaine, part of the Gendarmerie National of France, participated in the historic Changing of the Guard ceremony alongside the King's Guard. As part of the celebrations of the 120th anniversary of the Entente Cordiale, the men and women of the Garde Républicaine would become the first non-British and non-Commonwealth soldiers to participate in the Changing of the Guard at Buckingham Palace. In France Number 7 Company, Coldstream Guards, stood alongside 1st Infantry Regiments, Garde Républicaine at the Elysée Palace, Paris. This moment showed the strength of the diplomatic ties between the United Kingdom and France and the friendship and trust that can be established between former adversaries.

Today, the men and women of the Household Division, in their many guises, continue to fulfil the role of Royal Bodyguards, be it on parade at Whitehall or on any number of operational duties required of them.

The Household Division is the sum of a millennia of service; first established by the Housecarls of Cnut the Great (c. 990–1035), embellished as the many Yeomen of Henry VIII, reborn as Foot Guards under Charles II and refined as warrior ambassadors of pomp and ceremony by Edward VII.

The Foot Guards, known for their adaptability, have once again embraced change. On 30 September 2022, the Guards Division was renamed the Guards and Parachute Division, a strategic decision to align with the evolving needs of the British Army. This new division, responsible for

Afterword

the training and administration of the regiments of Foot Guards and the Parachute Regiment, reflects the British Army's elite forces coming together to prepare for the challenges of a dynamic strategic landscape. This includes the return of beards and the inclusion of women in their fighting ranks, demonstrating their readiness to adapt and evolve.

Meanwhile, the Household Cavalry are also busy preparing for the many challenges of modern military operations. Today, the Household Cavalry Regiment (HCR) is again preparing for significant change as it begins honing its reconnaissance skills with the new General Dynamics Ajax. The Ajax, a state-of-the-art reconnaissance vehicle, will replace the venerable CVRT family of vehicles. This upgrade is crucial in the division's modernization efforts, enhancing their ability to gather and analyze battlefield information. The Ajax is set to be fully operational by 2030. It is important to note that the new Guards and Parachute Division does not replace the Household Division, which continues to be commanded by the Major General commanding the Household Division and proves the worth of work carried out by all.

As the men and women of the Household Division and the Royal Household continue to carry out their State Ceremonial and Public Duties, they remain steadfast symbols of national pride. They are first among equals and bearers of a rich history with a deep sense of pride. Their instantly recognizable presence is a testament to their rightly earned reputation for élan and their unique connection to the nation's history, a privilege that few can claim.

BIBLIOGRAPHY

Anderson, D., *The Falklands War 1982*, Osprey Publishing, 2002

Ascoli, D., *A Companion to the British Army*, Book Club Associates, 1984

Bidewell, S., *The Royal Horse Artillery*, Leo Cooper Ltd., 1973

Braddon, R., *All the Queen's Men: The Household Cavalry and the Brigade of Guards*, Hamish Hamilton, 1977

Bruce, A., Calder, J. & Cator, M., *Keepers of the Kingdome; The Ancient Offices of Britain*, Seven Dials, Cassell & Co., 2000

Bruce, A., Calder, J. & Pigott, M., *The Queen's Birthday Parade; Trooping the Colour*, Julian Calder Publishing, 2020

Carman, W. Y., *Richard Simkin's, Uniforms of the British Army; The Cavalry Regiments*, Webb & Bower, 1982

Carman, W. Y., *Richard Simkin's Uniforms of the British Army: The Infantry Regiments*, Webb & Bower, 1985

Chappell, M., *The Guards Divisions 1914–1945*, Osprey Publishing, 1995

Corps of Army Music (CAMUS), *The Music Makers: A Photographic Record of The Bands of the British Army,* Ministry of Defence (UK)

Cussans, T., *Kings & Queens of the British Isles*, Times Books, 2004

Dunstan, S., *The Guards: Britain's Household Division*, Windrow & Green, 1996

Feiling, K., *A History of England; From the coming of the English to 1918*, Macmillan, 1966

French, D., *Military Identities: The Regimental System, the British Army, & the British People c. 1870–2000*, Oxford University Press, 2005

Bibliography

Gander, T., *Encyclopaedia of the Modern British Army*, Patrick Stephens Ltd., 1986

Gibbs, B. & Simkin, P., *The Guards*, Macmillan Press Ltd, 1972

Gladwin, I, *The Sheriff: The Man and his Office*, Gollancz, 1974

Goold Walker, G., DSO, MC, *Honourable Artillery Company; 1537–1987, Third ed.*, Honourable Artillery Company, Armoury House, 1986

Grant, C., *The Coldstream Guards*, Osprey, 1971

Griffin, P. D., *Encyclopaedia of Modern British Army Regiments*, Sutton Publishing, 2006

Harris, T., *Restoration: Charles II and his Kingdoms*, Penguin Books, 2005

Hills, R. J. T., *The Royal Horse Guards (The Blues)*, Leo Cooper Ltd, 1970

Hills, R. J. T., *The Life Guards*, Leo Cooper Ltd., 1971

Hills, R. J. T., *The Royal Dragoons,*, Leo Cooper Ltd., 1972

Hunt, R. & Mason, D., *Camera at War: The Normandy Campaign*, Purnell Book Services Ltd., 1976

Jebb, M., *The Lord-Lieutenants and their Deputies*, Philimore, 2007

Kightly, C., *The Customs and Ceremonies of Britain*, Thames & Hudson, 1986

Legge-Bourke, H., *The Household Cavalry on Ceremonial Occasions*, Macdonald, 1952

Legge-Bourke, H., *The Queens Guards; Horse and Foot (New Edition)*, Macdonald, 1965

Mahon Bt, W., Colonel Sir et al, *Up the Micks!*, Pen & Sword Books, 2016

Miller, J., *The English Civil Wars: Roundheads, Cavaliers, and the execution of the king*, Robinson, 2009

Paget, J., *The Yeomen of the Guard; Five Hundred Years of Service, 1485–1985*, Blandford Press, 1984

Ponting, C., *The Crimean War: The truth behind the myth*, Pimlico, 2005

Reese, M. M., *The Royal Office of Master of the Horse*, Threshold Books Ltd., 1976

Retallack, R. I., *The Welsh Guards*, Frederick Warne, 1981

Richards, A, *The Flag: The story of David Railton MC and the Tomb of the Unknown Warrior*, Casemate, 2017

Rosse, Captain the Earl of & Hill, Colonel E. R, *The Story of the Guards Armoured Division*, Pen & Sword Books, 2021 (orig. 1956)

Sellwood, A. V., *The Saturday Night Soldiers*, Wolfe Publishing Ltd., 1966

Shakespeare, W., *Henry V*, 1599

Skilton, W., *British Military Band Uniforms: The Household Division*, Midland Publishing, 1992

Skipper, B., *Operation Market Garden; A Bridge Too Far*, Pen & Sword Books, 2022

Skipper, B, *Battle of the Bulge: The last counter offensive in the West*, Pen & Sword Books, 2022

Taylor, J. & Denning, I., *Reflections of a Regiment: The Honourable Artillery Company and the Great War in Pictures*, Honourable Artillery Company & Third Millenium Publishing, 2016

Tute, W., Costello, J. & Hughes, T., *D-Day*, Sidgwick & Jackson, 1974

Warner, P., *The British Cavalry*, J.M. Dent & Sons Ltd, 1984

Westlake, R., *The Territorial Battalions: A Pictorial History, 1859–1985*, Guild Publishing, 1986

White-Spunner, B., *Horse Guards*, Macmillan, 2006

Whiting, C., *Siegfried: The Nazis last stand*, Leo Cooper, 1983

WEB RESOURCES

www.army.mod.uk/
www.arrse.co.uk
www.alanharding.com
https://archives.parliament.uk
www.arundelcastle.org
https://assets.publishing.service.gov.uk
https://babel.hathitrust.org
www.bankofengland.co.uk
www.berkshirehistory.com
www.blenheimpalace.com
www.britishempire.co.uk/
www.britishforcesinpalestine.org/
www.cambridge.org/

https://coldstreamguards.org.uk
www.college-of-arms.gov.uk
www.commandoveterans.org
https://corpsofdrums.com
http://cwrs.russianwar.co.uk
www.defenceimagery.mod.uk/
www.english-heritage.org.uk/
https://englishmonarchs.co.uk/
http://guardsmagazine.com
www.guardsparathepathfinders.co.uk/
www.grengds.com/
www.thegazette.co.uk/
https://hac.org.uk/
www.hcavfoundation.org
https://history.blog.gov.uk/
https://householdcavalry.co.uk
www.householdcavalryconnect.com/
www.householddivision.org.uk/
www.horseandhound.co.uk/
www.hrp.org.uk
https://iloi.org/the-immortal-seven-invitation-to-invade
www.internationalheraldry.com
www.jstor.org/
www.kbgsrca.co.uk/
www.lightcavalry.org/
www.longbow-archers.com
www.longlongtrail.co.uk
www.museumoflondon.org.uk
www.nam.ac.uk
www.nafd.org.uk/
www.napoleon.org/
www.napoleon-series.org/
www.parliament.uk
www.paradata.org.uk

www.parksandgardens.org/
www.pegasusarchive.org/
www.pikemen.org.uk/
https://quod.lib.umich.edu
www.rct.uk
www.royal.uk
https://scotsguards.org/
https://theguardsdepot.co.uk/
www.trooping-the-colour.co.uk/
www.uniformology.com
https://vickersmg.blog/
www.warhistoryonline.com/
www.westminster-abbey.org
https://willowhaynerecordsltd.blob.core.windows.net
https://wyedeanstores.com
www.yeomenoftheguard.co.uk
www.yorkshirecorpsofdrums.com

LIST OF MONARCHS FROM 1066

House of Godwin
1066   Harold II, Harold Godwineson or Harold Godwinson (c. 1022)

1066   Edgar II, Edgar Ætheling (c.1052–1125). Elected King by the Witan in 1066. Disputed and uncrowned, Edgar II was the last male member of the Royal House of Cerdic of Wessex

House of Normandy (1066–1135)
1066–1087   William I, William the Conqueror (c.1028)

1087–1100   William II, William Rufus (c.1057)

1100–1135   Henry I, Henry Beauclerc (b.1068)

House of Blois (1135–1154)
1135–1154   Stephen I, Stephen of Blois (c.1096)

1141   Empress Matilda (1102–1167). Disputed claim and uncrowned, Matilda ruled between April 1141 and November 1141 during the Anarchy, a civil war that took place in England and Normandy between 1138 and 1153.

1152   Count Eustace IV of Boulogne (c.1130–1153) was appointed co-king by his father Stephen I to guarantee succession to the throne.

House of Plantagenet (1154–1485)
Angevin kings of England
1154–1189   Henry II, Henry Curtmantle (b.1133)
1189–1199   Richard I, Richard the Lionheart (b.1157)
1199–1216   John, John Lackland (b.1166)
1216–1217   Louis, Louis the Lion (1187–1226). Disputed and uncrowned.

Main line of Plantagenets
1216–1272   Henry III, Henry of Winchester (b.1207)
1272–1307   Edward I, Edward Longshanks (b.1239)
1307–1327
  (abdicated)   Edward II, Edward of Caernarfon (1284–1327)
1327–1377   Edward III, Edward of Windsor (b.1312)
1377–1399   Richard II, Richard of Bordeaux (b.1367)

House of Lancaster
1399–1413   Henry IV, Henry of Bolingbroke (b.1367)
1413–1422   Henry V, Henry of Monmouth, (b.1386)
1422–1461   Henry VI (1421–1471)

House of York
1461–1470   Edward IV (1422–1483)

House of Lancaster (restored)
1470–1471   Henry VI (1421–1471)

House of York (restored)
1471–1483   Edward IV (1422–1483)
1483   Edward V (1470–483)
1483–1485   Richard III (b.1452)

House of Tudor
1485–1509   Henry VII (b.1457)

List of Monarchs from 1066

1509–1547   Henry VIII (b.1491)
1547–1553   Edward VI (b.1537)
1553   Jane, Lady Jane Grey (c1536–1554). Disputed.
1553–1558   Mary I (b.1516) and Philip I of Naples (1527–1598)
1558–1603   Elizabeth I (b.1533)

House of Stuart

1603–1625   James I (b.1566). James adopted the title *King of Great Britain,* though this was not formally recognised until the 1707 Acts of Union.
1625–1649   Charles I (b.1600)

The Union of the Crowns in 1607 ensured England, Scotland and Ireland shared a monarch.

First Interregnum (1649–1660)

Between 1649 and 1653, there was no Head of State, as England was ruled directly by the Rump Parliament with the English Council of State acting as executive power during a period referred to as the Commonwealth of England.

1653–1658   Oliver Cromwell (b.1599)
1658–1659   Richard Cromwell (1626–1712)

House of Stuart (restored)

1660–1685   Charles II
1685–1688   James II (1633–1701)

Second Interregnum 1688–1689

The second interregnum took place as a result of James II being ousted by Parliament. This was followed by the Convention Parliament who elected James' daughter Mary II and her husband William, a nephew of James II, co-regents, in what became known as the Glorious Revolution.

House of Stuart and Orange
1689–1654   Mary II (b.1662)
1689–1702   William II, William of Orange (b.1650)
1702–1707   Queen Anne, Queen of England and Scotland (b.1665)

Acts of Union
The Acts of Union 1707 was a pair of Parliamentary Acts passed during 1706 and 1707 by the Parliament of England and the Parliament of Scotland to put into effect the Treaty of Union agreed on 22 July 1706. The acts joined the previously separate sovereign states of the Kingdom of England and the Kingdom of Scotland and allowed both to maintain separate legislatures but with the same monarch while creating the Kingdom of Great Britain.

1707–1714   Queen Anne, Queen of Great Britain

House of Hanover
1714–1727   George I, George Louis (b.1660)
1727–1760   George II, George Augustus (b.1683)
1760–1820   George III, George William Frederick (b.1738)

On 1 January 1801, the Kingdom of Great Britain and the Kingdom of Ireland merged, creating the United Kingdom of Great Britain and Ireland.

1820–1830   George IV, George Augustus Frederick (b.1762)
1830–1837   William IV, William Henry (b.1765)
1837–1901   Queen Victoria, Alexandrina Victoria (b.1819)

House of Saxe-Coburg and Gotha becoming the House of Windsor 17 July 1917
1901–1910   Edward VII, Albert Edward (b.1841)
1910–1936   George V, George Frederick Ernest Albert (b.1865)

List of Monarchs from 1066

Upon the secession of southern Ireland in 1922, the title of the union was changed to the United Kingdom of Great Britain and Northern Ireland.

1936	Edward VIII, Edward Albert Christian George Andrew Patrick David (1894–1972). Abdicated.
1936–1952	George VI, Albert Frederick Arthur George (b.1895)
1952–2022	Elizabeth II, Elizabeth Alexandra Mary (b.1926)
2022	Charles III, Charles Philip Arthur George (b.1948)

INDEX

Abbey, Westminster, 10, 81, 89, 100, 122, 160, 181–182, 184, 186, 191, 195, 200–202, 204–205
Adams, John Quincy, 183
Admiralty, Board of, 48–49
Afghanistan, 277, 283, 284, 285
Albert, Prince Consort, 161, 177, 181, 198
Ancaster, 39–40
Anglesey, Earl of, 46
Anne, Queen, 27–28, 30, 81, 172, 196, 223, 296
Anne of Denmark, 37
Anne, Princess Royal, 199, 202
Arthur, Prince, 238

Battle of the Boyne, 218
Battle of Crécy, 56
Battle of East Stoke, 71–74
Battle of Hastings, 38, 110
Battle of Stamford Bridge, 8
Battle of Waterloo, 44, 175, 229
Bearskin, 11, 43, 77, 144, 145, 176, 180, 232, 233, 243
Beaufort, Henry Somerset Duke of, 56-57

Becket, Thomas, 21–22
Beefeater, 71, 78, 80
Bernard Montgomery, 63, 259, 262
Blue Ensign, 190
Blues and Royals, 64, 131, 135, 141-144, 175–179, 222, 231, 273–275, 279, 281–283
Body Guard of the Yeomen of the Guards, 153
Bohun Family, 41
Bolingbroke, Henry, 20–21, 50
Brigade of Guards, 127, 149, 188, 190, 197, 221, 225–226, 237, 242–243, 254–255, 261, 273-274
Brocas, John (de), 55–56
Buckingham, Duke of, 41, 48, 155
Buckingham Palace, 12–14, 58, 122–123, 130, 136, 147, 154–156, 158, 163–165, 167–168, 178, 180–182, 188–189, 200, 202, 204–205, 208, 244, 286

Cambridge, 35, 52, 82, 91
Cambridge, Prince Adolphus, Duke of, 114

Index

Cambridge, Prince George, Duke of, 128, 177
Cambridge, Prince William, Duke of Cambridge, 131, 162
Camilla, Queen, 135, 205, 208
Canada, 149, 222–223, 283
Canterbury, 16, 22, 82, 190
Cenotaph, The, 183–184, 188–189, 190–192, 202, 255
Charles I, 26, 48, 76, 124, 163, 166, 209, 222, 295
Charles II, 26, 29, 37, 40, 63–64, 68, 76, 83, 104, 123, 142-143, 146, 154, 159, 161, 168–169, 172, 195, 213, 216, 219, 222, 286, 289, 295
Charles III, 21, 33, 40–41, 49, 64, 97, 103, 119, 131, 181, 199, 205, 297
Charles IV of Spain, 227
Church of England, 23, 215
Clarendon, Earl of, 25
Cold War, 140, 272, 277
Coldstream Guards, 32, 54-55, 91, 114, 119, 122, 128, 146–147, 170–173, 176, 178, 189, 190, 195, 199, 202, 208, 213–214, 219, 223–224, 227–228, 230, 232, 237, 246–248, 254, 258–262, 267–268, 286
Commander-in-Chief, 173
Confessor, Edward the, 21
Constable of the Tower, 43, 105, 157
Constantinople, 234
Cornwallis, Charles, 224–225
Coronation, 204–208
Crichton, George Arthur, 55
Crimean War, 59, 118, 171, 237
Cromwell, Oliver, 26, 38, 161, 169–170, 209–212, 295
Cromwell, Richard, 295
Cumberland, Duke of, 125, 221

Danish Battleaxe, 8
Deputy Lieutenant, 105–106, 108–109, 270

Earl Marshal of England, 17, 41, 96
Edward the Elder, 204
Edward I, 98, 294
Edward II, 34, 55, 195, 294
Edward III, 17-18, 24, 55, 61, 93–95, 294
Edward IV, 26, 294
Edward V, 294
Edward VI, 35, 72, 295
Edward VII, 54, 57, 65, 103, 149, 162, 164, 178, 198, 205, 241, 242, 286, 296
Edward VIII, 55, 57, 93, 180, 199, 255, 297
Elizabeth I, 35–36, 75, 195–196, 218, 295
Elizabeth II, 13, 49, 52, 54, 57, 67, 70, 80, 85, 91, 96, 103, 114, 124, 138, 147, 152, 162, 180–181, 194, 199–204, 205, 297
Ely, Bishop of, 26
Emma the Pony, 202
English Heralds of Arms in Ordinary, 93

Falkland, Lucius Cary, Viscount, 33
Falklands War, 274, 276–277, 282

299

Fawkes, Guy, 36, 75, 162
Field of the Cloth of Gold, 22, 68
First World War, 55, 62, 66, 69, 118, 124, 139, 149, 179, 183, 243, 255, 256, 260
FitzGilbert, John, 45
Foot Guards, 32, 43, 60, 69, 77, 114, 115, 119, 120, 121, 122, 124, 128, 129, 130, 141, 142, 144–145, 146, 152, 154, 158, 171, 172, 173, 176, 177, 178, 179, 180, 207, 213, 214, 215, 219, 220, 221, 224, 225, 226, 227, 228, 229, 230, 232, 237, 238, 239, 241, 243, 244, 245, 248, 254, 272, 286, 287
Francis I of France, 22

George I, 28, 30, 161, 172, 219, 296
George II, 31, 123, 126, 146, 173, 219–220, 296
George III, 124, 147, 155, 173–174, 176, 221–222, 224–225, 233, 296
George IV, 40, 44, 81–82, 102–103, 156, 158, 161, 175, 196, 233, 296
George V, 55, 66, 81, 162, 178, 182-183, 186, 190, 192, 193, 199, 243, 245–246, 254–256, 296
George VI, 55, 57, 65, 66, 114, 180, 199, 204, 254, 261, 297
Glyndŵr, Owain, 51
Gold Stick-in-Waiting, 63–66, 81–82, 131, 135, 170, 199, 207
Granby, Marquis of, 222
Grenadier Guards, 11, 128, 133, 137, 146, 149, 153, 155, 177, 188–189, 191–192, 199–200, 202–203, 228, 236, 255, 259, 261, 266, 271, 284
Guards Armoured Division, 245, 256, 261–262, 270
Guards Division Memorial, 124
Guards Museum, 7
Guard of Honour, 80, 149, 164, 167, 188, 191, 192, 200, 203

Hakewill-Smith, Sir Edmund, 62–63
Hardrada, Harald, 8
Henry I, 25, 38, 110, 293
Henry II, 22, 24, 45, 60–61, 110, 294
Henry III, 45, 47, 50–51, 53, 98, 157, 159, 294
Henry IV, 20–21, 32, 46, 94, 294
Henry V, 26, 87, 90, 91, 94, 294
Henry VI, 46, 61, 94, 294
Henry VII, 29, 71, 90, 94, 153–154, 294
Henry VIII, 22, 34, 38, 41, 47, 48, 68, 71, 74, 77, 79, 93, 97, 104, 122, 160, 286, 295
High Sheriff, 108, 109–112
His Majesty's Body Guard of the Honourable Corps of Gentlemen at Arms, 68–70, 75, 154, 200, 254
Honourable Artillery Company, 7, 69, 109, 136, 137, 152, 197, 240, 243, 284
Honourable The King's (or Queen's) Champion, The, 100–103
Howard, Henry (Earl of Surrey), 34
Horse Guards Parade,
Household Brigade, 230

Index

Household Cavalry, 7, 59, 64, 65, 67, 69, 119, 120, 122–125, 128, 131, 134, 141–144, 155, 159, 175–180, 201–202, 206–207, 214, 220, 228–229, 233, 239, 240, 241, 243–245, 252, 264, 268–271, 273–275, 287

Household Cavalry Composite Regiment, 238

Household Cavalry Mounted Regiment, 113, 129, 142–143, 205, 271, 275

Household Cavalry Regiment, 283, 287

Household Division, 10, 67, 113, 120, 121, 124, 125, 131, 134, 136, 140–142, 152, 153, 165, 166, 179, 181, 200, 202, 204, 206, 207, 209, 255, 286–287

India, 42, 62, 65, 66, 69, 137, 240

Iraq, 150, 284, 285

Ireland (inc. Northern), 10, 13, 17, 20, 28, 30, 33, 42, 43, 44, 48, 50, 59, 67, 72, 92, 93, 102, 106, 109, 139, 150, 170, 210, 216, 218, 219, 226, 275, 277, 284, 295, 296, 297

Irish Guards, 144, 149–150, 155, 178, 207, 241, 244, 255, 263, 274–276

James VI and I, 30, 36, 75, 103, 161, 162, 195, 196, 295

James II, 27, 80, 106, 170, 172, 215–216, 219, 295

James II of Scotland, 80

John of Gaunt, 17-20
John, King of England, 294

Kesselring, Albert, 63
Kipling, John, 255
Kipling, Rudyard, 124, 243, 255
King's Body Guard of The Yeomen of The Guard, 71
King's Bargemaster, The, 164
King's Troop, The, 7, 114–115, 125, 128, 131, 135, 136, 138–140, 159, 165, 180, 189, 197, 200, 201, 203, 206
Kitchener, Lord Horatio, 65, 241, 244, 245, 255
Knights of the Garter, 158

Leicester, Earl of, 17, 98
Life Guards, 64, 76, 131, 135, 141, 142–144, 154, 170, 173, 175, 176, 179, 230–231, 238, 271, 272, 283
Lincoln Castle, 61
Lincoln, Earl of, 72–74
London District, 114, 123, 131, 136, 155, 166, 179, 180, 181, 182, 188, 190, 199, 204, 244, 254,
Long Range Desert Group, 260
Lord Chamberlain of the Household, 53–55
Lord Great Chamberlain, 15-17, 37–40, 47, 89, 162, 165
Lord High Admiral, 15, 16, 17, 48–49
Lord High Chancellor, 15, 16, 21–25
Lord High Constable of England, 17, 41–44

Lord High Steward of England, 16, 17–21
Lord High Treasurer, 15, 17, 25–28
Lord Keeper of the Privy Seal, 15, 17, 33–37
Lord President of the Council, 15, 17, 29–33, 82
Lord, John RSM, 11, 266
Lord Lieutenant, 28, 33, 41, 42, 43, 52, 82, 104-109, 111, 155, 224
Louis VI, 38
Louis XIV, 171, 214

Major General's Review, 2, 113, 115, 129, 130
Marlborough, Duke of, 172, 173, 219
Mary, Queen of Scots, 35
Massed Bands, 120, 122, 125, 129, 130–134, 136, 145, 149, 189, 190, 191, 200, 207, 270
Master of The Horse To His Majesty, 25, 41, 49, 55–57, 58, 131, 196
Maude, Sir George Ashley, 59
Military Knights of Windsor, 60, 61–63, 88
Monck, George, 170, 195, 213
Monmouth, Duke of, 64, 83, 172
Montgomery, Field Marshal Bernard, 63, 259, 260, 262, 264–265, 267, 270
Mounted Bands, 131, 134–135
Musical Ride, 114, 125

Napoleon, 43, 174, 182, 225, 226, 227, 234

Neville, Ralph, 46
Newark-on Trent, 71, 73
Norfolk, Duke of, 34, 35, 45, 46, 47, 96, 98
Normandy, 8, 38, 45, 86, 101, 263, 293
Northampton, Earl of, 34, 36
Nottingham, 20, 71, 73, 104

Officer of Arms, 47, 89–92, 92, 95, 96, 98, 99, 100, 160
Officers of The Royal Household, 49
Ormonde, Duke of, 172, 173
Oxford, Earl of, 19, 20, 35, 37, 38, 39, 73, 74

Parker-Bowles, Andrew, 67, 275
Pembroke, Earl of, 45
Philip II of France, 60
Prince of Wales, 14, 31, 51, 65, 68, 93, 109, 151, 161, 162, 174, 199, 200
Privy Council, 15, 29, 30, 31, 33, 36, 108, 111

Queen Anne, 27, 28, 30, 81, 172, 196, 223, 296
Queen Camilla, 135, 205, 208
Queen Mary, 90, 217, 218
Queen Mother, Elizabeth, 194, 199, 204
Queen Victoria, 44, 75, 82, 83, 124, 168, 197, 296

Railton, Reverend David, 183–186, 188, 192, 194

Index

Richard I, 40, 45, 60, 61, 294
Richard II, 17, 19, 45, 46, 50, 98, 101, 294
Richard III, 19, 71, 72, 90, 95, 294
Royal Artillery, 7, 52, 133, 135, 137, 151, 198, 206
Royal Collection Trust, 14
Royal Company of Archers, 67, 80–84, 200
Royal Family, 13, 14, 47, 48, 57, 59, 107, 115, 124, 129, 130, 131, 135, 136, 156, 164, 167, 191, 192, 200, 201, 202, 203, 204, 227
Royal Horse Artillery, 7, 59, 128, 136, 138, 180, 189, 206
Royal Horse Guards, 88, 173, 222, 223, 230, 238, 260, 271, 274
Royal Household, 7, 10, 12–16, 23, 25, 34, 37, 38, 45, 49, 50, 53, 56, 58, 59, 69, 74, 76, 87, 90, 91, 97, 99, 100, 122, 123, 126, 128, 141, 146, 148, 152, 153, 155, 160, 163, 164, 165, 173, 175, 179, 180, 1081, 182, 201, 203, 242, 255, 287
Royal Marines, 152, 200, 201, 207, 274, 278, 279, 282
Royal Mews, 14, 53, 58
Royal Navy, 31, 48, 179, 198, 199, 200, 201, 206, 207, 214, 225, 274, 278, 279, 281, 282

Scotland, 19, 28, 34, 36, 42, 44, 46, 48, 63, 67, 80, 81, 82, 83, 100, 104, 106, 107, 108, 108, 149, 170, 199, 201, 207, 210, 213, 216, 218, 219, 221, 295, 296

Scots Guards, 122, 128, 148, 149, 150, 170, 171, 173, 176, 177, 178, 190, 216, 228, 230, 232, 236, 240, 247, 248, 258, 259, 260, 279, 280, 281, 282
Second World War, 62, 69, 91, 99, 124, 125, 137, 146, 147, 150, 254, 256–271, 271, 283
Sefton, 275
Selassie, Emperor Haile, 57
Shakespeare, William, 17, 41, 87
Silver Stick-in-Waiting, 63, 64, 67
South Africa, 62, 65, 127, 178, 239, 240, 241
South Sea Bubble, 30
Sovereign's Bodyguard, 67, 68, 71, 78, 84, 88, 154
St. Edward's Crown, 21
State Ceremonial, 10, 13, 14, 47, 50, 54, 57, 58, 59, 60, 64, 68, 69, 75, 76, 78, 80, 81, 87, 89, 100, 114, 118, 119, 122, 125, 140, 141, 142, 145, 148, 151, 153, 156, 162, 180, 181, 182, 188, 242, 243, 254, 255, 273, 287
State Funeral, 44, 47, 88, 100, 123, 180, 183, 188, 194–203, 204
Stephen of Blois, 38, 41, 45, 101, 293
Stokes, Vern, 119, 199, 208
Sudan, 155, 239

Tower of London, 21, 43, 60, 78, 105, 136, 137, 156, 157, 164, 254
Trooping the Colour, 10, 120, 121, 122, 125, 127, 128, 129, 136, 179 181

Utrecht, Peace of, 32

Victoria Barracks, 154, 155
Victoria Cross, 191, 194, 237, 240, 246, 248, 251, 254, 261, 268

1st Duke of Wellington, Field Marshal Arthur Wellesley, 41–44, 56, 113, 122–123, 157, 174, 177, 182–183, 228–231, 233, 235, 238
2nd Duke of Wellington Lieutenant-General Arthur Richard Wellesley, 56
Wellington Arch, 201–202
Wellington Barracks, 122, 136, 142, 147, 154
Welsh Guards, 131, 133, 151, 179, 207, 244, 246, 262, 275, 279–282, 284

Westminster Abbey, 10, 81, 89, 100, 122, 160, 181, 182, 184, 186, 191, 195, 200, 201, 202, 204, 205
William I (the Conqueror), 38, 86, 101, 156, 158, 204, 293
William I of Scotland, 80
William II, 293
William III, 76, 81, 133, 155, 171, 176, 217, 218, 222, 296
William IV, 44, 61, 77, 82, 103, 142, 156, 176, 178, 196
Windsor Castle, 59–62, 87, 88, 100, 103, 137, 138, 154, 158, 167, 202, 210, 296

Yeomen of the Guard, 68, 75–80, 153, 162, 196, 200, 207, 270,
Yeomen Warders, 77, 78, 156, 157